Soul

PROVIDER

Sissy—

Blessings+

Fr Edward Ryf

Also by Edward L. Beck

God Underneath:
Spiritual Memoirs of a Catholic Priest

Unlikely Ways Home:
Real-Life Spiritual Detours

Soul
PROVIDER

❋

Spiritual Steps

to

Limitless Love

❋

Edward L. Beck

IMAGE BOOKS | DOUBLEDAY

New York   London   Toronto   Sydney   Auckland

Published in the United States by Doubleday, an imprint of
The Doubleday Publishing Group, a division of
Random House, Inc., New York
www.doubleday.com

A hardcover edition of this book was originally published
in 2007 by Doubleday.

IMAGE, DOUBLEDAY, and the portrayal of a deer drinking
from a stream are registered trademarks of Random House, Inc.

Frontispiece: The Heavenly Ladder, *photograph © Erich
Lessing/Art Resource, NY*

Book design by Donna Sinisgalli

Library of Congress Cataloging-in-Publication Data

Beck, Edward L., 1959–
Soul provider : spiritual steps to limitless love /
Edward L. Beck.
p. cm.
1. Spiritual life—Christianity. 2. John, Climacus, Saint,
6th cent. Scala Paradisi. I. Title.
BV4501.3.B425 2007
248.4—dc22
2007015122

ISBN 978-0-385-51553-5

PRINTED IN THE UNITED STATES OF AMERICA

1 3 5 7 9 10 8 6 4 2

First Paperback Edition

For Chris, Jayne, and Jack Beck,

soul providers

for one another

and for me

In memory of my mother,

Geraldine Maureen McGuiness Beck

(1937–2007)

Contents

Author's Note

Some of the names and characteristics of people in the following pages have been changed to protect their identities.

Unless otherwise noted, the Scripture quotes are from The New American Bible (Iowa Falls, Iowa: World Bible Publishers, 1986).

Quotes from *The Ladder of Divine Ascent* by John Climacus, edited and translated by Colm Luibheid and Norman Russell (Mahwah, NJ: Paulist Press, 1982).

We would rather be ruined than changed.
We would rather die in our dread than
climb the cross of the moment
and let our illusions die.

—W. H. Auden

Before the Climb

By the time we were on our way to the Sinai desert, I was weary of archeological ruins and artifacts. As part of a study program I had spent two months in Israel looking at old buildings and contemplating their historical significance. The expanse and desolation of the Sinai desert were a welcomed relief. As we camped out under a night sky that glowed like trillions of crushed diamonds, the psalmist's words resonated: "When I see your heavens, the work of your fingers, the moon and stars that you set in place—What are humans that you are mindful of them, mere mortals that you care for them?" (Psalm 8:4–5).

Although I was more enraptured by the stark beauty of the sky and the luminous granite rock than I had been by the ancient buildings, we had one more edifice to visit. We were making a pilgrimage to Saint Catherine's Monastery in the southern part of the Sinai Peninsula, the oldest monastery in the world. It had been constructed by order of Emperor Justinian between 527 and 565 CE at the foot of Mount Moses, where the great prophet had received the Ten Commandments and an epiphany of God in the Burning Bush.

We arrived in late morning with the sun already high in

the sky, beating down on the imposing granite walls surrounding the monastery, which looked like a burnished fortress at the foot of the parched mountain. Some gardens and orchards outside the walls extended like a long triangle into the desert and created a startling oasis amid the rock.

When we entered the gates a minicity of buildings awaited us: churches, chapels, monks' cells, a library, icon gallery, and even a mosque (supposedly built around the tenth century to appease the early Arabic rulers of Egypt and the local Muslims who served the monks). I soon discovered that the monastery has one of the largest collections of ancient illuminated manuscripts in the world, as well as one of the most impressive collections of icons, numbering over two thousand. It was the icons that left a lasting impression.

Although not well versed in the spirituality of icons, I had always liked the art form. The exaggerated stylistic depictions seemed more appropriate than realistic ones for images that cannot, and perhaps should not, be captured in their totality. The icon leads one to contemplate that which it symbolizes. The Christian Orthodox traditions venerated and worshipped icons, believing that the honor paid to the image passes to the prototype. At the monastery this reverence for the icons was on full display, as monks bowed before the sacred images and as countless candles illumined their shiny gold-leaf and subtle colors.

One icon stood out from the rest for me. I had seen reproductions of it, but apparently this was the original. It represented a ladder positioned vertically at a forty-five-degree angle, reaching up to the sky. Numerous men, presumably monks, were ascending the many rungs of this ladder to heaven. At the top a celestial welcoming committee was headed by Jesus Christ, who had his hand extended to the arriving monks. But farther down the ladder, black-winged demons appeared to be picking off some monks on the rungs with sticks and weapons resembling bows and arrows. It was an arresting image, leading me to speculate as to why some of the monks were falling prey to the demonic nymph-like figures.

I stood in front of the icon for a long time, unsure why I was so captivated by it. I assumed that the icon was based on the biblical text of Jacob's Ladder from the book of Genesis:

> Jacob left Beersheba and went toward Haran. And he came to a certain place and stayed there that night, because the sun had set. Taking one of the stones of the place, he put it under his head and lay down in that place to sleep. And he dreamed that there was a ladder set up on the earth, and the top of it reached to heaven; and behold, the angels of God were ascending and descending on it! And behold, the Lord stood above it and said, "I am the LORD, the God of Abraham your father and the God of Isaac; the land on which you lie I will give to you and to your descendants."
>
> (GENESIS 28:10–13, RSV)

A guide informed me that the icon was from the twelfth century and was inspired by a classic work by a monk, Saint John Climacus, who had actually lived at Saint Catherine's Monastery. Born around 525, Climacus had come to the desert at age sixteen to be a monk at Mount Sinai and had lived in various hermitages. When he was about seventy-five years old, after forty years of living in one hermitage, Climacus was chosen to be the abbot of Mount Sinai at Saint Catherine's Monastery. Having been entrusted with the pastoral care of the monastery, Climacus was advised by a fellow monk to write a discourse that would help those in his charge to reach spiritual perfection. Climacus, known to be a holy monk who had achieved a high level of spiritual acuity, was considered to be someone who could impart spiritual wisdom and advice through such a written manual. During his four years as abbot, he wrote his classic work, *The Ladder of Divine Ascent.*

While I vaguely remembered having heard about the work when studying theology in graduate school, it wasn't until I returned to the United States some months later, that finally I read John Climacus's *Ladder of Divine Ascent.*

Though I was not initially enamored with the antiquated language or with some of the dualistic notions Climacus seems to espouse, the general themes captivated me and glistened with relevancy. The timelessness of the topics was uncanny— perhaps the best litmus test for a spiritual classic—prompting me to wonder how a seventh-century text written for desert monks could retain its relevancy through these many centuries.

Some years later a thirty-day retreat that I had planned gave me the opportunity to test the efficacy of my arcane spiritual guide. I decided that John Climacus and the thirty steps to spiritual fulfillment that he proposes in *The Ladder of Divine Ascent* would form the structure for my retreat. His book and my Bible would be my only companions on my sacred journey. I set out not sure what to expect and not even confident that the climb would be one worth taking.

The experience surpassed all of my expectations. Meditating on one of the thirty steps each day of my retreat was one of the most formative spiritual experiences I have ever had. Each step seemed to take me deeper into the reality of Spirit with which I so wanted to communicate. I was encouraged to face my vices and demons, assured that they didn't have the power to overcome me, and then to move on. With the virtues and limitless love at the top of the ladder beckoning me forward, by the end of my thirty-day climb, I had changed. And I knew it. The following pages bear testimony to that.

The structure of this book is straightforward, based on the thirty steps that are visually represented by the rungs of the famous ladder. Climacus chose thirty steps to represent the thirty years in Christ's life before he begins his active ministry. (In Christian literature those years often are referred to as the *hidden* years, while the last three years of Jesus' life in ministry are the *active* years.) Of Climacus's thirty steps, sixteen are vices to overcome and fourteen are virtues to acquire—a clearcut structure for a book on spiritual mastery.

The following pages demonstrate the continued relevancy of Climacus's steps. Most are perennial virtues and vices that have also been considered elsewhere in spiritual literature. They have endured because they hold universal truths that can lead to transformative insights. Perhaps that is why *The Ladder of Divine Ascent* is still the most popular work in all of Eastern Christendom and is read every Lent in Orthodox monasteries throughout the world.

Take your time on this climb. Climacus himself says that one cannot "climb the entire ladder in a single stride." Climb, walk, sit, stand, kneel, or do somersaults; I'm not sure it much matters. The structure is simply a means to an end: union with God, the source of all love. Get there however you can. As you savor the beauty of this divine ascent, may God provide for your soul, and may the secret wisdom of these steps reveal to you the path to limitless Love.

Love Song

How shall I hold my soul so yours and mine
Don't touch? What path around you can I take
To get to other things? I would mislay
My soul among the clutter left behind
In quiet darkness, far enough away
That it not resonate when your depths shake,

But everything that touches me and you
Takes us together, just as bowing two
Draws from a pair of strings a single sound.
What is the instrument on which we are strung?
And what musician holds us in his hand?
O sweetest song.

—RAINER MARIA RILKE

(TRANSLATION BY LEONARD COTTRELL,

USED WITH PERMISSION)

Step 1

❋

Renunciation / Offer It Up

Renunciation remains sorrow,
though a sorrow borne willingly.

—CHARLES DICKENS

Those of us who wish to get away from Egypt, to escape
from Pharaoh, need some Moses to be our intermediary
with God.

(CLIMACUS, STEP 1)

At eight years old I am facing one of my earliest life crises. Where is my Moses when I need him? My Pharaoh mother, whom there is no escaping, thinks—no, is sure—that it is time for me to give up the pillow and blanket that I have had almost since birth. Although the pillow is flattened and worn, and the blanket is stained and hole-ridden, they are nonetheless prized possessions, giving comfort and security in a sometimes merciless world.

"But why do I have to get a new pillow and blanket?" I plead. "I like these." My supplication falls on deaf ears. Like an arms-folded Yul Brynner in dark eyeliner and a cobra head-dress, my mother has made up her mind.

"Don't be so ridiculous," she says with no small measure of disdain. "How could you be so attached to a pillow, for God's sake?"

"*And* a blanket," I correct her.

"*Whatever,*" she says heartlessly as she wrests both from my clutching fingers. "You'll see. The new ones will be much better. New is always better."

Well, then, how about a new mother? I think.

> *Renunciation—is a piercing Virtue—*
> —EMILY DICKINSON

It would seem that renunciation is not a virtue of the young. In fact, even the more mature tend to stumble on this first "spiritual step." Despite the precariousness, however, the fruits of voluntary renunciation have been extolled throughout the centuries, indeed the millennia. In advising relinquishments more significant than pillows and blankets, all of the major religious traditions promote renunciation as necessary for spiritual maturation.

Buddhism says that renunciation of the self and the world leads to the deathless state of Nirvana. In Hinduism renunciation (*sanyas*) of desires and attachment is necessary to become a true *sanyasi* (enlightened disciple), with the Bhagavad-Gita saying that renunciation is the highest form of spiritual discipline and is considered the goal of life (12.12).

In Judaism the renunciation necessary to adhere to the Ten Commandments, such as not coveting another's wife or goods, produces a law-abiding Jew, while the Koran of Islam suggests, "What is with God is better than diversion and merchandise. God is the best of providers" (62.11).

And finally, in Christianity, followers are urged to deny their very selves, take up their crosses, and follow in the footsteps of Jesus, who renounces all for the sake of the Kingdom (Matthew 16:24, Mark 8:34, Luke 9:23).

And yet despite these testimonies to the virtue of renunciation, many of us manage to avoid renouncing *anything*, especially things we like. The indisputable unpopularity of self-denial in a can't-I-have-everything? culture may give a clue, however, as to why renunciation endures as a spiritual virtue: because it flows against a mainstream society that, left to its base instincts, often avoids the virtuous. While this is not always true, the lack of examples of voluntary renunciation makes their appearance all the more noteworthy.

Once I was traveling on a fully booked flight from the West Coast to New York. The plane's departure had been delayed for over two hours, and tempers were flaring. As finally we were boarding, I witnessed an interchange between a smartly attired businessman and an elderly woman with a cane. She was leaning against a wall as the first-class passengers were entering the plane.

"Don't you want to board first?" the businessman asked her.

"Oh, no, I'm not in first-class," she responded.

"Yes, but you have difficulty walking, and you have a cane," he said. "Please, go ahead." He motioned her forward with a sweep of his hand.

"Well, okay, I guess I can. Thank you."

She limped ahead of the businessman and a few annoyed-looking first-class passengers and handed the smiling agent her coach-seat boarding pass. The businessman followed with his first-class boarding pass.

When I finally boarded and was passing through the first-class cabin, I noticed the somewhat dazed woman sitting in a first-class seat on the aisle, sipping a sparkling water with lime and looking like she had hit the lottery. I didn't see the businessman anywhere—until I reached my seat, midway down the plane. He was jammed into a middle seat in the next to last row, not sipping anything.

With renunciation life begins.
—NATALIE CLIFFORD BARNEY

In his *Nicomachean Ethics,* the ancient Greek philosopher Aristotle suggested that the moderation needed to achieve "the good" is hard work because it requires saying no to desires and passions that, unchecked, become all-consuming. According to Aristotle, the cultivation of renunciation is necessary to live the virtuous life, the only kind of life that leads to true happiness.

Other epochs have looked more kindly on renunciation than ours does today. In the Middle Ages renunciation was a revered spiritual virtue, especially in the Christian tradition, because the focus wasn't all on *this* world. The world to come held just as important a place in people's consciousness. For many this world was of little importance when compared to the more significant and eternal future world. Therefore, one renounced aspects of this world hoping to acquire something more lasting in the next.

The growing influence of science and technology in the nineteenth and twentieth centuries caused us to perceive the world differently and perhaps to focus less on the next world. The physical world, perceived with our senses, was presented as the only "real" world; while the worlds of spiritual consciousness came to be thought of as pious, fabricated constructions that collapsed under empirical, scientific scrutiny. Supposed advancement encouraged embracing the progress of science and technology and forgetting about that *other* world.

Exclusive focus on scientific exploration and technology might be advisable if one believes that science and technology are paramount and have produced only good things. But that is a debatable supposition. Global warming, the hazardous by-product of unguarded technological "advancement," is but one example that suggests caution in an unbridled embrace of technological supremacy. Here it can be argued that sometimes even scientific advancement encourages renunciation. The emergence of the environmentally friendly hybrid car is but one example. Why would one who can afford a fast and sexy car choose instead to drive a less speedy but more environmentally responsible vehicle? Only for a higher good, it would seem. Perhaps renunciation, even in the worlds of science and technology has relevance for us yet.

> But to secure a rocklike foundation, those with a mind for
> the religious life will turn away from everything, will
> despise everything, will ridicule everything, will shake off
> everything. Innocence, abstinence, temperance—these
> make a fine thrice-firm foundation.
>
> (CLIMACUS, STEP 1)

Saint John's words seem extreme to our modern sensibilities. Turn away from *everything*? Despise *everything*? While we may not want to embrace such radical renunciation, might we want to turn away from *some* things, to despise *some* things? It seems evident that to do so might be beneficial. Many Catholics were raised hearing the phrase "offer it up." It means that you should do something you don't want to do for the sake of someone else or for some higher good. While it is not a notion easily pitched to a self-absorbed adolescent, or even to a gregarious adult, voluntary relinquishment *can* change us for the better.

When I was working on my master's degree in theology in Chicago, I became involved with Bread for the World, an organization that attempts to raise consciousness about world hunger. The organization offered statistics suggesting that, while the United States produced only 20 percent of the world's goods, it consumed roughly 80 percent of them. The figure baffled me when I considered the billions of people in Asia and other parts of the globe, as compared with our measly 250 million. The organization asked us to voluntarily stop eating meat to protest that what we so heedlessly consumed was denied to most of the world's population. I stopped eating meat for five years. I remember going home once to have dinner at my parents', when they were serving roast beef, and I passed the platter without taking any.

"I don't understand this hunger strike that you are on," my mother said. "What good is your not eating meat going to do the starving babies in Africa? It's not like I'm going to send this roast beef to them."

"No," I responded. "But maybe next time you'll buy a smaller roast beef because you know I won't be having any."

"No, I won't," she said. "Because I know you. Eventually you're going to change your mind and move on to some other fad. Why don't you give up movies and plays instead? Now, that's something I could see. At least your blood iron wouldn't be affected. Plus, you'd save some money."

Maybe she was onto something.

In Catholic teaching the notion of "offering it up" was multilayered. If not "offering it up" for some higher value, it was suggested that you offer up an unpleasant or undesirable personal event for the sake of "the poor souls in Purgatory." It meant that in some way your sacrifice or endurance of something enabled the good of another, possibly even someone's exit out of Purgatory and through the pearly gates of Heaven. While such religious language is dated and rarely used anymore, some value may still lie beneath the verbiage. Isn't it true that the basis of love is the desired well-being of someone else, even above our own good? And in loving, isn't it sometimes necessary for me to do without so that someone else may benefit from my renunciation? How else does one explain the self-sacrificial love so often present in parenting and in marriage?

In classic Ignatian spirituality (*The Spiritual Exercises of St. Ignatius*), "inordinate attachments" must be renounced in order to move deeper into relationships of love with God and others. Ignatius doesn't suggest that we give up all of our attachments but that we beware the "snares" of power, privilege, position, and possessions, which can become "inordinate attachments." The failure to renounce the inordinate attachment produces an imprisonment of the soul. In modern parlance, we cannot truly be free while inordinately tied to our bank accounts, our jobs, our homes, or our reputations, to name just a few.

While the above personal attributes are not inherently bad, renunciation suggests cultivating a detachment from the ephemeral so that an attachment to what lasts might be fostered. Thus, in denying ourselves some things, we enable an attachment to a loftier good. Renunciation is not, however, an end goal, lest we revel in a self-centered satisfaction of all we have given up; rather it is a *step* to something or someone else, allowing us to turn our attention toward a greater good, or perhaps to goodness itself.

Through love one acquires renunciation and
discrimination naturally.

—RAMAKRISHNA

One year a friend of mine who is an avid Yankees fan finally got much-anticipated tickets to the final game of the World Series. He was like a kid who had been given every toy in the store, and yet his glee boiled down to two paper tickets that assured his entrance into a sports stadium—granted, at a most auspicious time. He was wearing his Yankees cap when I ran into him on the street the day of the big game.

"You must be so excited," I said. "What time are you leaving?"

"Oh, I'm not going," he said, looking down.

"You're not going?" I said, sure that I had missed a sentence, or paragraph for that matter.

"Nah," he said. "I gave the tickets away."

"Gave them away? Are you crazy? You've waited years for this."

"Yeah, but I met someone who's waited even longer and who might not ever see another Series."

He wouldn't say any more than that. Wouldn't tell me to whom he gave the tickets, or why there was such urgency. But I remember thinking, *I wonder if I could do that.* Not necessarily with baseball tickets—that would be easy. But with something I really wanted. Really coveted. I thought about it for a long time.

Aside from its character-building potential, renunciation can also promote a healthy realism. It may remind us that in our lives we easily choose wrongly, lose our way, or foster attachments to things that are not good. Superficialities, masquerading as "goods," unwittingly can muscle themselves into a disproportionate place in our lives. We may find ourselves attached to food, alcohol, possessions, or even certain relationships. For some, these attachments can even advance to addictions. The classical ascetic practice of renunciation is designed to help us combat the tendency to allow certain loves of our lives to become disordered. For example, a disordered love of food leads to gluttony; of money to greed; and so on.

The theological term for such disordered love is concupiscence. Saint Thomas Aquinas, one of the theological stalwarts in the Christian tradition, identifies concupiscence as one of the results of Original Sin. Concupiscence allows one to turn toward a "mutable good," one that is fleeting, such as the pleasure of sex, eating, or some other transitory activity, rather than to be attached to the true and lasting immutable good, namely, God. While we should not deny the enjoyment of mutable goods, they must be appreciated in proper proportion and not embraced inordinately. Only the Supreme Good deserves that privilege.

Unlike concupiscence, renunciation is an aspect of the virtue of temperance, one of the four cardinal virtues. Temperance is that virtue that deals with our deepest drives and inclinations. While allowing that our human drives can be good and healthy parts of our nature, temperance suggests we not let them dominate our lives. When these lesser goods, such as food, sex, money, or even relationships, are not kept in check through the virtue of temperance, we can lose our freedom to them. For instance, a lack of temperance in the area of sexuality may lead to promiscuity or abuse, or even to violence.

Renunciation is therefore a kind of purification and asceticism that does not exist for its own sake but rather for the sake of higher goods. Thus, I renounce excessive use of alcohol so that I don't destroy my marriage or my work. Or I renounce consumerism so that I don't lose my soul to what money can buy. Granted, some people may renounce more easily than others, and those who have the added burden of addictions must cope with unique physical and psychological factors as well. For them voluntary renunciation may not be possible alone, and additional help and support may be needed.

In view of John Climacus's *Ladder of Divine Ascent*, renunciation lightens us and frees us so that we can climb less encumbered, ascending without restraint toward the good. Renunciation exists for the sake of freedom. It liberates us and ultimately allows us to love more wholeheartedly. Who of us doesn't want that?

> *The man who renounces the world because of fear is like burning incense, which begins with fragrance and ends in smoke.... but the man who leaves the world for love of God has taken fire from the start, and like fire set to fuel, it soon creates a conflagration.*
>
> (CLIMACUS, STEP 1)

Questions for the Climb

1. Is there something (or someone) to which (or whom) you feel "inordinately" attached?
2. What would be most difficult about lessening that attachment?
3. Have you recently given up something voluntarily for the sake of a higher good?
4. What did it feel like when someone gave up something for you?

*He who would be serene and pure needs but
one thing—detachment.*
—MEISTER ECKHART

I sit in a hermitage in the hills of Big Sur, California, high
above the Pacific Ocean. My home for these thirty days of retreat is a one-room trailer with none of the creature comforts
to which I am accustomed. No television, no computer, no
CD player, no telephone—no one else but me and the wilderness of these beautiful mountains and that great pool of blue
below. I am literally *detached* from all that is familiar. And yet,
am I really? Exteriorly I am, but interiorly I am not. My attachments to things and people scream at me. I miss, I want, I
crave. And I almost give up. At the end of my first week as I
pack my bags to leave early, I contemplate excuses to give the
guest master monk who resides in the plushier (relatively
speaking) hermitage one mile away. How can I tell him I have
a family emergency if there's no way for my family to contact
me? Perhaps I should just be honest and tell him that I'm not

spiritually ready for this kind of detachment. But it is only the first week. I sit on my bag and then on my feelings. A few more days, and then I'll see . . .

And in a few days, that's exactly what happened. I began to see. To see differently, more clearly, I think. What I saw was that my attachments became less important, less indispensable than at first I had felt. It didn't happen because of something changing on the outside but because of something that was slowly changing on the inside. The simplest things brought me great pleasure: the way the sun crept up to awaken me through the canopy of trees; the sounds of birds delighting in their morning feed; the expanse of an ocean that seemed to know no limits; the fog that hung so low it made the mountaintop feel like a celestial garden. All these things were there my first week, but by my third week, I *knew* they were there. I began to loosen my grasp of things that mattered less, to be open to more significant things that I knew better than to try to grasp.

> *Obedience is detachment from the self, the most*
> *radical detachment of all.*
> —BEDE GRIFFITHS

Detachment requires a nongrasping stance toward life—to be able to behold and revere without having to possess. But how hard that is. In our insecurity and neediness, we think attachment secures our happiness. We want what is ours, and we want it totally and completely. As children we are loath to share, because if we do, we think that somehow we have less, which, of course, we do—physically. But paradoxically, sharing produces its own abundance in a magnanimity of spirit that trumps anything our hands can hold. In the end, we have more.

During my time in the hermitage at Big Sur, I found detachment in the silence and solitude. It helped me to see more clearly because it reduced the clutter and noise—proverbially, it allowed me to step back from the wood and see the trees. Beginning my time feeling empty and unfulfilled, I had an ache in my stomach. By focusing on everything and everyone I was missing, the missing overshadowed all else. As time progressed, however, the emptiness led me to an experience of solitude that was full, calling me to be more present, attentive, and even more loving. I'm not sure quite how that happened, only that it did. The space somehow let "the breath of heaven," as one poet called it, infuse the ordinariness of earth until it no longer appeared ordinary at all, but rather full of wonder and beauty and promise.

In Hinduism the concept of dharma is inherently connected to detachment. One does what is called for in one's "state in life" with love, skill, and attention, but without concern for the results or fruits. So, for example, one becomes a doctor in order to serve humanity, not for the prestige and wealth that it may bestow. Deepak Chopra has popularized the beliefs of the Hindu tradition in his many books, including *The Seven Spiritual Laws of Success.* In that book, Chopra names Detachment as Law 6. He claims that in order to acquire anything in the physical universe, you must relinquish your attachment to it. This doesn't mean that you give up "the intention to create your desire. [But rather] you give up your attachment to the result." Otherwise, desire continues to possess you.

In 395 CE Saint Gregory of Nyssa, a Father of the Church, said it in another way: "As soon as a man satisfies his desire by obtaining what he wants, he starts to desire something else and finds himself empty again; and if he satisfies his desire with this, he becomes empty once again and ready for still another.

And this never stops until we depart from this material world . . . the soul should fix its eye on its true good and not be immersed in the illusion of the present life."

An illusion of the present life is that it will last forever. In the Vedantic tradition (Hindu belief), one of the five reasons given for why people suffer is that they're attached to that which is impermanent and insubstantial, including their own lives. So, a fear of death is an inordinate attachment to a life that cannot be indefinitely sustained. If death is the Big Detachment and is unavoidable, coming to terms with it can free you of the fear it can induce. Detachment therefore helps you to live a freer life.

*We are able to laugh when we achieve
detachment, if only for a moment.*

—MAY SARTON

There is a classic Zen story about two celibate monks who are on pilgrimage together. As they approach a raging river, they see a beautiful, distressed young woman standing on the bank, afraid to make the crossing. The younger monk picks the woman up, puts her on his shoulders, and wades into the river as the older monk looks on, horrified but saying nothing. When the three reach the other side, the monk puts the grateful woman down safely, and the two monks continue on their journey in silence. Hours go by without the two speaking. The older monk is obviously angry and upset. He finally looks at the younger monk and says, "How could you have done that?" "Done what?" says the other monk, surprised. "How could you have carried that woman? You know we are to have nothing to do with women and yet you intimately carried her on your shoulders." "My dear brother," replies the younger monk,

"I set that woman down on the shore of the river hours ago. Why are *you* still carrying her?"

While detachment is indeed more a mental reality than a physical one, it is not necessarily the goal, but rather a by-product or result of becoming more free, more alive, more centered in one's "true self," as the famous Trappist monk Thomas Merton might have said. Detachment is more a description of the one who is enlightened, not a prescription for how to attain enlightenment. You become more detached as you grow in freedom and love.

Sometimes the enlightened person might find it easier to detach because the end goal of love is already present. My friend Judy tells the following story.

Once I was traveling back from Boston by plane. As the boarding was nearly complete, a couple of women with old and weathered faces wrapped in shaggy babushkas came on the plane and guided about half a dozen children to open seats and then took seats themselves. A young girl, probably about eight years old, was told to sit next to me. Her face was lovely. Something about her demeanor—she was sad but resolute—told me that this was going to be no ordinary trip. I asked where she was from and wasn't surprised when she spoke a few words in a foreign language and shrugged her shoulders. I'd studied Russian in college and the words were of that ilk, but nothing I recognized. I thought about how those old women looked and remembered what was going on in the world at the time.

"Kosovo?" I asked. She nodded yes.

As the flight wore on, I became obsessed with the

idea that I wanted to give her something. Though I was sure that money would be valuable, I was also certain it would be taken away. I looked through the purse that I was carrying. There was a small box I had gotten from the jewelry counter of a high-end store. Inside were two gold clips with semiprecious stones to hold back the hair that always fell in my face. I'd been delighted when I'd spied them under the counter glass, because I'd had difficulty finding pretty clips that actually held my hair. I really liked them.

The girl's hair was cut in a short flip with long bangs, not much different than mine. I gave her the box and said, "For you." She motioned, clearly asking "For me?" I nodded yes. She opened the box, and her eyes widened. I gently put the clips in her hair.

It was the smile on her face that I'll never forget. My whole body felt warm. I felt good for days afterward. I'll never forget her, and whenever I hear the name Kosovo, I think of her. I felt that God had given me the opportunity to make that girl happy, even if it was only for a little while. Sure, I had to part with clips I liked, but it was nothing in comparison to what I received. I wasn't sure which of us felt better during the rest of that plane trip, as we continued to exchange happy glances.

> *There is no detachment where there is no pain.*
> *And there is no pain endured without hatred*
> *or lying unless detachment is present too.*
> —SIMONE WEIL

While it is sometimes difficult to detach from *things,* perhaps there is no greater challenge than to remain detached in our personal relationships. We cannot appreciate people's value if our goal is to possess them, because then we only view them in terms of what they can do for us. Detachment allows another person to be, and allows us to contemplate another's goodness, to prize his or her uniqueness, not as a stepping-stone to something else but simply because he or she is.

In the Christian tradition, chapter 20 of the Gospel of John gives us insight into how detachment and love go hand in hand. Mary Magdalene has gone to the tomb of Jesus, the one whom she loved, only to find that the stone covering the tomb had been taken away and that the tomb is now empty.

> But Mary stayed outside the tomb weeping. And as she wept, she bent over into the tomb and saw two angels in white sitting there, one at the head and one at the feet where the body of Jesus had been. And they said to her, "Woman, why are you weeping?" She said to them, "They have taken my Lord, and I don't know where they laid him." When she had said this, she turned around and saw Jesus there, but did not know it was Jesus. Jesus said to her, "Woman, why are you weeping? Whom are you looking for?" She thought it was the gardener and said to him, "Sir, if you have carried him away, tell me where you laid him, and I will take him." Jesus said to her, "Mary!" She turned and said to him in Hebrew, "Rabbouni," which means Teacher. Jesus said to her, "Stop holding on to me [sometimes translated "do not cling to me"], for I have not yet ascended to the Father. But go to my brothers and tell them, 'I am going to my Father and your Father, to my God and your God.' "

(JOHN 20:11–7)

Don't we all want to hold onto and cling to people whom we love? Sometimes even for good reasons. Our love can become all-consuming. But when Jesus says "Stop holding on to me," although he is inviting Mary to a relationship of detachment with him, it need not be less loving. It must have hurt her, as detachment sometimes does, but that doesn't seem to be his intent. Rather, he seems to be inviting her to a new way of knowing and loving him. He doesn't say "Don't ever touch me," or "Discard me and have nothing to do with me." Simply "Stop holding on to me," because he must leave to love in a new way if the fullness of love is to be known.

Like the bonsai tree or the bound feet of Chinese women of years past, constricted love cannot grow. There is no place for it to move. But when we cultivate a detachment in our loving, we choose not to bind or constrict others. We give them (and us) permission to grow, to flourish, to become their (and our) best selves. Detachment becomes a way of holding people with open hands, allowing them to be an integral part of our lives but not strangling them or attempting to possess them. In fact, such freedom in loving may encourage others to draw closer to us, willing to be held, confident they won't be consumed.

Sometimes this lesson takes a long time to learn. In the counseling room or the confessional, I've talked to many people who have struggled to love more freely, more openhandedly. I remember a woman who began dramatically by saying "I cannot live without him. I'll kill myself if he's not in my life." I learned that she was talking about a boyfriend with whom she had been living for two years. He had met someone else and was soon moving out. She was distraught.

"I know he's my soul mate," she continued. "How can I live without my soul mate?"

"But obviously he must not feel the same way," I said. "He seems to want to go on living without you."

"He doesn't realize what he's doing," she countered. "He can't see what a mistake this is."

"Whether it's a mistake or not," I said, "he's leaving, and you are going to have to learn to live without him. Why give him that kind of control over your life? You have a life separate from his."

"But I don't feel like I do. He has become my life."

"Then you may have to try to get your life back."

While perhaps I had the "right" words, I knew then that she didn't feel I was right at all. I also knew from experience that the words were easier to say than the reality was to live. When a relationship becomes all-consuming and obsessive, it creates a prison that is not easily escaped. We learn to live comfortably within the boundaries of bars we think protect us, but in reality they only limit us—and others. Attachments blind us from seeing and living truthfully because we become obsessed with having, with gratifying ourselves, with wanting to be secure. We lose our freedom. And others feel its loss, as well. There is a hackneyed saying that has been strewn across one too many banners, probably because its inherent truth remains relevant: *If you love someone, set him free. If he returns to you, he is yours forever. If he doesn't, he never was.* Overly simplistic? Surely, yet who can argue with the truth of its appeal?

There is one attachment that spiritual teachers have no qualms encouraging: the attachment to God. While attachment to things and people may produce restlessness and unhappiness, the attachment to God alone produces peace and fulfillment. Saint Augustine said it best: "O God, our hearts are restless until they rest in Thee." Yet even Augustine, and other spiritual teachers, struggled to live the truth of those words. In his *Ascent* John Climacus says, "For those sailing the tides of spirituality know only too well that the religious life can be a harbor of salvation or a haven of destruction, and a pitiable sight indeed is the shipwreck in port of someone who had safely mastered the ocean" (Step 2).

While we may not ever completely master this ocean, the second step encourages us to look honestly at the impermanence and fragility of all we have and are. Recall the 2004 news headlines that reported a catastrophic tidal wave caused by a monumental earthquake in the middle of the Indian Ocean which claimed upward of 250,000 lives from the shores of Asia and East Africa. People who simply had been going about their normal daily tasks were swept away in an instant. How else to live but with an openhandedness that receives what we are given and freely gives back what is taken?

Once upon a time there was a monk traveling down a road who had a pearl in his sack. In the village through which he was traveling there was a man asleep who had a dream that there was a monk who had a pearl in his sack. When he awoke, he interpreted his dream to mean that he was to have that pearl. So he ran to the road, found the monk, and said, "Give me the pearl." The monk said, "What pearl?" And the man said, "I had a dream that you have a pearl in your sack." And the monk said, "As a matter of fact, I do." And he looked into his sack and there, between an old prayer book and a crusty piece of bread, was a pearl. The monk took it out of his bag and held it in his hand, saying "Do you mean this one?" The man said, "That's it!" for the pearl was as big as the monk's fist. The monk freely gave the pearl to the man, who snatched it and ran home. When he reached his house, he locked his door, pulled down his shades, put the pearl on a shelf, and sat and stared at it. But the more he stared at it, the more confused, the more restless he became. Until, finally, he could stand it no longer. He ran back to the road, found the monk, and gave him back the pearl, saying "I don't want it." And the monk said, "Well, then, what *do* you want?" The man said, "I want the wealth that gave you the power to give the pearl away." Don't we all?

Questions for the Climb

1. Have you ever detached from "creature comforts" for an extended period of time? What was the result?
2. What has been the most difficult aspect of detaching from relationships?
3. Do you think that freedom and "openhandedness" is the only way to live relationships of love? Why or why not?
4. How does detachment aid your relationship to God?

Step 3

*

Exile / I Want to Go Home

I have loved justice and hated iniquity;
therefore I die in exile.

—POPE GREGORY VII

When my mother was five years old, she and her sister were placed in an orphanage by my grandmother, who no longer felt she could properly care for her daughters.

"What was that like?" I once asked my mother.

"It was awful," she said. "Suddenly I didn't have a home. Everything familiar was ripped from me. I felt very alone, even with my sister there, and wondered if I'd ever be able to go home again."

I suppose that is what it feels like to live in exile: to be removed from all that is familiar and safe and to live in a place of uncertainty and insecurity. Can you imagine a reason why anyone would deliberately choose that? Saint John Climacus can. He deems exile a good and even desirable spiritual step, defining it in this way: "Exile is a separation from everything, in order that one may hold on totally to God." As such, exile is similar to renunciation and detachment, for as Climacus writes, "Detachment is good and its mother is exile" (Climacus, Step 3).

There is also another aspect of exile worth considering: exile as a place of purging and recognition. Let us return to the beginning. The Garden of Eden in the Book of Genesis represents the place of primordial "at homeness" and "at oneness" that still we seem to yearn for. After Creation, Adam and Eve were at home in a world replete with all they could possibly desire. They were at one with themselves, each other, the natural world around them, and their God. What a desirable state of being—to want for nothing. But, of course, there was a catch. (Otherwise, there would be no story.)

Paradoxically, Adam and Eve became restless in their satiated lives and eventually wanted the one thing they were told they could not have. When they reached beyond their capacity, for the symbolic apple from the Tree of the Knowledge of Good and Evil and attempted to "become like God," they were exiled from the Garden. In exile they learned what it is to want.

All of humanity has been trying to get back to that Garden ever since: to return to "paradise lost," to restore right relationship with self, others, nature, and God—to come home again. Exile is a spiritual step because it gives us a deeper appreciation of home. Unfortunately, many of us live in exile longer than we would choose. We feel fractured and dislocated. Rather than deal with that pain, we attempt to bypass it, perhaps reaching beyond our capacity. As such, Adam and Eve's sin is no stranger to us.

He who does not prefer exile to slavery is not
free by any measure of freedom.
—KAHLIL GIBRAN

The children's classic *The Secret Garden,* by Frances Hodgson Burnett, helps to illustrate the restoration from exile for which we long. First published in 1911 and later made into a film and Broadway musical, it is the story of Mary Lennox, whose world has been destroyed by the time she arrives at her uncle's mysterious mansion on the moors. A cholera epidemic in the Indian village in which she was born has killed her parents and the beloved Indian servant who cared for her.

Soon after coming to live with her uncle, Mary discovers an overgrown and neglected walled garden. Her uncle, traumatized by the sudden death of his wife, who died giving birth to their son Colin, had emotionally abandoned the infant and buried the keys to the garden his wife had so loved. Colin grows up to be a hateful and spiteful boy given to tantrums, while his father loses his zest for life.

The once-lush garden is now overgrown and all are forbidden to enter it, until a robin leads Mary to the garden's hidden key. It is in this garden, which slowly comes to life again, that Mary, Colin, and the uncle eventually find the path to physical and spiritual health.

The Secret Garden, steeped in biblical and mythical symbolism, is a classic because of its timeless themes of redemption and rejuvenation. Readers and commentators have suggested that the stern uncle and Mary's parents represent the fallen adult world, while the children represent the possibility of returning to a more innocent and vibrant life. It is a story of lives interrupted and broken by tragedy, loss, and grief, and how the unlikely heroine, Mary, helps to restore life. As the abandoned garden is rediscovered and brought back to life, a powerful metaphor of coming out of exile, of coming home again, is born. When we find the key to the doorway of that garden of possibilities—a Garden of Eden, now reclaimed and rejuvenated—it no longer matters where we actually (literally) live. As the story says, "We all learned that the secret garden is everywhere, and all we need are the eyes to see it."

"Eyes to see it" may, indeed, be what is lacking. Sometimes we are blind to the fact that we exist in exile. We become accustomed to living a disconnected life and forget what it feels like to be at home with ourselves and with others. The current pace of corporate America and our technology-"enhanced" world seems to promote exile as a necessary state of being for success. *Live on the edge. Push yourself beyond the limits. Be number one.* News reports of our lives on the go tell of sleep deprivation, poor nutrition, unhealthy stress levels, sexual dysfunction, and the collapse of relationships too burdened by the frenetic pace of our lives. We ache for wholeness and "home," but many of us aren't sure how to get there. The third step of Climacus invites us to consider our own experience of exile and to reflect upon where our dislocation comes from.

> *We all carry within us our places of exile,*
> *our crimes and our ravages.*
> —ALBERT CAMUS

In the history of Judaism, the Exile is second in importance only to the Exodus. During the seventy years that the Israelites were in exile in Babylon, they underwent profound social and religious changes. Separated from their beloved homeland and familiar external religious symbols, the Israelites were forced to rely on their deep communal bonds and their identity as a people chosen by God. The prophecy of a Davidic dynasty that would last forever needed to be reinterpreted, however, in light of a kingdom that had been crushed and leveled. Had God's promise to them been broken? Or had the Israelites failed to live up to their part of the bargain? Believing the latter to be true, the people (and their prophets) began to see the Exile as a punishment for their sinfulness. "Home" would be restored only when they once again lived in right relationship with the God who had promised land and fidelity.

Perhaps the same is true for us. We live in exile as long as we do not respect and nurture the gift of home and the promise of fidelity. That home need not be a geographical place, but it must be a location of peace and connectedness within ourselves and with others. An article in the December 2001 issue of *The Economist* profiles a group of women living in exile in Hong Kong: Filipinas who have left their homeland in order to provide for their families. These domestic helpers make up 40 percent of Hong Kong's non-Chinese population. Reports indicate that they live in cramped quarters and are often treated poorly by their Chinese "masters." One would expect that, separated from their loved ones and from all that is familiar to them, the women of this Filipina Diaspora would be a sad and resentful lot, but that is not the case. Surprisingly, a weekly ritual seems to play a key role in keeping their spirits high and even joyful.

Each Sunday thousands go to the central business district of Hong Kong to "picnic, dance, sing, gossip, and laugh. . . . They hug. They chatter. They smile. Humanity could stage no greater display of happiness." This weekly ritual of connectedness seems key to allowing the women to retain a sense of joy and peace, even in exile. In the article, Felipe de Leon, professor of Filipinology at Manila's University of the Philippines, says, "They really are happy." He concludes that Filipino culture is the most inclusive and open of all those he has studied and stands in stark contrast to the cultures of the West.

Filipino culture is based on the notion of *kapwa,* a Tagalog word meaning "shared being." "In essence," de Leon says, "it means that most Filipinos, deep down, do not believe that their own existence is separable from that of the people around them." Because they know how to connect deeply, they are less lonely. The Sunday gathering in the Hong Kong square is a weekly mass celebration of that connectedness. Even though the women speak various dialects, there is no exclusivity. Strangers move from group to group as welcomed guests, celebrating on this "one day of freedom" when the true Filipina spirit can be liberated. "Togetherness is happiness," suggests de Leon.

The social gathering in the public square occurs after Sunday Masses, where the predominantly Catholic Filipinas celebrate another ritual of their connectedness. Ninety-seven percent of Filipinos believe in God, while 65 percent report feeling "extremely close" to Him. That is double the percentage of the two runners-up in the survey: America and Israel. Faith seems to be another crucial factor in how the Filipina community retains a sense of home even in a foreign land. Could there be some connection between a life of faith and the ways in which we create a sense of home even in the midst of external alienation?

I have some missionary friends living in voluntary exile who would answer yes to that question. One such friend is Finbar Maxwell, a Columban priest from Ireland who has lived in Pakistan for twenty-two years. He says this:

> I trust that Pakistan is where I am meant to be, insofar as we can have any certainty over such things, but were it not for faith, I certainly would not be living here, and my life would have been very different. My own missionary journey took me to Pakistan at an early

age, and it took some time to grow into Pakistan, to feel that I belong here. Sometimes I feel very much a part of the culture and place, especially now that the Urdu language is so familiar, but sometimes I feel that there are aspects of the culture that I will never be able to fully enter into. At times I feel a bit like an exile, like a tree grafted onto the trunk of another one, growing together as something like one, sharing the same place and atmosphere, the same life, but being different, too.

One thing that tends to mark us as Columbans is our tendency to gravitate toward the margins, whether of communities, cultures, or faiths. Being an exile among exiles is almost our calling, choosing to be there. After a while, being on the margins becomes a comfortable place to be. I tend not to feel afraid in such places, maybe because I feel at home in myself and also, certainly, because I know that God is there—or *here*. I love that line of Maya Angelou from *I Know Why the Caged Bird Sings*: "From then on, wherever I went, I knew that I no longer needed to be afraid, because I knew there was no place God is not."

"No place God is not." What a wonderful notion. One need not go to Pakistan to realize that, but it is easily forgotten. We may even feel exiled from this omnipresent God during stressful times in our lives. When hardship or tragedy befalls us, we may wonder if God has abandoned us. The biblical character of Job certainly felt as though God had. In Job's lament in chapter 29 at the suffering that befalls him, he says, "Oh, that I were as in the months of old, as in the days when God watched over me; when his lamp shone upon my head, and by his light I walked through darkness; as I was in my autumn days, when the friendship of God was upon my tent; when the Almighty was yet with me, when my children were about me; when my steps were washed with milk, and the rock poured out for me streams of oil!" (29:2–6, RSV), Job feels exiled from the presence and protection of a God he once knew. For much of the book, he struggles to get back to that place of favor, to restoration.

We, too, know that feeling at various times in our lives. The sudden appearance of a life-altering illness, the dissolution of a plagued marriage, the loss of a child, and the betrayal of a trusted confidante are but some experiences that may cause us to lose a sense of home and the safety and security we usually associate with that place. We can feel like a stranger in our own homes when family problems threaten to pull us apart. Our most intimate relationships can become vehicles of alienation, resentment, and aloneness when we fail to communicate in love. But there can be a positive side even to such dreaded experiences.

I know how men in exile feed on dreams.
—AESCHYLUS

The uncomfortable place of exile can become our impetus to work toward the restoration of relationships until our sense of home is restored. Recall Climacus's words: "Exile is a separation from everything, in order that one may hold on totally to God. . . . Detachment is good and its mother is exile." We come to understand that ultimately we are indeed alone in relationship to our God and our world, but that aloneness need not mean isolation. As individuals we live connected, however temporarily, to people and places who become home for us, as we struggle to attain a more lasting home than brick and mortar can provide.

After my mother and her sister had been in the orphanage for several months, my mother's grandmother arrived and took them to their mother, Caroline, who was working in Coney Island and living with a man she had met. Their grandmother ushered my mother and aunt up to the counter where Caroline was serving hamburgers and ice cream sodas and said, "Here, they are your children. They don't belong in an orphanage. You take care of them."

"What was that like?" I asked my mother.

"We were frightened at first, because we didn't know if my mother was going to take us back. But she did, without any questions about our time away from her. And even though she took us back to an apartment we had never seen before, as soon as we walked in, it felt like home, because she was there. 'Home Sweet Home' isn't just a phrase on a plaque when you know what it is to be without a home. I don't think I ever took that for granted again." Exile encourages us not to either.

Questions for the Climb

1. Have you ever felt like a stranger in a foreign (or familiar) land? What was it like?
2. What creates a sense of "home" for you?
3. Do you think "exile" can ever be a good thing?
4. When have you felt most exiled from God? How did you make your way home again?

Step 4

* * *

Obedience / Do You Hear What I Hear?

One act of obedience is better than
one hundred sermons.
—DIETRICH BONHOEFFER

What's so good about obedience anyway? Its virtue has been drilled into us since we were little children. We have all been raised to obey our parents, an edict that even the Ten Commandments espouse. As we grow older, the need to obey laws is continually stressed, while the alternative, disobedience, potentially lands us in jail. In the military obeying orders is sacrosanct, the highest obligation of military personnel. Court martial can be the result of failing to honor that duty. In fact, much of the structure of society seems to hinge on obedience of one kind or another.

Yet disobedience is alluring for many of us. Isn't it more fun to revolt? It seems rebellious, cool, and sometimes even a bit dangerous. When I first decided to become a religious and realized that obedience was one of the vows I would have to take, I had a moment of pause. Having been reared with the notion that the good priest, brother, or nun simply did what the superior said without questioning, I wondered about my ability to comply. After all, the superior's voice was said to be God's voice, and one simply obeyed—or so I was told. If the superior sent me packing to Timbuktu, I was to go without questioning. This might present some problems.

Religious obedience has a long history in the Christian tradition, beginning with the obedient servant Jesus, who was "obedient unto death," according to the Scriptures. In his chapter on obedience in *The Ladder of Divine Ascent*, Climacus quotes a wise monk as saying "Like Christ our God, gird your loins with the towel of obedience, rise from the supper of stillness, wash the felt of your brethren in a spirit of contrition, and roll yourself under the feet of the brethren with humbled will."

Climacus tells many stories of monks' encounters with obedience in relation to the religious superior of the monastery, a theme long honored in Eastern and Western monasticism. Much later Saint Ignatius of Loyola, the founder of the Jesuits, wrote a letter on obedience that remains his most celebrated and widely read. Written in 1553, it was Ignatius's attempt to discipline some of his religious (especially those in the Portuguese province) who were apparently acting in a manner not in accord with the rules of the Jesuits. His letter sums up well the idea of religious obedience:

The superior is to be obeyed not because he is prudent, or good, or qualified by any other gift of God, but because he holds the place and authority of God, as Eternal Truth has said: *He who hears you, hears me; and he who rejects you, rejects me* [Luke 10:16]. . . . You do not behold in the person of your superior a man subject to errors and miseries, but rather Him whom you obey in man, Christ, the highest wisdom, immeasurable goodness, and infinite charity, who, you know, cannot be deceived and does not wish to deceive you.

This may seem a hard notion to accept given that we know of some religious superiors who have not warranted obedience, such as some of the prelates in the pedophilia scandal that rocked the Roman Catholic Church. Does their failure negate the wisdom that so many feel Saint Ignatius possessed?

> *I know the power obedience has of making things easy which seem impossible.*
> —SAINT TERESA OF AVILA

During my first year of formal religious life, when I was a novice in the monastery, I had the unenviable task of washing the common bathroom every couple of days. Eight white porcelain sinks that lined the wall under a high window were separated from the urinals and toilet stalls in the adjacent room by a wooden door that swung like that of a busy kitchen.

A bar of orange Dial soap sat in the indented porcelain of each of the sinks. These were heavy-duty washbasins, nothing like the pedestal or fancy wood-cabinet sinks you see today. The soap scum and mushy buildup from the orange bricks made the sinks look unsightly soon after I cleaned them. The water from the sinks would rest in the indentations, causing the soap to become soft and sloppy and drip down the sides of the sinks.

I became frustrated. No matter how often I cleaned the sinks, the lava-like soap would soon begin to cascade down the side of the shiny porcelain, mocking my efforts. Radical action was called for. I decided to buy soap dishes. At the local market not far from the monastery, I plopped down my money for eight plastic soap dishes—not ordinary receptacles, but rather white plastic tubs with a top layer of grated plastic that allowed the water to seep into the plastic tub below. The soap, therefore, could dry fully while the excess water was caught and stored in the tub below. No more mushy, running soap on my watch.

I threw out the soggy messes I found in the bathroom after returning from the store and opened eight new soap bars. I placed them in their new plastic homes, turned out the bathroom lights, and waited for the kudos I was sure would follow from my fellow monks. *Au contraire.*

The monastery began buzzing about the new soap dishes all right, but it was not what we call "good buzz." It seemed that the monks thought I had overstepped the boundaries of religious poverty by buying the $1.49 plastic soap dishes. "What next? Lavender-scented aromatherapy?" one of them had sneered to an agreeing cleric. (This while Johnnie Walker Black scotch was kept in good supply in the liquor cabinet under the sink in the recreation room. Go figure.) I was called into the novice director's office.

"Do you have any idea where the new soap dishes came from?" asked Father Raphael, a kind man with a large nose and old-fashioned, black plastic glasses. Visible only from the neck up, he sat behind a desk covered by mounds of papers and books.

"Yes. I bought them. The sinks always looked dirty. Now they look clean. The soap dishes make perfect sense."

"Did you get permission before you bought them?"

"Well . . . no. I didn't think it was necessary. They're only—"

"Where did you get the money to buy them?"

"I actually took it out of my own budget money." (We received $25 a month to spend for our personal needs.)

He closed his eyes and moved his two index fingers to his nostrils as he leaned back in his ratty leather chair. He looked as though he were weighing something dire.

Finally he spoke with his eyes still closed. "You will bring the soap dishes back to the store."

"But, I can't do that. I threw their cardboard wrappings away. I didn't even save the receipt." It had seemed like a no-brainer to me.

"Well, then you will remove them from the sinks and store them in the supply cabinet."

"But that makes no sense."

"It doesn't have to make sense. Just do it. And next time, get permission."

I wondered if this was some kind of test of my obedience. Saying nothing more, I shuffled down the hall to the bathroom like a dog with its tail between its legs, removed the eight soap dishes, and put them in the closet. For the rest of the year I had to clean up dribbling soap, while resenting the fact that perfectly able drip-busters sat unused in a closet two feet away. (When I visited the monastery six months after I had left, the soap dishes were back on the sinks. I surmised that, since there were no longer novices to clean the bathroom, the monks had caught on quickly to the benefit of soap dishes.)

Is this example testimony that Saint Ignatius was wrong about the wisdom of superiors and the unquestioning obedience they were due? Or is obedience more than blind adherence to the will of a superior or to some rules? Can obedience, even when not understood or seemingly nonsensical, lead us to a deeper truth about ourselves?

It may be helpful to recall that the root etymological

meaning of "obedience" is to listen. In spiritual parlance, it means to listen to the movements and promptings of God, believing that God wishes to communicate with us and desires some response to that communication. The discipline of "discernment" as explored by Saint Ignatius of Loyola in his *Rules of Discernment* is based on the principle that God has a specific will for our lives. Our task is to listen attentively to discern that will and then, in obedience, to live in accord with it. Implicit in this discernment is the supposition that "listening" is not done in isolation or in a spiritual bubble, but rather with others in a communal context. Therefore, other people help us to hear the voice of God by their perceptions and insights. This discernment doesn't refer to decision making about the superficialities of everyday life but rather to the weightier issues of life, the major concerns and turning points: *Should I get married or stay single? What profession should I pursue? Do I have a religious vocation? How much of my money should I donate to charity?*

Obedience is inextricably linked to discernment because one is invited to obey the result of a healthy and well-informed discernment. "To obey" is to listen to the deepest stirrings of our hearts and to act in accord with those stirrings, believing that God moves there. Such discernment is not necessarily a choice between good and bad; often it is a choosing among many goods. What path is God inviting me to take? becomes the primary question.

> *Rebellion against tyrants is obedience to God.*
> —BENJAMIN FRANKLIN

The classic scriptural text on obedience comes from the Book of Genesis. Commonly referred to as the Test of Abraham, it is a story of the call to blind obedience even when empirical data and human emotion might dictate otherwise.

> After these things God tested Abraham, and said to him, "Abraham!" And he said, "Here am I." He said, "Take your son, your only son Isaac, whom you love, and go to the land of Moriah, and offer him there as a burnt offering upon one of the mountains of which I shall tell you."
>
> (GENESIS 22:1–2, RSV)

God is asking Abraham to kill his son without asking any questions. The command seems particularly cruel because God has made Abraham and Sarah wait twenty-five years for the birth of their beloved son. When he is finally born, Abraham and Sarah name him Isaac, which means "laughter," because they laughed in disbelief when God told them they would have a son in their old age and they laughed again with joy when he arrived. Now God wants Abraham to kill "laughter."

This is the same God who in chapter 12 of the Book of Genesis commands Abram (who becomes Abraham) to

> "Go from your country and your kindred and your father's house to the land that I will show you. And I will make of you a great nation, and I will bless you, and make your name great, so that you will be a blessing."
>
> (GENESIS 12:1–2, RSV)

In other words, leave everything and everyone who is familiar to you and trust that I will bring blessing from your obedience.

In chapter 12 at least there is some reward for the obedience—a great nation of descendants. In chapter 22 there is only the command, no promises, no reward. If Abraham obeys the command of God to slaughter his only son, it will be for the sake of obedience only. To see if Abraham is capable of this radical obedience, God gives him the most unthinkable and seemingly absurd command. God is calling Abraham to embrace an apparent contradiction: Having promised to build a family that will bless the world through Isaac, God is now asking Abraham to kill the very one from whom the blessing is to come. If Abraham obeys God, doesn't it make it impossible for God to keep God's promise? Obedience seems to lie in the willingness to embrace this apparent contradiction and paradox. What kind of God would require such a thing?

The basic lesson of the text seems to be an exhortation to trust in a wisdom and insight that goes beyond our own. It is reminiscent of God's response to Job from the whirlwind when Job questions his seemingly meaningless suffering. "Because I'm God and you're not" is God's implicit answer. End of story. It is a call to accept that we don't always have the answers. Similarly, God has to be sure that Abraham trusts God's wisdom more than he trusts himself. Only then can God keep the promise to Abraham and bless the world through his descendants.

I don't yet possess this kind of radical trust, but I admire it. And I've met people whom I believe do possess it. In my better moments I perceive that God can indeed speak to me through others, even through a religious superior who seems to have no clue about the advantages of soap dishes. I now realize that my encounter in the novitiate wasn't about soap dishes at all. It was about teaching me sensitivity to the feelings and concerns of others, even when I might disagree with them. The obedience to something I didn't understand and certainly didn't agree with pushed me to reflect upon the hidden value that Father Raphael, the novice director, was attempting to communicate to me. There is wisdom in consultation, in respecting the feelings of others, in not thinking I am always right. To truly listen means that I open myself to hear the wisdom and experience of others and allow them to influence my actions.

Having acknowledged that, sometimes obedience means standing alone in our convictions even after consultation with others. Civil disobedience has long been revered as an admirable choice if one cannot in conscience obey what appears to be an unjust or ill-informed law. While one may need to pay the consequences for civil disobedience, "to thine own self be true" continues to resonate with us. Many would argue that this perspective must remain an option in religious traditions, as well. I agree.

> *Woe to him that claims obedience when it is*
> *not due; woe to him that refuses it when it is.*
> —THOMAS CARLYLE

The post–Vatican II Roman Catholic Church has taught that one's individual conscience is the highest moral barometer, superseding any man-made Church law. Our absolute moral obligation is to follow our conscience and never to act against it. This presumes, however, that we take time to inform our conscience, that we take time to listen. In the Catholic Church part of that listening is a willingness to seriously consider the teaching of the Church, believing that it must be an integral part of our discernment. If we believe that God's will is often communicated through the faith community, we must consider the teaching of the leadership that guides and helps to inform that Church community. That listening is key to obeying the deeper voice of our souls, a voice we believe has its origin in God's deepest dream for each of us: happiness and fulfillment.

Perhaps obedience doesn't seem like such a bad thing, after all, when we perceive it as leading us to a deeper life and union with God. While there is a vast chasm between soap dishes and sacrificing your only son, obedience on any level may be a step toward spiritual fulfillment and limitless love, because it can lead us into the dream for fulfillment that God has for us. Perhaps we are doing God's will best when our own deepest dream is in accord with God's dream for us. That is when we truly hear what God wants us to hear.

Questions for the Climb

1. What is the hardest thing for you about obeying?
2. Do you believe God has a "will" for you that requires obedience?
3. How do you attempt to listen to God?
4. Have you ever engaged in civil disobedience? Was it to listen to a higher call?

Step 5

＊

Repentance / "Sorry" Seems to Be the Hardest Word

*Of all acts of man repentance is
the most divine.*
—THOMAS CARLYLE

I was late for a meeting with a friend I hadn't seen in twenty years. We were rendezvousing in the lobby of the Times Square hotel in which he was staying, and, of course, Times Square was the mess it usually is: horns blaring, people scurrying like ants, and, worst of all, MTV kids blocking the sidewalk and screaming at the top of their lungs at the newest boy band that was waving at them like royalty from their studio perch above the mayhem. My usually rapid gait had been slowed to a resentful shuffle. As I neared the corner of 45th Street, there he stood—a John the Baptist wannabe, with the same message, in fact. Not wanting to make eye contact, I only glanced at him. He had a scraggly gray beard, long, unwashed hair, and a black overcoat that was, surprisingly, in pristine condition. And then there was the placard: REPENT! NOW! The letters were scrawled in red paint that had run, making them look like blood, on a white piece of oaktag that he raised high above the madding crowd with a thin strip of unfinished wood. He looked as though he were leading a battle charge.

I maneuvered to get around him but, seeming to sense that I was an unwilling convert, he would have none of it. He made a bee-line for me as I lowered my head and tried to get lost in the crowd that I now appreciated. He held a tattered black Bible that he massaged gently with his thumb.

"Do you know Jesus as your personal Lord and Savior, young man?"

He was standing right in front of me, blocking my passage. (At least he called me young.) I didn't answer, pretending I thought he was talking to someone else.

"*You,* sir, do you have a personal relationship with Jesus Christ?" he persisted.

I looked up, unable to ignore him any longer.

"What?" I said, though I'm not sure why, since I had clearly heard the question.

"Do you have a personal relationship with Jesus?" he repeated more forcefully. A woman bumped me from behind, letting me know in her own not-so-gentle way that I was blocking the path.

"Yes, I do," I said. "I do, thank you," I walked around him and started to make my way down the street.

"Hey," he called to me. I looked back. "Isn't it wonderful?" His eyes were glowing.

"Not always," I answered truthfully.

I continued walking and was about a hundred feet from him when he shouted, "Well, then, *repent,* blue eyes, and it *will* be always."

> *Remorse is impotence; it will sin again. Only*
> *repentance is strong; it can end everything.*
>
> —HENRY MILLER

Repent is a loaded word. It doesn't mean simply to change your mind, or even to say you're sorry. Those conditions may be part of the process of repenting, but repentance is a more all-encompassing endeavor. In fact, most of the major religious traditions view repentance as key in the process of spiritual transformation. In Christianity repentance is at the very heart of the proclamation of Jesus. John the Baptist, preaching in the wilderness of Judea, sets the stage even before Jesus arrives on the scene: "Repent, for the kingdom of heaven is at hand" (Matthew 3:2). Jesus takes up the message in the very next chapter: "From that time Jesus began to preach, saying, 'Repent, for the kingdom of heaven is at hand'" (Matthew 4:17). Much of the rest of his message in the Gospels is about how we do that.

In Old Testament Judaism repentance is a major theme with regard to the sins of the people and their leaders. Recall King David, who repents before God with all his heart when his sins of adultery and murder were exposed, or the repentance of Nineveh in the Book of Jonah—the reading for Yom Kippur, the Jewish fast dedicated to repentance and atonement. (Interestingly, in the New Testament, Jesus compares himself to Jonah, who succeeded in influencing the Gentiles while failing to achieve equal success with his own people [Matthew 12:39–41].) *Teshuvá* (repentance) is the key concept in the rabbinic view of sin and forgiveness. It must come from the heart.

The Arabic word *Tawbah* (repentance) literally means "to return." In Islam repentance means the act of leaving what Allah has prohibited and returning to what he has commanded. The month of Ramadan, the holiest month in the Islamic calendar, is dedicated to this process.

Even more interesting than the primacy of repentance in the religious traditions is the similarity of the process in each. In the major religions of Christianity, Judaism, and Islam, true and total repentance requires five general elements:

1. Recognition of one's sin
2. True remorse
3. Desisting from the sin
4. Restitution where possible
5. Confession

Admittedly, the process isn't an easy one. As spiritual masters and traditions suggest, repentance is hard work. For John Climacus, acts of repentance are attempts at the transformation of the whole person. Following in the Patristic tradition, Climacus suggests that repentance is not simply a matter of emotions, sorrow, or regret for some sin. It is rather a way the person changes his or her whole purpose and life. It is an active changing of mind and flesh. In characteristically harsh terms, Climacus sometimes speaks of the process as a battle. He writes that, just as a soldier's enemy has spent years in training to defeat him, so has an individual's flesh grown accustomed to its fallen and sinful state. Active combat is needed to resist this propensity. Repentance is part of that arsenal.

> *When a child can be brought to tears, and not*
> *from fear of punishment, but from repentance*
> *he needs no chastisement.*
> —HORACE MANN

Using the listed 5 steps as a framework, an actual experience of repentance may help us to navigate a sometimes difficult and complex process.

On September 14, 2001, I was volunteering in a triage center close to Ground Zero in New York City. The horrors of the previous three days had begun to sink in and people were attempting to make sense of the devastation. I and some other religious leaders and counselors were meeting with people who were asking to speak to someone for counsel. I was told by one of the young volunteers that a woman who had asked to speak to a priest was waiting in a counseling room. When I walked in, the look on her face betrayed a woman who had experienced firsthand the loss emblematic of September 11. Her eyes were red and swollen. Her hands were shaking slightly as she tried to wring them still.

Recognition of One's Sin

"I want you to know that I'm a married woman. I've been married for fifteen years. But for the last five years of my marriage, I've been having an extramarital affair." Unable to meet my gaze, she looked at the desk between us. "But you should also know that I had no regret about this affair. Well, until recently." She began to cry, dabbing her eyes with a shredded tissue.

"My husband checked out of the marriage a long time ago. He was always working. Never there for me. Emotionally, physically, and psychologically distant. The whole nine yards. Father, I'm sure you've heard this more times than you care to remember. When I met the guy I began the affair with, he was everything my husband wasn't. He saw *me,* acknowledged *me.* He knew I existed. In a crazy way, I convinced myself that the affair actually helped me stay in the marriage, because at least now I was getting something I needed that my marriage wasn't providing."

She went on to say that her perspective began to change as her daughter got older. That's when the guilt settled in. She would have to make excuses to her daughter about where she was going and with whom. She even asked her daughter to keep their secret that mommy was away some afternoons.

"I began to see that I couldn't live this double life anymore. When my daughter turned six, I felt that I had to make a choice one way or the other, for her sake, really. And maybe for mine, too. I had to end the marriage or end the affair. I couldn't do both anymore. And since the marriage came first, I thought maybe it deserved one more shot."

She called up the man with whom she was having the affair and told him that she wanted to meet him for breakfast the following morning. She planned to tell him she was ending the affair.

"I was so angry all that day. And the anger was directed at my husband. Here I was, planning to give up someone who brought me love and joy, but nothing in my marriage had changed. I resented it. And I resented my husband."

When her husband came home from work that evening, she picked a fight with him, letting loose all of her rage. They argued most of the night, screaming so loudly that the neighbors began banging on the walls for quiet. They were arguing in their bedroom when the anger escalated out of control.

"I picked up a vase from the nightstand and threw it at his head, just barely missing him. It shattered into a hundred pieces all over the rug. He looked at me like I had lost my mind. And maybe I had. I was exhausted. We went to bed without speaking."

During the silent breakfast the following morning, her

daughter, who seemed to be getting a cold, accidentally spilled her cereal all over the kitchen floor.

"And I lost it. I smacked her hard across the face. I can't believe. . . ." She started crying again and shaking her head, unable to go on.

Her husband grabbed their daughter and told his wife that she must be losing her mind. He said he'd take their daughter to work with him and put her in the day care center because he couldn't send her to school like this. Then he left.

True Remorse

"I knew I would have to deal with all of that later, but the only thing on my mind was getting into the city for that breakfast and telling him the affair was over. I knew that if I could take that step, I could maybe save my marriage. I got dressed and began driving into Manhattan."

She was listening to the radio as she exited the Brooklyn Battery Tunnel. A reporter was saying that it appeared as if a plane had flown into the World Trade Center building.

"I didn't want to believe what I was hearing, but somehow I knew right then that everything had changed. And I was right. My husband worked in that building, and he's dead." She stopped speaking for a moment and began staring at the wall, expressionless. After a few moments she said, "And my daughter was evacuated from the day care center close by, but I couldn't find her for twelve hours. So I didn't know if she was dead or alive, either. But thank God, she's all right."

She looked at me with tears streaming down her face. "How could I have known that that would be the last time I would see him? I mean, I threw something at his head! And my daughter . . . What kind of monster am I? I am so sorry, but it's just not enough. He's gone and I can never even tell him. That's the worst part. I will always have to live with that."

Desisting from the Sin

Granted, this woman had no choice but to desist from "the sin" because her husband was now dead. But she had decided to end the affair before that. She had come to the realization that she could no longer live a lie. She needed authenticity and to reclaim something that she had lost.

"I know that I can't see the guy I was having the affair with anymore, even though in some sense I can now. I would never feel right about being with him ever again. I don't think I ever did feel right about it, even though I tried to convince myself. I knew that it was always wrong. But now it would just be *really* wrong. I'd feel like I'm betraying my husband and daughter even more now. I can't explain it."

Restitution Where Possible

"Nothing I can do will bring my husband back. I know that. But I have a sense now that I have to make it up to my daughter. To be a better mother. So much of me wasn't there for her in the first years of her life. I was so busy trying to fill my own life. I want to do what's right from now on."

Confession

The act of her telling me about this tragedy and the resultant epiphany was itself the "confession," but there was more confession yet to come. She said that she needed also to tell other important people in her life about what had happened so that she wouldn't have to carry her burden all alone. She wanted validation from people she loved that she was still loveable despite her transgressions. She said she would talk again about the affair, the fighting, and the death of her husband. I hoped that with each retelling she might heal just a bit more from something from which she may never heal totally.

What makes repentance so difficult is the total life alteration demanded. It is not just about making amends for something we may have done wrong. It is rather the deep realization that an aspect of our life or our relationships is disordered and that conversion is necessary if we are to be in right relationship again—with ourselves and with others. With this view, Climacus's definition of repentance is striking: "Repentance is the renewal of baptism and is a contract with God for a fresh start in life." I think the demands of repentance and real relationship with God are what caused me to answer the modern-day John the Baptist in Times Square the way I did.

"Do you have a personal relationship with Jesus?"

"Yes, I do."

"Isn't it wonderful?"

"Not always."

It is not easy to follow Jesus, because he is perfect love. Love has its demands. And perfect love is really demanding.

"Well, then, *repent*, blue eyes, and it *will* be always."

Easy for him to say. Hard for me to live.

Questions for the Climb

1. Do you find asking for forgiveness easy or hard? Why?
2. Do you find forgiving someone else easy or hard? Why?
3. Have you ever done something that you think is beyond forgiveness?
4. Do you experience a link between the forgiveness of God and others?

Step 6

⁕

Remembrance of Death / Six Feet Under

*The fear of death follows from the fear
of life. A man who lives fully is prepared to
die at any time.*

—MARK TWAIN

Nobody wants to die. Well, at least most people don't. You have the occasional suicide, but most attribute that to psychological illness. But if we don't want to die, do we really want to live forever? Think about it: *Forever*. Might we not one day get tired of it all? Final rest could seem like a good thing.

Elina Makropulos seems to think so. She is the protagonist in a play by Karel Čapek, the most important Czech writer of the first half of the twentieth century. In his play *The Makropulos Case*, Elina has lived 342 years, thanks to an elixir of eternal life created by her alchemist father. She takes the formula when she is 42 years old and stays that age for the next 300 years. Her unending life becomes boring, however, because everything that could possibly happen to her already has. All is now joyless. She refuses to take the elixir again because she realizes that human life should not last too long. She decides that the termination of life is what allows life to keep its value. At the end of the play she sinks lifeless to the floor.

Is it true that death gives meaning to life or, at least, informs life? Saint John Climacus writes, "Just as bread is the most necessary of all foods, so the thought of death is the most essential of all works . . . The man who lives daily with the thought of death is to be admired, and the man who gives himself to it by the hour is surely a saint." The knowledge of our mortality is therefore an incitement to live more fully. When we realize that we have a limited time to revel in the gift of human life, we are infused with an urgency that an endless life might not offer. There is only so much time to climb that beautiful mountain, or swim in that pristine ocean, or appreciate the sound of that bird calling to its mate. More significantly, our time with those whom we love is limited. Why waste the time with the nonessentials: family feuds that last for years, long-held grudges, opportunities at loving never taken? Some famous sayings may be hackneyed and clichéd, but their truth is nonetheless real: *We only go around once. This is not a dress rehearsal. Carpe diem. Smell the roses. Go for the gusto. You will not pass this way again.* The reason why these words resonate is because our experience validates their truth.

> *Mortality weighs heavily on me like*
> *unwilling sleep.*
> —JOHN KEATS

Psalm 90 may hold further wisdom for us:

> *A thousand years in your eyes*
> *are merely a yesterday,*

But humans you return to dust,
saying, "Return, you mortals!"
Before a watch passes in the night,
you have brought them to their end;
They disappear like sleep at dawn;
they are like grass that dies.
It sprouts green in the morning;
by evening it is dry and withered.

Our life ebbs away under your wrath;
our years end like a sigh.
Seventy is the sum of our years,
or eighty, if we are strong;
Most of them are sorrow and toil;
they pass quickly, we are all but gone.

Teach us to count our days aright,
that we may gain wisdom of the heart.

(VV. 3–6, 9–10, 12)

Teach us to count our days aright, that we may gain wisdom of the heart. The psalmist suggests that to realize one's mortality is wisdom. It is to know that we pass through this life at a relatively rapid pace and that our place in the universe is fleeting, not as monumental as we might think it is. And yet many of us trust that we are significant to the Creator of the universe and to the people with whom we share our little place in this vast and complex world. The *wisdom* seems to be to live fully and lovingly, knowing the shortness of our life.

When my friend Henry's nineteen-year-old son Marco was diagnosed with lymphoma, it was a shock to all of us. Henry, Marco, and I were having lunch before a scheduled doctor's appointment where Marco was to have an unusual lump in his neck checked.

"Here, feel my neck, Father Edward," said Marco after we had ordered our salads. "It's kind of hard." I didn't like the way it felt. Henry must have noticed my concern.

"What's the matter with you?" said Henry. "Kids get those kinds of things all the time when they're maturing."

"Yeah, I'm sure," I said. "I'm just glad you're getting it checked." We were silent for a few moments.

"Why, what's the worst it could be?" Henry finally said.

"Lymphoma," I said, though I really didn't believe it could possibly be that.

The next two years were a roller-coaster ride of hope and disappointment. After going into remission for more than a year, the cancer returned with a heartbreaking virulence. Marco endured radical chemotherapy that destroyed not only some cancer cells but much of the life and vitality so character-istic of him. His skin actually became charred from the anti-cancer toxins, causing his complexion to darken, making him almost unrecognizable.

Henry and Marco's mother, Ann, stood by his bed for hours. Family members traded twenty-four-hour shifts, so that Marco would never have to be alone. Henry began reading *A Course in Miracles* and praying for just that, a miracle. He sat by Marco's bedside, telling him of some of the insights into life that he was gleaning from his reading.

When it seemed that the end was near, I canceled a retreat I was giving in the Midwest and flew home to be with Marco and his family. Even then Henry never acknowledged that Marco was dying. "He's going to be fine. I know Jesus can and will perform a miracle here. It's going to happen." When it didn't happen, I saw something die in Henry, too. Baptized

Catholic, he had always had his struggles with the Church, but he had returned to it full force after the baptism of his daughter and a promise to God to be faithful if God would be faithful in return. It now seemed as though God had broken the promise, so Henry was free to abandon it, as well.

The funeral Mass at which I presided and preached was the last time I saw Henry in a Catholic Church. (It didn't help his disillusionment when, because of a diocesan rule prohibiting family eulogies at funerals, Henry was refused permission to deliver a eulogy in the same church in which he had celebrated the Initiation sacraments with his son.) He blamed the Church, but he also blamed God. He returned to *A Course in Miracles* in an effort to find answers and to justify his son's death, even though he refused to acknowledge Marco's absence as death.

"He's not dead. No one really dies. He's just living in a different way. And we have to be trained to be able to see that." Was this denial, or was it a valid perspective? Was it simply a way to continue to hold on to Marco, or was Marco really now holding on to Henry? Whichever it was, Henry's life did indeed change when Marco was no longer physically present. Henry's visits to Marco's grave (the only time Henry *ever* leaves his cell phone in the car) have become a ritual of connecting with Marco's spirit, which Henry senses lives on in tangible ways. He sees signs from Marco every day.

Henry's relationships with his other children have also deepened as a result of Marco's death. I sense Henry has come to realize the fragility of life as we know it and the necessity to live it as consciously and fully as we can. He recently bought a house by a lake in suburban New Jersey just so he could "feel the peace of watching the sun rise over the water and see the beauty of it all."

Life is a sexually transmitted disease and the
mortality rate is one hundred percent.

—R. D. LAING

When the sisters of Lazarus are mourning the death of their brother in the Gospel of John, Jesus says this to them: "I am the resurrection and the life; whoever believes in me, even if he dies, will live, and everyone who lives and believes in me will never die. Do you believe this?" (John 11:25–26). I think Henry believes it. The central teaching of resurrection in Christianity greatly impacts our perspective on mortality and physical death. As Saint Paul writes in his first letter to the Corinthians, "Death is swallowed up in victory. Where, O death, is your victory? Where, O death, is your sting?" (15:54–55).

All of the major religious traditions have some notion of an afterlife that lessens the sting of death. While in Buddhism there is no belief that an individual soul lives on, there is an understanding that what one does in this lifetime determines what happens in the next life and on through time, without end. Similarly, in Hinduism there is a belief in reincarnation, which is determined by one's karma. In Islam Paradise is gained in the next life through good works and obedience to the Koran in this life. And while Judaism is focused primarily on the here and now and not on an afterlife, traditional Judaism teaches that death is not the end of existence, for there is still a messianic age to come.

So then, if we do get to live forever, why fear death? Perhaps what we fear are the unknown aspects of death. There are varying hypotheses and religious beliefs about what happens after we die, but nobody has come back to tell us. We are not sure at all about the particulars of an afterlife. What if we don't make it to "Heaven" and instead are bound for that other place we are loath to mention? The threat of the flames of eternal damnation is enough to give anyone pause. It is also hard to accept a notion of a disembodied soul living on because we have no point of reference by which to understand that reality.

A man who won't die for something
is not fit to live.
—MARTIN LUTHER KING JR.

Pious depictions of Heaven have us reunited with all of our loved ones, even with our pets. We will eat, drink, and be merry forever. While such an anthropomorphic understanding of Heaven might be comforting, it does little to realistically address what a soul united to God might actually be like. One less pious friend says he believes Heaven will be like "one never-ending orgasm" (perhaps akin to the seventy virgins promised the righteous Muslim). He claims *that* belief alone is enough to keep him on the straight and narrow. But is it really? Would we want that *forever*? Recall Elina's concern from Čapek's play. She gets bored with it all. Even the good things become tiresome if we continue to experience them with no cessation. Endless eating, drinking, and orgasms may seem attractive from a distance, but close-up they are human activities that easily run their course and most probably have nothing to do with a soul's afterlife. So then, what does it mean to *live forever*? And do we really want to?

I, of course, cannot answer those questions with certainty. Nobody can. Life is mysterious enough without believing we can also figure out all of the ambiguities of death and afterlife. While my own Catholic Church has some detailed teachings about death and afterlife in its catechism, the nuances of the particularities of life after death remain a mystery. Rather, I prefer to say that a God of Love is the creator and sustainer of the universe. We come from the life and love force of that God and will eventually return to it. After physical death, when our spirits exist wholly and completely within that spirit of Love, we will feel most completely and utterly alive. It won't be boring or numbingly cyclical because it will be a perpetual state of rest that knows no wanting or imperfection. Our loved ones from this life and the love we have given and received will be a part of that experience of Ultimate Love. My justification for such an articulation finds its genesis in the first letter of Saint John:

> Beloved, let us love one another, because love is of God; everyone who loves is begotten by God and knows God. Whoever is without love does not know God, for God is love. . . . No one has ever seen God. Yet, if we love one another, God remains in us, and his love is brought to perfection in us . . . God is love, and whoever remains in love remains in God and God in him. In this is love brought to perfection among us, that we have confidence on the day of judgment because as he is, so are we in this world. There is no fear in love, but perfect love drives out fear because fear has to do with punishment, and so one who fears is not yet perfect in love.
>
> (1 JOHN 4:7–8, 12, 16–18)

The "remembrance of death" is a good thing because it encourages us to make this love a part of our lived experience now, while we still can. Many believe that the love experienced in the afterlife will be proportionate to the love we share and experience now. The remembrance of death is also a good reality check for what is really important in life. In death all distinctions are obliterated. It won't matter if you were attractive or ugly, successful or a failure, rich or poor, gay or straight, Ph.D. or high school dropout, black or white. We will all die the same. What will matter is the love. And six feet under is too late to remember that.

Postscript to Step 6: As I was making final preparations for the publication of this manuscript, my mother died unexpectedly while visiting me in New York. (Just two weeks ago, as of this writing.) Over three days she became progressively more ill until I had to take her to the emergency room of a local hospital. Tests concluded that she had a previously undetected, massive, cancerous tumor in her lungs that was constricting her breathing. She died three days later on Passion Sunday with my father, my brother, and me by her bedside in the intensive care unit.

As I reread the previous chapter, written before this tragic event, the words bear even more significance for me now. I wrote them some months ago. Now I live them. I hold on to the spiritual truth of life that does not end. I want to *feel* that for my mother and for those of us who miss her. Life as we know it is so very fragile. And it is indeed swept away in an instant. I have to believe that the deep love we shared lives on in the spirit of my mother. That belief is what enables me to say yes to more life, to more love.

Questions for the Climb

1. Do you think about death? Do you fear it? Why?
2. What do you think the afterlife is like?
3. When you have experienced the death of a loved one, does your faith help you in the experience? Why or why not?
4. Do you think you live life fully?

Step 7

✳

Sorrow / Good Grief

To be always fortunate, and to pass through life
with a soul that has never known sorrow, is to
be ignorant of one half of nature.

—SENECA

One of the classic feasts in the liturgical calendar of the Roman Catholic Church occurs on September 15, the feast of Our Lady (sometimes known as Mother) of Sorrows. It has long been an important feast in my own Passionist community, and its inspiration can be traced to the Gospel of John with the account of Mary at the cross of Jesus. "Standing by the cross of Jesus were his mother and his mother's sister, Mary the wife of Clopas, and Mary of Magdala. When Jesus saw his mother and the disciple there whom he loved, he said to his mother, 'Woman, behold your son.' Then he said to the disciple, 'Behold, your mother.' And from that hour the disciple took her into his home" (John 19:25–27).

Long before the crucifixion, at the Presentation of the Infant Jesus in the Temple, Simeon prophesied that a sword would pierce Mary's soul so that the thoughts of many hearts would be revealed (Luke 2:35). Devotion to the Mother of Sorrows flowered in the Middle Ages, as evidenced by the medieval hymn "Stabat Mater": "At the Cross her station keeping, stood the mournful Mother weeping. Close to Jesus to the end." And in Christian art one of the most recognizable images is that of the Pietà, the sorrowful mother holding the dead body of her Son taken down from the cross.

Why has this image of the sorrowful mother captured the imagination of believers and nonbelievers for centuries? What is it about *sorrow* that we find intriguing, perhaps even alluring? And why would *sorrow* be one of the spiritual steps necessary to loving more fully?

Some contemporary sorrowful mothers might give us a clue. The Mothers of the Disappeared in Argentina first marched in protest on April 30, 1977, demanding an account of the thousands who had disappeared at the hands of the rightist military dictatorship that took power in 1976. The mothers estimated that thirty thousand of their children had disappeared or had been detained. On that first Thursday, fourteen of the women marched to the Plaza de Mayo, across from the presidential palace in Buenos Aires. Two months later, after weekly demonstrations, three mothers were allowed to see the minister of the interior, a general who acknowledged that people had disappeared but claimed that he did not know who had taken them. Wearing their trademark white scarves, the dissatisfied mothers continued to march every Thursday, demanding answers and justice. And they have been marching for thirty years since. While some of the leaders of the rightist junta have been jailed for the atrocities committed, the fate of thousands who disappeared remains unknown to this day.

What is striking about the sorrow of the Mothers of the

Disappeared is that it was not turned inward. Rather, their personal experience of sorrow was directed outward and became a vital force in addressing this and many other injustices. They earned a UNESCO Prize for Peace Education in 1999 and have continued to inspire women's groups worldwide. In 2000 they began the Popular University of the Mothers of the Plaza de Mayo, which has one thousand six hundred students who focus on political and social human rights. In addition, they joined in protests against Argentina's economic policies in December 2001 and have criticized Argentina's foreign aid dependence and restrictions imposed by the International Monetary Fund.

What is redemptive about their sorrow is that it led them to compassion, to a heartfelt understanding of the injustices and sufferings of people not connected to their original cause. This is perhaps nowhere more striking than in their connection to another group of mothers—from New York. Inspired by the long-suffering mothers of Argentina, the Mothers of the New York Disappeared have organized in their own fight for justice. Theirs is a campaign against the draconian Rockefeller drug laws of the 1970s that mandated harsh prison terms for the possession or sale of relatively small amounts of drugs. Approximately 18,300 drug offenders are serving lengthy minimum sentences in New York prisons, many of them offenders with no history of violent behavior. Of these, 93 percent are African American or Latino. Their mothers are fighting for their release in a "Drop the Rock" (referring to the Rockefeller drug laws) campaign that has extended all the way to Argentina. In February 2004 the mothers from New York met with the Argentinean mothers in an effort to publicize what they perceive as one more social injustice. The New York mothers received a verbal and written endorsement from the Madres de Plaza de Mayo.

*There is an alchemy in sorrow. It can be
transmuted into wisdom, which, if it does not
bring joy, can yet bring happiness.*
—PEARL BUCK

To know sorrow or to mourn is to have a realistic view of life and to realize that one is connected to the suffering of the world. A true spirituality of sorrow leads to compassion. One story that shows up in various forms in many religious traditions is about a woman overcome with grief at the death of her husband. She has tried everything to get over her loss, but nothing has worked. Someone suggests that she go and visit a spiritual master who may be able to help. When she tells him of her grief, the spiritual master says that he believes that he can help her, but he has a request. He tells her to go from house to house and to ask for one lentil bean from the inhabitants. But there is a catch. She can take the bean only from a house that has *not* known loss or sorrow. At each house she hears a story about how a wife, husband, child, or mother or father had died. Everyone seems to have experienced some kind of loss or grief. Slowly the woman realizes that death and mourning had visited each house, and she returns to the spiritual master without so much as one bean but with her grief beginning to heal.

Sorrow and grieving can be turned inward or outward. The above story suggests that outward is better. Sorrow can close us down or open us up. Being opened up is better. The spiritual path of sorrow seems clear when it becomes an avenue of communion with others. Conversely, sorrow's most deadening impact can be the isolation it sometimes fosters. "Nobody knows the troubles I've seen . . ." laments an old Negro spiritual. Sometimes it can indeed seem that way. We feel utterly alone and disconnected, sure that no one has experienced the depth of our misery. But, of course, others have—and worse misery than ours. Comparisons in this regard, however, are odious. If we play the can-you-top-this-suffering game, we are sure to lose and wind up feeling even worse about ourselves. Rather, the spiritual path of communion with the sorrow and sufferings of others provides strength in that solidarity. "No one gets out of life alive," the saying goes. That universality is the ultimate leveler. The key is how we respond to life in the midst of sorrowful circumstances that are often beyond our control.

> *You were a stranger to sorrow; therefore Fate*
> *has cursed you.*
> —EURIPIDES

A missionary friend of mine working in Pakistan, Finbar Maxwell, reminds me that in the Urdu language of the subcontinent, the word for empathy is *hamdardi,* which literally means "we share the same pain." To grow in empathy we need to understand and move through our own sorrow and suffering in order to stand in solidarity with others in theirs. In his classic book *Man's Search for Meaning,* Victor Frankl reflects on his and others' experiences of the concentration camps during the Holocaust of World War II. He writes, "To live is to suffer, but to survive is to find meaning in one's suffering." It's an important point, yet it is not an easy thing to do. In the midst of suffering we are often so consumed by it that we can see little else, least of all meaning. Only in hindsight can we absorb wisdom from the experience.

A widow of September 11 learned this lesson the hard way. Kathy Trant was the wife of Dan Trant, a forty-year-old Cantor Fitzgerald employee who was killed in the attacks on the World Trade Center. Newspapers reported that she received $4.2 million from the Federal Victims Compensation Fund— actually, she received $2.1 million and another $3 million from friends and family. In four years she went through $5 million, much of it on frivolous spending. She spent $70,000 to take six friends to the Super Bowl and $30,000 for a trip for twenty to the Bahamas. Home repairs took on new meaning as she spent $1.5 million to nearly triple the size of her suburban New York home, including $350,000 on the backyard alone, adding a full basketball court and a heated swimming pool and hot tub. She has a $500,000 shoe collection and gowns by Versace and Capelli that cost $5,000 each, as well as handbags costing $5,000 per bag. (To be fair, she didn't spend all of the money on herself. In addition to the group vacations mentioned, she also gave $15,000 to a former housekeeper to buy a home in El Salvador.)

While the ethics of such lavish spending can be debated, especially given how the money was obtained, a more nagging question in our context might be *why?* Why would a grieving widow spend such a huge sum of money given to her to compensate the loss of a husband whom she loved? One answer might be all-consuming sorrow. Kathy Trant was quoted as saying "It's blood money that I don't want. I want my husband back." She entered a deep depression after his death and used alcohol and antidepressants in an effort to dull the pain. She also used her charge card. Rather than allow the sorrow to take hold and work its way through in the normal process of grieving, Kathy tried to circumvent the process by buying herself happiness and peace of mind again. While she maintains that she simply didn't want the money and that she wanted her husband back, if that were true, she could have disbursed the money in more charitable ways. Rather, apparently, she used the money to dull the sorrow. Her hard lesson was that it didn't work. She wound up a lot less wealthy and just as sad.

In her classic work *On Death and Dying,* Elisabeth Kübler-Ross suggests that the initial stage of grief is denial. We deny in all sorts of ways. Perhaps buying our way out of sorrow is one of them. But we can buy for only so long before we run out of money and realize that the sorrow remains. Instead, sorrow must be befriended. Hard as it is, we must give sorrow a place in our hearts, even allow it to pierce our hearts at times, if eventually we are to be released from its grip and move into the world of empathy and compassion. John Climacus presents a more dramatic view: "Mourning which is according to God is a melancholy of the soul, a disposition of an anguished heart that passionately seeks what it thirsts for, and when it fails to attain it, pursues it diligently and follows behind it lamenting bitterly."

> *Genius is sorrow's child.*
> —JOHN ADAMS

Ladies in Lavender is a poignant film based on a short story by William J. Locke. Set between the First and Second World Wars, the film stars Maggie Smith and Judi Dench as two elderly sisters who live quietly in the coastal countryside of Cornwall, England. Their placid existences are turned upside down by the mysterious appearance of a young man who washes ashore near their house after a night of heavy storms. Battered by the waves and rocks, but still alive, the young man is brought to the sisters' house, where they nurse him back to health.

Although he speaks very little English, we eventually learn that the gifted man is Andrea, a Polish refugee and a master violinist who brings an unintended gift to Ursula, the sister played by Judi Dench. The gift is an opportunity to overcome the sorrow of unrequited love. Ursula, perhaps the embodiment of Yeats's line, "tread softly, because you tread on her dreams," is an elderly virgin who has long mourned a lost love. Andrea rekindles the spark of that dormant love. The audience is invited not only to witness Ursula's pain and sorrow, but also to become more conscious of some of its own losses and sorrows and to find the "gold in the shadow," as Jungian psychologist Robert Johnson might put it. The "gold in the shadow" here is mined and brought to the surface by the unwitting "gentleman caller" who gives an old woman a chance to feel love again and in the process to know joy, even in her sorrow. Although, given the ages and circumstances of Ursula and Andrea, the love must remain unrequited, the possibility of love in sorrow shines forth. The movie illustrates what is perhaps the ultimate goal: to find joy amid the sorrow.

> *Sorrow can be alleviated by good sleep, a bath*
> *and a glass of wine.*
> —SAINT THOMAS AQUINAS

In Sister Wendy Beckett's small book *Meditations on Joy,* she comments on famous and not-so-famous paintings that speak to the theme of joy. One meditation accompanies a beautiful and dramatic painting by El Greco titled *View of Toledo.* The painting shows the gray-stoned town of Toledo in the middle distance as it curves and straddles a hill. In the foreground are lush fields and vibrant trees. The sky is black with some white storm clouds, through which peeks a sliver of blue sky. Sister Wendy writes: "Joy is not a constant condition. Most people manage a settled cheerfulness, but this, however admirable, has nothing to do with joy, which flashes suddenly upon our darkness. Like the lightning in El Greco's painting, joy not merely illuminates our interior landscape but transforms it."

Maybe this hints at why Climacus presents *sorrow* as the seventh step on the ladder. He does not seem to suggest that we embrace sorrow as an end in itself—there would be no virtue in that—but rather that we "go through" the sorrows of our lives to find a certain joy that may emerge, or "peek" its way through, much the way the blue sky of El Greco's painting does. This is a joy that Sister Wendy suggests is anything but a "settled cheerfulness." Rather, it is something that "illuminates our interior landscape" and that can live even amid the little deaths of the pains and sorrows of our lives. We need to embrace the sorrows if we are to truly know the joys, for as Climacus suggests, "When we die, we will not be criticized for having failed to work miracles. We will not be accused of having failed to be theologians or contemplatives. But we will certainly have some explanation to offer to God for not having mourned unceasingly." I would add to that . . . for the sake of joy.

Questions for the Climb

1. What has been your deepest sorrow?
2. How have you found joy in the midst of sorrow?
3. Has sorrow led you to compassion?
4. Can joy exist without sorrow?

Step 8

*

Anger / Mad about You

*Holding on to anger is like grasping a hot coal
with the intent of throwing it at someone else;
you are the one who gets burned.*

—BUDDHA

I was rushing to get to downtown Manhattan for a dinner appointment with two friends, one of whom is often late. As I was leaving my office to race to the subway, a gentleman standing outside asked if he could see me for about fifteen minutes. I looked at my watch, knowing that I didn't have fifteen minutes to spare if I was to make it to the restaurant on time.

"Gee, I'm sorry, but I'm on my way to an appointment," I said, failing to mention that it was a restaurant appointment.

"Oh," he said, looking a bit disappointed.

"Can you call me and make an appointment?" I said.

"Sure, but the problem may be solved by then. But that's okay. Don't worry about it."

But I *did* worry about it—the whole train ride downtown. *What if the guy really needed to talk to a priest about something important? What was more important, him or being on time for a dinner? But would it be fair to keep Henry and Norbert waiting?*

I arrived at the restaurant on time, to find Henry already waiting at the table with a glass of wine.

"Hi, Norbert not here yet?" I said.

"No, and I haven't heard from him. But his office is only two blocks away, so he should be here any minute."

It was a very long minute. Half an hour later, and he *still* wasn't there. I could feel my temperature rising. He had done this so many times before with seemingly little remorse. *What makes him think his time and his life is more important than ours? I rushed here for nothing. He's so self-centered. It's always about* him.

By the time Norbert sauntered through the door of the restaurant, I was loaded for bear. He could tell by the look on my face that I wasn't happy.

"What's the matter with you?" he said all too glibly.

"No, the correct question is, what's the matter with *you?* What makes you think you can just keep us waiting here for over half an hour, with not so much as even a phone call? Who the hell do you think you are? You do this *all* the time."

"Fine, I apologize," he said with a sigh and without one shred of sincerity.

"No, you really don't apologize, because you don't give a crap."

"Look, I didn't have to rush from work for this. If you keep it up, I'm going to leave."

"Well, that would be your choice."

He didn't leave, but we hardly spoke the rest of the meal. I attempted to make forced, polite conversation, wanting to salvage the meal for Henry's sake, but Norbert was hardly co-operative. He dug his heels in, convinced that I was overreacting to his tardiness, while I cooled my heels, unwilling to dismiss yet one more late and unrepentant arrival. We didn't speak for weeks afterward.

Anger as soon as fed is dead.
'Tis starving makes it fat.
—EMILY DICKINSON

The climb on the ladder of John Climacus takes a bit of an unexpected turn with the eighth step. While the first three steps are concerned with a "break with the world," and the following four focus on the practice of the virtues, the next *sixteen* are classic struggles against the "passions," including the battle with the traditional Seven Deadly Sins. In that sense, this eighth step and the fifteen to follow are aspects of life to overcome before we can continue to move onward up the ladder to fulfillment. Gaining insight into how these realities can prevent one from advancing in the life of love is the goal.

Anger is one of the Seven Deadly Sins, a list that has its origins in the monastic movement, first in the cloisters of the Eastern Church. In the fifth century, John Cassian of Marseilles introduced the rules of Eastern monasticism to the West and with them a listing of *eight* deadly sins, a list later modified by Pope Gregory the Great (who dropped *accidia*—ennui—as one of the sins). Pope Gregory's list of the Seven Deadly Sins is the one with which we are currently familiar. In the secular text of the "Parson's Tale" in the *Canterbury Tales*, Geoffrey Chaucer attempts to universalize these sins and extend their reach beyond the monastic walls by using them as examples of the ordinary behavior of landlords, merchants, children, and other townsfolk. Chaucer refers to the deadly sins as "the trunk of the tree from which all others branch."

Whether anger is the trunk or a branch, there is no denying that its roots run deep in us. While a minor fight in a restaurant might not seem to warrant extreme anger, often the buildup of such everyday confrontations affects us most. From talk radio to the congested highways of our cities, anger rears its ugly head. I once read a definition of anger as "a disorderly outburst of emotion, connected with the inordinate desire to do damage, or hurt, or take revenge." We need only have experienced unbridled road rage to know the truth of that definition. Yet is it the only truth? What about good anger, or justified anger? We have been conditioned to believe that anger must be managed or controlled, but is it ever to be embraced or even celebrated?

Jesus may teach us something in this regard. He makes it quite clear in the Gospel of Matthew that he is not a fan of anger: "But I say to you, whoever is angry with his brother [or sister] will be liable to judgment, and whoever says to his brother [or sister] 'Raqa' [an insult] will be answerable to the Sanhedrin, and whoever says, 'You fool!' shall be liable to the fire of hell" (Matthew 5:22).

Yet there are examples of this peace-loving Jesus getting angry:

> When it was almost time for the Jewish Passover, Jesus went up to Jerusalem. In the temple courts he found men selling cattle, sheep and doves, and others sitting at tables exchanging money. So he made a whip out of cords, and drove all from the temple area, both sheep and cattle; he scattered the coins of the money changers and overturned their tables. To those who sold doves he said, "Get these out of here!"
>
> (JOHN 2:13–16A, NIV)

Another time he went into the synagogue, and a man with a shriveled hand was there. Some of them were looking for a reason to accuse Jesus, so they watched him closely to see if he would heal him on the Sabbath. Jesus said to the man with the shriveled hand, "Stand up in front of everyone." Then Jesus asked them, "Which is lawful on the Sabbath: to do good or to do evil, to save life or to kill?" But they remained silent. He looked around at them in *anger* and, deeply distressed at their stubborn hearts, said to the man, "Stretch out your hand." He stretched it out, and his hand was completely restored. Then the Pharisees went out and began to plot with the Herodians how they might kill Jesus.

(MARK 3:1–6, NIV; EMPHASIS ADDED)

Jesus is no doubt angry in these passages but it seems as though both the motivation for and the result of the anger are crucial to evaluating the justification for it. In the case of the moneychangers in the temple, Jesus was railing against those who were taking advantage of the poor and at the money-changers' blatant disrespect for God's house of worship. In the encounter with the man with the shriveled hand, Jesus is angered by the Pharisees' inability to allow compassion to transcend man-made law. The Pharisees are putting protocol above human need. Jesus' anger in both instances is a righteous anger.

John Climacus, however, doesn't seem to be discussing this kind of anger when he writes: "Angry people, because of their self-esteem, make a pitiable sight, though they do not realize this themselves. They get angry and then, when thwarted, they become furious. . . . So then, anger the oppressor must be restrained by the chains of meekness, beaten by patience, hauled away by blessed love."

For every minute you remain angry, you give
up sixty seconds of peace of mind.
—RALPH WALDO EMERSON

Climacus's description of anger does not seem to point to an emotion that is good for the soul. It is the kind of anger that can eat us up inside, the kind of anger that destroys souls. I remember giving a retreat for a group of nuns in the Midwest, and one asked to speak to me privately. She had been having some health issues—stomach problems and an inability to sleep. Doctors were at a loss at what to prescribe, though they thought that perhaps she had a stomach ulcer that eluded treatment.

"Do you feel bad most of the time?" I asked.

"No, I wouldn't say most of the time. It comes and goes." She was in her seventies and had some trouble making eye contact with me. Perhaps it was a vestige of the era when nuns didn't look at priests head on, and vice versa.

"Do you notice any pattern to when you feel more ill?"

She hesitated, looking out at the window behind me. I could tell she wanted to speak but something was preventing her from doing so.

"Sister?"

"Well . . . I think it may have something to do with a sister that I live with here. I've just been thinking that recently."

"What about her?" I said.

"We don't get along. And we haven't for many years."

"Have you spoken to her about what the problem is?"

"No."

"May I ask why?"

"A couple of years ago that woman publicly humiliated me." The nun sat straight up and began waving her index finger. "And from that day onward I've felt this way about her. I can't stand her. I'm embarrassed to say it to you, Father, but even now, when the woman walks in the room, I can feel my face flush." As a matter of fact, it was flushing as she said those words to me.

I was silent for a moment, trying to let this acknowledgment and insight sink in.

"Okay, now, Sister, tell me something. What about if you were to sit down with her and tell her what you've been feeling and why? To try to move beyond it after these years have now passed. Could you do that?"

"I'm not sure," she said, wringing her hands on her lap.

"Why not?"

She looked at me straight on and said, "Because it would give her the upper hand then. She was the one who was wrong. Not me. *She* should be the one to ask me about it. *She* should be the one to apologize."

"You may be right, Sister, but she may not even be aware how much you've been affected by what she did. Instead of dealing with the cause of this anger, you're allowing yourself to get sick over it."

"That's not a conscious choice."

"But it is *now* if you still refuse to confront her about why you are so angry."

I never asked the nun what the humiliation was. It didn't really matter. Its effect did, however. She had chosen to allow one instance to affect eighteen years of her life without confronting it head on. I left the convent not knowing if she ever took my advice, but later I thought that maybe she had needed to hold on to that anger. Sometimes it's easier than letting it go. Once you let anger go, you not only have to deal with its cause, you also have to relinquish it as an excuse for what may be wrong in your life. Then you have only yourself to deal with. And some of us would rather have anger as our protector.

> *Anger is a killing thing: it kills the man who angers, for each rage leaves him less than he had been before—it takes something from him.*
>
> —LOUIS L'AMOUR

As we know all too well, anger negatively affects not only individuals but whole societies. We need look no further than the horrific events of September 11 to see that. The anger of militant Islam against the United States was on full display as the World Trade Center towers came crashing down, surprising many in the United States who had not fully understood the extent of anti-American hatred. While Ayatollah Khomeini's slogan "Death to America" was heard round the world in bombings of U.S. embassies, planes, and ships in the years following his ascent to power in Iran in 1979, it was not until the attack on our own shores that the message was finally driven home.

This perception of anger gone awry in the Islamic world is particularly disturbing when we consider the teachings of Muhammad, who spoke regularly against being angry. Yet militant Islam justifies its anger and violence through claims that the United States has stolen Muslim resources, exploited its labor, and undermined its religion. A holy jihad, these Islamists argue, is the only sensible response.

Herein lies the problem with anger. While it can be argued

that some anger is justified, such as the righteous anger against injustice, the proper channeling of the anger must be debated. No one would dispute, for example, that the race riots of the 1960s in the United States were the result of anger too long unacknowledged; however, Martin Luther King Jr. preached another way to channel that anger: nonviolent resistance. King realized that violence on the part of civil rights workers would simply lead to violent counterattacks from segregationists. The cycle of violence is self-perpetuating. Anger indeed needs an outlet, for anger turned inward is self-destructive. (In fact, psychologists suggest that as the classic definition of depression.)

> When angry, count to four;
> when very angry, swear.
> —MARK TWAIN

The major problem with the nun who got sick from her anger was that she had turned her anger inward, refusing to give it voice. In that sense, anger does indeed become a deadly sin, in that it slowly kills us from the inside out. People who harbor anger as a result of a bloody divorce or a contested will sometimes speak of the same slow death. Some doctors are convinced that unresolved anger can cause migraines and even cancer. So what do we do with all of this malady-inducing anger?

The choice of life takes the path of love. The path of love does not pretend that everything is hunky dory and that injustice does not exist. Rather, the path of love calls us to acknowledge the injustice and then to work to address it in creative and loving ways. While physical violence, revenge, and ill will are never acceptable options on the path of love, anger need not be totally excised from that path, for a righteous anger can be a step toward a loving response. Righteous anger can be constructive, but festering anger never is.

Minor as the restaurant altercation with Norbert was, my anger had begun to fester. Four weeks after our acrimonious dinner, I decided to call him. I had hoped he would call, since I perceived him as having been at fault, but a friend suggested that I take the first step, so I reluctantly dialed the phone. Our conversation went this way.

"Hello."

"Hi, Norbert. It's Edward."

"Oh, hi. Haven't spoken to you in a while."

"No, but I thought maybe it was time."

"Uh-huh."

"Does that mean you think it's time, too?" I asked.

"Yeah, I guess so," he said. I could tell he was still a bit tentative, not knowing what this call would mean.

"Well, I wanted to tell you that I feel bad about our fight in the restaurant, but I was just really mad, and you didn't seem to care or to acknowledge that maybe my anger was justified."

"I think I just got defensive right away because I could tell from your face you were mad. I fought back without listening. I shouldn't have done that. Sorry."

"Yeah, and I should have told you more reasonably why I was so angry. We should have talked about it rather than yelled about it. I'm sorry, too."

"Well, we can talk about it now, can't we?" he said.

"Yes, we can," I said. And we did.

> *On the eighth step the crown is freedom from anger. He*
> *who wears it by nature may never come to wear another.*

But he who has sweated for it and won it has conquered
all eight together.

(CLIMACUS, STEP 8)

Questions for the Climb

1. Do you think that you deal with anger well? Why?
2. Has anger ever made you sick?
3. Have you experienced righteous anger?
4. Is it okay for you to be angry at God?

Step 9

＊

Malice / Look Out, Girl, 'Cause I'm Gonna Get You

*It is deplorable that homosexual persons have
been and are the object of violent malice in
speech or in action. Such treatment deserves
condemnation from the Church's pastors
wherever it occurs. . . . The intrinsic dignity of
each person must always be respected in work,
in action and in law.*
—JOSEPH CARDINAL RATZINGER,
NOW POPE BENEDICT XVI

*Malice: A desire to harm others or to see others suffer; extreme ill
will or spite.* It may be surprising to discover that one of the
steps on the ladder of Saint John Climacus is a disposition so
at odds with the spiritual pursuit. At first we might not even
recognize malice as part of us, but upon reflection we may realize that we are indeed capable of malice. We benefit by ex-
ploring our potential for malice, if only to unmask its insidious
power.

I once heard a spiritual teacher say that one of the avenues to forgiveness is to realize that we are all capable of all of it— "it" being the worst action or thought that we could imagine. His point was that our heart expands to permit forgiveness only once we acknowledge that, given a "perfect storm" of circumstances, we, too, could perpetrate the same act by which we feel hurt or betrayed. When we recognize that we are capable of *all of it*, judgment subsides and compassion emerges, enabling understanding and forgiveness. Making peace with that potential for malice helps to disarm its power and, ultimately, to banish it from our lives. "Never imagine that this dark vice is a passion of no importance for it often reaches out even to spiritual men" (Climacus).

Many years ago I saw the effects of malice played out in dramatic relief while acting in an Off-Broadway show. The lead was a talented girl who had as much ambition as talent. During the auditions she had competed with another girl. There were multiple call-backs with both girls going head to head to enable the creative team to make their final choice. During breaks from the long and grueling process the girls seemed strained, each saying that the delayed decision had unnerved her. With the rest of the show having already been cast, the girls obviously were feeling the pressure.

The day the role was awarded I happened to be with Colleen, the girl who lost out. Her agent called to break the bad news to her, but also to tell her that she was being offered the role of understudy for the lead as well as a small part in the play. The classic *All About Eve* scenario could not have been staged more perfectly. Colleen cried when she hung up the phone.

"How could they have chosen *her*?" she asked me. "You were there for some of the auditions. You know I was better than she was. I don't understand it." I felt sorry for her and not quite sure what to say.

"Well, sometimes they're looking for one particular thing," I finally replied. "And maybe she had it. It's not better than, just different. There'll be other roles. You're so talented."

"Yeah, well, what if there *aren't* other roles?" she said. "Can you tell me for sure that this wasn't my one shot? *Can you?*" Tears streamed down her cheeks.

"No, I can't tell you anything for sure. But I highly doubt this was your only chance for a lead. If you are meant to do this, it will happen. You just have to keep at it. It will be okay. It will." I tried to hug her, but she turned away from me.

"Could you please just go? I need to be alone for a while," she said, facing the wall.

"Sure," I said. "I'll see you at rehearsals tomorrow. Give me a call if you need to talk." I touched her shoulder and left without her turning to face me.

Colleen was late for rehearsals the next day and barely spoke to anyone. She did the minimum of what she had to and left as soon as we ended.

"God, she's such a sore loser," I heard the victor say in the hallway during a fifteen-minute break.

It turned out that Colleen was more than just a sore loser. The next day, before rehearsals began, the director called everyone to the stage to tell us that rehearsals would be suspended indefinitely because Justine, the lead, had been injured in a car accident. Some cast members gasped, and then everyone fell silent.

"How badly injured is she?" one of the girls finally asked.

"Bad enough," the director said. "She'll be hospitalized for several weeks."

"What about Colleen? Can't she step in until then?" another cast member asked.

"No, I'm afraid not," said the director. "It seems as though she was driving the car that hit Justine. They're trying to determine now if it was an accident or not. In any event, Colleen won't be returning to the show. That's all the information I have. We'll be in touch if we find a way to proceed. Thank you."

The show never did go on. Colleen was eventually convicted of running down Justine deliberately and sentenced to a short jail term and community service. I met with her once to talk about what had happened. She said that she had been so overcome with anger that she just lost her mind and wanted to hurt Justine in whatever way she could. She said it felt like she was a possessed woman.

Malice sucks up the greater part of her own venom, and poisons herself.
—MICHEL DE MONTAIGNE

Malice is not a light emotion that we can simply brush off. We must pay attention to *extreme ill will.* When our anger reaches such fever pitch that we consider actually hurting another person, we need serious counseling or spiritual guidance. Ideally, it doesn't take jail time to make us realize that.

I think John Climacus understood the negative power of malice; that's why he includes it as a step to be negotiated on his ladder toward more perfect love. "The holy virtues are like the ladder of Jacob and the unholy vices are like the chains that fell off the chief apostle Peter. The virtues lead from one to another and carry heavenward the man who chooses them. Vices on the other hand beget and stifle one another" (Climacus, Step 9).

Remember, Climacus was writing specifically for monks; it is striking to note that no one is exempt from human emotions that have the potential to inflict harm and destruction. "A malicious hesychast [hermit/monk] is like a lurking snake carrying about its own deadly poison" (Climacus, Step 9). Having lived in a few monasteries myself, I can attest to the existence of malice, even among the holy monks whom we think should know and act better. I've witnessed this especially in power struggles for leadership within the community. While in our piety we attest that our leaders are elected by the movement of the Holy Spirit, the movement of some conniving monks also can have a hand in ecclesiastical politics. Good reputations have been marred by bold lies told so that certain candidates might advance while others are forced to retreat in unwarranted shame. I remember one instance when a fabricated psychological illness and the sexual impropriety of one of the candidates were implied to make sure that he never made it to the winner's circle. It was vicious and cruel, especially within the confines of a monastic cloister. But malice knows no boundaries.

I have sat in a counseling room with wounded people attempting to recover from bloody divorces. Their hurt and pain is raw. Their malice toward the demonized spouse is sometimes hard to witness. "I wish he were dead." "His next wife should get cancer." "If I had the chance, I'd cut off his penis myself." "If she begged me to take her back, I'd spit in her face." These are some of the comments that I've heard supposedly practicing Catholics make—and to a priest, no less. I can only imagine what they say when no self-censoring exists (assuming, of course, that a white collar encourages some modicum of restraint).

Family rifts are not the exclusive preserve of troubled marriages. Often such vitriol extends to siblings who are embroiled in protracted legal squabbles about estates and contested wills. I have also been privy to my share of those take-no-prisoners bouts. I recall one man who systematically drugged his unwitting brother to make him appear incompetent to share in the financial largesse of their parents' will. It is shocking how people with lifelong histories of familial connection can be driven to the point of such extreme actions. Malice invades hearts and turns them black. Vigilance is needed to protect against such cooption.

So then, how do we protect our hearts from such a metamorphosis? Religious traditions have long maintained the need to guard against evil taking up residence. The purpose of prayer, spiritual exercises, examination of conscience, and spiritual direction is to assure connection with the soul/spirit dimension of our lives. The unexamined spirit soon becomes no spirit at all.

If malice or envy were tangible and had a
shape, it would be the shape of a boomerang.

—CHARLEY REESE

In chapter 3 of the Gospel of John Jesus tries to teach this truth to Nicodemus, a religious leader who comes to see Jesus "at night," (a signal that Nicodemus is in darkness). Jesus says to him, "Truly, truly, I say to you, unless one is born anew, he cannot see the kingdom of God" (3:3, RSV). Nicodemus is confused and assumes Jesus is talking about physical birth, but Jesus explains: "Truly, truly, I say to you, unless one is born of water and the Spirit, he cannot enter the kingdom of God. That which is born of the flesh is flesh, and that which is born of the Spirit is spirit. Do not marvel that I said to you, 'You must be born anew' " (3:5–7, RSV). Jesus is attempting to get Nicodemus to see that we are both flesh and spirit, and unless we attend to the spiritual dimension of our lives, it grows dark and inaccessible. It is our spiritual dimension that allows us to choose goodness instead of malice.

Jesus goes on to say: "And this is the verdict, that the light came into the world, but people preferred darkness to light, because their works were evil. For everyone who does wicked things hates the light and does not come towards the light, so that his works might not be exposed. But whoever lives the truth comes to the light, so that his works may be clearly seen as done in God" (3:19–21).

Jesus points to an important dynamic of the soul. When we have something to hide, we run away from being exposed. We choose the anonymity of darkness, lest our deeds be discovered. When malice invades our hearts, we may choose to disguise it, fearful of the destructive force that it is. Movement toward the light and toward disclosure of the less than perfect parts of ourselves may assist in our dealing with negative passions, such as malice, that can easily overtake us in the darkness of our secrecy and shame.

> *With malice toward none, with charity for all,*
> *with firmness in the right as God gives us to see*
> *the right, let us strive on to finish the work we*
> *are in, to bind up the nation's wounds . . .*
> —ABRAHAM LINCOLN

I once had a girl come to speak to me who felt terrible malice toward her more popular sister. But it was a forbidden emotion because she was supposed to love her sister. After all, her sister was a champion tennis player, bright, well respected, and a nice person. How could the girl not like her? Of course, the malice she felt had more to do with herself than with her more popular sister, but until she was able to acknowledge the extent of her malice, she was unable to be released from it.

"I wish bad things would happen to her, like she would break her leg on the tennis court," she said. "But I could never tell anyone that I really feel that way. It just seems so wrong. And I think I'd feel just terrible if it actually happened."

"Do you think maybe you feel that way because she gets more attention than you do?" I said.

"Probably," she said. "But she deserves more attention than I do. She's more talented than I am."

"But if you keep on comparing yourself, you'll always feel like the loser. Maybe if you focus on your unique gifts, then hers won't be such a threat."

We worked for a number of months on getting her to recognize her assets and to delight in them. While the negative feelings toward her sister were not totally expelled, after a while the malice disappeared. She no longer wished her sister ill and was well on the road toward a better relationship with her sister.

"If after great effort you still fail to root out this thorn of malice, go to your enemy and apologize, if only with empty words whose insincerity may shame you. Then as conscience, like a fire, comes to give you pain, you may find that a sincere love of your enemy may come to life" (Climacus, Step 9).

*Gossip is always a personal confession
of malice or imbecility.*
—JACK HOLLAND

Last, as a religious priest I feel some obligation to say something about malice present in the midst of religious traditions that profess to act otherwise. I will never forget the vitriol of one religious group for another that I experienced in one of the most sacred spots in the religious world—the Church of the Holy Sepulchre in Jerusalem. I was studying in Israel for three months and had come to expect the animosity that I witnessed between the Jews and the Palestinians. What I did not expect was a similar enmity between various sects of Christianity, all on display in the Church of the Holy Sepulchre, which marks the spot where the resurrection of Jesus was supposed to have occurred.

I remember praying at the spot of the Resurrection and hearing angry yelling. I turned to the guide for some explanation.

"Oh, pay no attention to that," he said. "They fight all day long. Always have, always will."

I learned that interdenominational wrangling occurred regarding everything from the restoration of the church to the proposed route of the Easter procession. The animosity between the Greek and Russian Orthodox and the Latins (Roman Catholics) extends back to the Great Schism between the Western and Eastern Churches in 1054. We might be tempted to say that animosity isn't the same as malice, until we trace the history and see that extreme ill will is indeed present. The Catholic Franciscans claim that the Greek Orthodox deliberately set the Great Fire in the Church of the Holy Sepulchre in 1808. A few Crusader tombs were destroyed, and the Franciscans still hold the Greeks responsible.

The church continues to be divided up among the various sects—Syrians, Greeks, Latins, Armenians, Ethiopians, Copts—with each having its own strict set of rules. If one group dares venture into the domain of another, all hell breaks loose.

"You can't have a Coptic priest sweeping the steps of the Armenian chapel without a riot breaking out," said one guide.

Ironically, members of a Muslim Turkish family serve as guardians of the church and hold the keys. They seem to be the only neutral ones whom the Christians trust.

My father, a former firefighter in New York City, once said to me: "Hate is a dangerous thing. It has no prejudice. It can affect everyone." Referring to the racial tensions in New York in the mid-1970s, he talked about riding on the back of the fire truck and having bricks thrown at him by people in the streets for no apparent reason.

"But why would people who didn't even know you want to hurt you?" I said.

"It wasn't me they wanted to hurt. It was what they thought I represented. Power, privilege, opportunity. Everything they didn't have. They were doing to us what they felt had been done to them."

Malice is like that. We can't be.

Questions for the Climb

1. Have you ever felt extreme ill will toward someone? How did you work through those feelings?
2. Do you believe that you are indeed capable of "all of it"?
3. Did you ever feel malice toward a family member? How did it differ from other times you have felt malice?
4. Does your spirituality/religion/faith help you to overcome feelings of malice? How or how not?

Step 10

*

Slander / Scandal Brewing

*Slander is a poison which kills charity, both in
the slanderer and the one who listens.*

—SAINT BERNARD

Have you ever had someone tell a lie about you? It's a pretty
helpless feeling. You can dispute the lie, but once it is uttered,
it cannot be taken back. It takes on a life of its own. Even if
shown to be untrue, the lie exists in memory, at times destroying reputations and lives. Perhaps this is why slander has been
seen as such a major offense by religious traditions. John Climacus begins his chapter on slander by writing "Slander is the
offspring of hatred, a subtle and yet crass disease, a leech in hiding and escaping notice, wasting and draining away the
lifeblood of love. It puts on the appearance of love and is the
ambassador of an unholy and unclean heart."

The admonition against slander also is included in the sacred Decalogue received by Moses from God on Mount Sinai.
The Eighth Commandment is: "You shall not bear false witness
against your neighbor" (Exodus 20:16). In the New Testament,

slanderers fare even worse than those who simply make false statements against another. Paul's letter to the Romans (1:30) seems to be an admonition to the early Church to refrain not only from false statements but from hostile and malicious speech against a neighbor. Slander in the early Christian community continues to be a primary concern of Paul in his other letters (2 Timothy 3:3, Ephesians 4:31, Colossians 3:8, 1 Timothy 6:4, 1 Timothy 5:13).

Margaret, a friend of mine, suffered the ill effects of slander in such a radical way that she needed to consult with a psychologist in order to cope. The slander came in the guise of sweetness that, beneath the surface, turned out to be bitter animosity and rage.

My friend, a respected professional in her field, had been working at a pharmaceutical company in California for a number of years when another woman, Judy, was hired as an associate in her office. Judy was single, not very attractive, yet bright and competent. She gushed with gooey sentiment every time she saw Margaret. "You are just so talented. Such a fine researcher. You're so lucky to have the high respect of your colleagues. And you're so pretty on top of it all."

While Margaret was appreciative and flattered by the compliments, something about Judy didn't sit well with Margaret. She chalked it up to quirkiness and social awkwardness and didn't give it much thought. Until things began to happen.

One day as Margaret was returning to her office, one of her male colleagues called after her.

"Hey, Margaret, got a minute?" It turned out to be more than a minute.

"I don't understand why she is trashing you this way," he said, after telling Margaret about an e-mail that Judy had sent to the whole office in which she had written about Margaret's incompetence and disorganization. Judy had to have realized that the contents of the e-mail eventually would make its way back to Margaret.

"She basically says that you shouldn't really have the position you have in the company," he went on to say, "and that we've all been blindsided by you. It's pretty severe in its tone."

"But why would she say something like that?" Margaret asked. "She's always so nice to me to my face."

"I don't know," he said. "But you better get to the bottom of it before this goes too far. This woman is out of control."

Margaret spoke to a few people, including her husband, about what she should do. Everyone agreed that she needed to confront Judy about the e-mail, but Margaret seemed powerless to do so.

"I wasn't sure what I would say to her," Margaret told me. "I suddenly felt intimidated by her and wondered if I could get through a face-to-face meeting with her without breaking down or blowing up. I decided it'd be best to let the higher-ups handle it."

But they didn't, dismissing it as "no big deal." "Probably just an e-mail that was fired off without much thought," said her boss. "Just let it go. It'll all be forgotten."

Margaret did try to forget it, but she was on her guard with Judy from then on. Judy's excessive sweetness continued. Margaret smiled back politely, knowing both were playing some kind of sick game in which Margaret wasn't sure of any of the rules or penalties.

Things seemed to settle down after a while, but then it all exploded with even more combustion.

"Margaret, I don't know if you're aware of this, but Judy is insinuating that you're using your female prowess to get the men in the office to like you."

Margaret and a male colleague were having lunch in the company dining room when he unloaded this bombshell.

"What? What are you talking about?" said Margaret.

"I'm telling you that she's hinting all over the place that you use your prettiness and sexuality to get what you want. And she's not very diplomatic about how she makes the accusations either."

"I can't believe she'd do such a thing. What does she have against me?"

"I have no idea. But you really can't let it continue. While I know that none of it is true, and I'm sure many in the office know it, too, she is systematically calling your reputation into question in every area. And once the damage is done, it will be very hard to repair it."

Margaret left the lunch feeling sick. She had no clue as to why Judy was out to get her. They had never had a confrontation or even a professional disagreement. She decided to seek counsel from a priest spiritual director.

"It seems very clear to me what's going on," he told her.

"Well then, please fill me in, because I'm at a loss," said Margaret.

"Look, it's pretty classic. She's threatened by you. And if she does you in, maybe she can feel better about herself."

"But she has no reason *not* to feel good," Margaret replied. "She's competent and extremely bright. She's a great researcher, better than I am, in fact. Why in the world would she feel threatened by me?"

"Margaret, open your eyes. You're pretty. She's not. You have a husband and great children. She doesn't. You get asked to lead seminars all over the country. She doesn't. You're hailed for your research. She has barely begun to make her mark. And you wonder why she's threatened by you?"

Obvious as it may have been to others, Margaret felt devastated and embarrassed, even though she had done nothing wrong. Wanting to avoid contact with Judy, Margaret began retreating from office functions and company gatherings. A mild depression set in that sent her to a therapist for six months. When Margaret finally felt strong enough to confront Judy about the accusations, Judy brushed it all off as complete misunderstandings, claiming that she had nothing but respect and admiration for Margaret.

When presented with specific instances of her slander, Judy merely said, "Well, you know people often have difficulty understanding what I'm really saying. I'm not always the best communicator. I really do have to work at that. Thanks so much for bringing it to my attention." In Margaret's opinion, Judy was one of the best communicators she had ever met. Unfortunately, what she communicated were defaming lies that caused a wide circle of hurt and suspicion that took years to get beyond. "Like the forked, two-edged tongue of the serpent, so is that of the slanderer, who at one dart pricks and poisons the ear of those who hear him, and the reputation of him who is slandered" (Aristotle).

> *It takes an enemy and a friend, working together, to hurt you to the heart. The one to slander you, and the other to get the news to you.*
>
> —MARK TWAIN

Margaret's spiritual guide named a fundamental truth regarding slander: It often is rooted in the need to tear down another so that the slanderer can build up him- or herself. Human insecurity can be a dangerous thing because often it is ameliorated, at least temporarily, by destroying someone else. If we can make another person look bad, or at least worse than we do, then maybe we can look better, or so goes the distorted reasoning.

In *An Experience Named Spirit,* the theologian and author John Shea characterizes this dynamic as the "shadow of the Envious Heart." The envious person never feels as though he or she has enough and is diminished whenever near someone who seems to have more. This heart is lured into a cycle of anxious striving and self-deception, and invariably it feeds on the oppression of others. As Shea says:

> This heart only knows who it is when it knows who it is not. . . . If it is our knowledge that makes us loveable, then we have a vested interest in other people's ignorance. If it is our wealth, we have a personal stake in other people's poverty. If it is our goodness, then other people must be designated sinners. If it is prestige, then other people must be downtrodden. We only know ourselves as loveable when other people do not have the possessions or qualities that make us loveable. Making ourselves loveable means making other people unloveable. All our efforts to build ourselves up mean that other people are automatically put down. . . . And so the envious heart schemes to take their pleasing qualities or possessions away from them. We torch a reputation for goodness to secure our own self-righteousness. We climb the economic ladder delighting in the fact we leave people behind on lower rungs. Those perceived as more pleasing we struggle to surpass or demean; those perceived as less pleasing we keep in their place. . . . We flaunt our higher position so that other people do not forget their lower status. We preen our beauty to remind the ugly of their mirror. We parade our learning so the empty-headed will not presume to question us.

(THOMAS MORE PRESS, 1983, CHICAGO, PP. 161–162)

If some people cannot attain self-esteem with the truth, they resort to slander. One religious luminary who understood slander's potential malignancy was Saint Francis de Sales (1567–1622). Bishop of Geneva and founder (along with Saint Jane de Chantal) of religious communities, de Sales is perhaps best known for his *Introduction to the Devout Life,* which religious scholars have called a masterpiece of psychology, practical morality, and common sense. In this treatise de Sales asserts that holiness is accessible to everyone. In part III he focuses on the practice of virtue as a path to holiness.

In chapter 29 of this part, entitled "On Slander," de Sales maintains that "slander is a kind of murder; for we all have three lives—a spiritual life, which depends upon the Grace of God; a bodily life, depending on the soul; and a civil life, consisting in a good reputation. Sin deprives us of the first, death of the second, and slander of the third. But the slanderer commits three several murders with his idle tongue: he destroys his own soul and that of him who hearkens, as well as causing civil death to the object of his slander."

De Sales goes on to say that one of the most insidious forms of slander is that done with affectation of goodwill or with dishonest pretenses of friendliness. (We need only recall Margaret and Judy to see the truth of his declaration.) We build up the person with one hand, so that our other hand can pull him or her down with even more force. He continues: "Witty slander is the most mischievous of all; for just as some poisons are but feeble when taken alone, which become powerful when mixed with wine, so many a slander, which would go in at one ear and out at the other of itself, find a resting-place in the listener's brain when it is accompanied with amusing, witty comments. 'The poison of asps is under their lips.'"

Some people fall into this manner of relating without even realizing the destruction they are causing. In Step 10 John Climacus says, "I have rebuked people who were engaged in slander, and in self-defense, these evildoers claimed to be acting out of love and concern for the victim of their slander. My answer to that was to say: 'Then stop that kind of love . . . If, as you insist, you love that man, then do not be making a mockery of him, but pray for him in secret.' "

> *Truth is generally the best vindication*
> *against slander.*
> —ABRAHAM LINCOLN

Often slander occurs as the result of making a judgment against a person. Slander may give that judgment the teeth that empirical evidence might not supply. We judge someone to be acting wrongly or inappropriately, so we take it upon ourselves to remedy those actions by whatever means are at our disposal. Sometimes slander is the sharpest arrow in our quiver. Yet both Francis de Sales and John Climacus speak against such judging and the slander to which it often leads. Climacus says, "Do not condemn. Not even if your very eyes are seeing something, for they may be deceived. . . . Do not start passing judgment on the offender—Judas was one of the company of Christ's disciples and the robber was in the company of killers. Yet what a turnabout there was when the decisive moment arrived!"

De Sales writes something similar: "If God's mercy is so great, that one single moment is sufficient for it to justify and save a man, what assurance have we that he who yesterday was a sinner is the same today? Yesterday may not be the judge of today, nor today of yesterday; all will be really judged at the

Last Great Day. In short, we can never affirm a man to be evil without running the risk of lying" (chapter 29).

The *Oxford English Dictionary*'s definition of "slander" is accompanied by its French equivalent: *sclaundre, esclaundre, es-clandre, escandle (scandal)*. Slander takes on another dimension when considering its etymology. As related to scandal, slander can be seen to have qualities that are both passive (something done to someone by another) and active (something done by the person him- or herself). Just as we are called not to slander another, we, too, are expected not to be scandalous (slanderous) in our own behavior.

Slander is a step on our ladder to contemplate because sometimes we find ourselves its victims and other times its perpetrators. Both are scandalous. Whatever side of the fence we find ourselves on, the outcome is the same: destruction. Whether we torch a reputation for our own purposes or we find ourselves maligned for the sake of someone else's designs, there is no good that comes from slander. Rooted in insecurity and detached from reality, slander begins as words uttered and ends in lives destroyed. The surest way to prevent that destruction is to imprison malicious words with utmost diligence—which brings us to Step 11.

Questions for the Climb

1. Have you ever been the victim of slander? What did you do about it?
2. Have you ever been a slanderer? What caused you to be so?
3. Have you ever masked slander with sweetness or supposed concern?
4. Does your faith/spirituality/morality help you to resist slander?

Talkativeness / Words, Words, Words

*Much talking is the cause of danger. Silence is
the means of avoiding misfortune. The
talkative parrot is shut up in a cage. Other
birds, without speech, fly freely about.*

—SASKYA PANDITA

Why is it that so few people seem able to listen? Could it be
that we are all too busy talking? "You Talk Too Much," a hit
song in 1960 by Joe Jones and the Dixie Cups, was a tongue-
in-cheek reminder that verbal overload is not a new phenom-
enon. We live in a word-saturated world, from the talking
heads on TV cable networks, to the annoying telemarketers
and computer-generated voices that disturb our evening
dinners. Everybody is prattling on about something—blah-
blah, blah-blah, yada, yada, yada. But is anybody listening?

Perhaps not wanting to be accused of verbosity, John Climacus gives a scant page and a half commentary on this step
in *The Ladder of Divine Ascent*. "Talkativeness is the throne of
the vainglory on which it loves to preen itself and show off,"

he writes. "I would prefer not to write too much about this, despite the urgings of my wily passions. . . . It is hard to keep water in without a dike. But it is harder still to hold one's tongue."

Observation suggests it is indeed hard for people to hold their tongues. Have you ever noticed how difficult it is for most people to stop talking and actually listen to what you are saying? Even dear friends seem to have a hard time listening. Before you can say *I*, they are already talking about *me* again. Just as you begin speaking you see that familiar glazed look, a precursor to the other person precipitously interjecting: "Well, that happened to me, too . . ." or "It makes me think of the time . . ." or "I know exactly what you're talking about because I'm in the same situation . . ." It can be maddening. (Of course, we probably do the same and are unaware of it.)

Published reports of a 2005 Medco Health Solutions study seem to support my anecdotal evidence. The study claims that the use of drugs to treat attention-deficit hyperactivity disorder in younger adults (ages twenty to forty-four) more than doubled from 2000 to 2004 and that spending on the drugs more than quadrupled. The use of medications for attention-deficit disorder grew faster in those years than the use of any other class of medication except treatments for rheumatoid arthritis. That trend seems to have continued in recent years.

So now, in addition to our children's inability to focus, science tells us that adults are scattered, as well. This comes as no surprise to some of us hoping to utter more than two sentences without being interrupted. While attention-deficit disorder is more complex than an inability to listen, it suggests a society so overstimulated that the normal rhythm of give-and-take relating is being compromised.

I have learnt silence from the talkative,
toleration from the intolerant, and kindness
from the unkind; yet strange, I am ungrateful
to these teachers.

—KAHLIL GIBRAN

I was staying with a priest friend in Florida for a few days in between preaching assignments. He owns his own home, a welcome respite from the rigors of his parochial ministry. Respite for him . . . hell for me. He had a remote control for everything and fingered them with a dexterity that was awe-inspiring.

"Philip, do you realize that you have two televisions, a radio, two computers, and a mini-DVD player all going at the same time?" I said.

He looked around at the panoply of technical wizardry lining his walls and tables and said, "Yeah, so?"

"But how do you *hear* anything?"

"I get bored easily," he said, and shrugged.

I am not suggesting that I am without my own distractions and diversions. At times I should resist my tendency to escape into the world of cinema and theater and linger longer in the pools of silence and reflection. I'm more focused when I take the time to be quiet, to reflect, to actively listen. But the spiritual discipline of silence is not easily cultivated in our noisy world. The type A side of me often wins out and spins me into activity that externally may appear more productive. This may be why religious traditions have long exhorted followers to allow silence to become part of their daily regimens. As it says in Ecclesiastes: "Be not hasty in your utterance and let not your heart be quick to make a promise in God's presence. God is in heaven and you are on earth; therefore let your words be few" (5:1–2).

Silence as a virtue is at the core of monastic (literally, "act of dwelling alone") spirituality, beginning with the solitary desert fathers and mothers of Eastern monasticism. Some of these monks were stylites, or pole-sitters, living on the tops of poles as a penitential, solitary experience. They believed that the predominant silence made the few words they might speak more valuable to hear. While their lifestyle seems extreme to us, numerous pilgrims sought out the pole-sitters for their sage counsel.

In today's Western monasticism, the monks who vow silence (at least for certain times during each day) believe that God comes to those who are disposed to listen. They refer to it as "active listening," which can occur only in the silence of one's heart. The Benedictine monk David Steindl-Rast calls this silence "God bathing." Another renowned monk, Thomas Merton, said that silence is "the mother of truth," while yet another famous contemporary Cistercian, Thomas Keating, called silence "God's first language." Monks learn that the space of silence can be more valuable than words, but to find inner quietude, one must make room for it.

The challenge is making room for it. In our busy lives perhaps we talk so much because we're not sure what else to do. Sitting still can seem like wasting time. Productivity has been so engrained in us that a contemplative stance toward life may seem wasteful or even lazy, until we discover that contemplation can be more productive than all our prattling and running around. Contemplation affords us the opportunity to be in the moment, to be attentive to what is, rather than perhaps missing what is right in front of us. Decisions that are prayed about, reflected upon, and revisited once again are surely more valuable than those we rush into with no forethought. An hour spent in prayerful contemplation may be more beneficial than eight hours of trying actively to "talk out" a problem.

> 'Tis better to be silent and be thought a fool,
> than to speak and remove all doubt.
>
> —ABRAHAM LINCOLN

Diane Perry, born in 1943 in London, learned this lesson from choosing a life she knew she was born to live but that others saw as unbalanced. Her story is told in a 1999 book by Vicki Mackenzie titled *Cave in the Snow.* The daughter of a fishmonger, Perry loved silence as a child and in her late teens was attracted to Buddhism. She went to India when she was twenty and became a Tibetan Buddhist nun, only the second Western woman to do so, and changed her name to Tenzin Palmo.

While spending twelve years in a Himalayan cave that was ten feet wide and six feet deep, Palmo meditated for twelve hours a day. She slept sitting up in her meditation box (perhaps a later form of pole-sitting) because there was not enough room to lie down, boiled snow for drinking water, and lived without heat and electricity. Despite the frigid temperatures and harsh conditions, she remained committed to this path of Enlightenment and saw the silence of meditation as the best way to travel that path. She has since journeyed the world helping women to claim their spiritual prowess while also raising money to build a monastery for Buddhist nuns in the Himalayas—perhaps a more inviting domicile than a cave.

Why would she live that way for twelve years? one might ask. Doesn't it seem extreme? Yes, it is extreme, but so is the amount of noise, distraction, and pollutants that enter our lives each day. It takes extreme measures to rid ourselves of them. While most of us will not go to the drastic lengths Palmo did, she teaches us a valuable lesson in how disciplining our bodies and our minds helps us to shut out the noise and to listen to the quiet.

The Quakers have always taken this advice literally. Silence shared in a Friends' Meeting is the medium for group discovery and discernment. The Spirit speaks in the gathered silence. The founder of the Quakers, George Fox, said, "Let your lives preach," a later interpretation of a famous quote attributed to Saint Francis of Assisi: "Preach the Gospel. If necessary, use words." George and Francis internalized well the words of Jesus in Matthew's Gospel: "Not everyone who says to me, 'Lord, Lord' will enter the kingdom of heaven, but only the one who does the will of my Father in heaven" (7:21). Elsewhere in Matthew's Gospel Jesus says: "In praying, do not babble like the pagans, who think that they will be heard because of their many words. Do not be like them" (6:7–8a).

> *Talking much about oneself can also be a*
> *means to conceal oneself.*
> —FRIEDRICH NIETZSCHE

It is not only the Christian Scriptures that advise against wordiness. In the Hebrew Scriptures, silence helps distinguish between authentic prophets and charlatans. False prophets are often loquacious, while true prophets speak only when uttering the truth. When the people sought Jeremiah's advice after the murder of Gedaliah, the prophet remained silent for ten days before conveying God's message (Jeremiah 42:1–7). It was in the silence that Jeremiah came to hear and understand the will of God.

The Book of Kings contains one of the best-known passages from the Old Testament in which God speaks in the silence:

> Then the Lord said, "Go outside and stand on the mountain before the Lord; the Lord will be passing by." A strong and heavy wind was rending the mountains and crushing rocks before the Lord—but the Lord was not in the wind. After the wind there was an earthquake—but the Lord was not in the earthquake. After the earthquake there was a fire—but the Lord was not in the fire. After the fire there was a tiny whispering sound. When he heard this, Elijah hid his face in his cloak and went and stood at the entrance of the cave.
>
> (1 KINGS 19:11–13)

It is tempting to think that we find God in the dramatic and the extraordinary rather than in the subtle and the quiet. Elijah's experience teaches us differently. It is also tempting to think that our words are more important than our gestures or our times of quiet. Religious traditions teach us differently. John Climacus says, "The lover of silence draws close to God." In the end, isn't that our ultimate goal?

Questions for the Climb
1. Do you think you are a good listener? Why?
2. Are you comfortable with silence?
3. What are your favorite distractions? Why?
4. Do you need silence to pray and be reflective?

*

Falsehood / The Truth about Mendacity

*All that one gains by falsehood is not to be
believed when he speaks the truth.*
—ARISTOTLE

When I first saw the play *Cat on a Hot Tin Roof,* Elizabeth
Ashley played the indomitable Maggie the Cat and Keir Dul-
lea played Brick, her liquor-tethered husband. Big Daddy,
Brick's father, was played by Fred Gwynne, an actor most remembered for his Herman Munster character from the popular TV series. The theme of mendacity was introduced early in
the play. Everyone seemed to be lying to everyone else. In a key
scene, Big Daddy asks Brick why he drinks so much, and Brick
responds, "Disgust." Big Daddy wants to know what Brick is
disgusted with, and Brick says, "Mendacity. You know what
that is? It's lies and liars . . . Not one lie, not one person. The
whole thing."

Big Daddy sinks his teeth into this notion. He, too, has
known his share of mendacity—in his family, in his marriage,

in his church, and in his social clubs—and he has adjusted to living with lies and pretense.

"Mendacity. What do you know about mendacity?" he yells back at Brick. "Boy, I've lived with mendacity. Now why can't you live with it? You've got to live with it. There's nothin' to live with but mendacity. Is there?"

Mendacity is the central theme of the play. The entire family and the doctor lie to Big Daddy and Big Momma about the seriousness of Big Daddy's illness. Big Daddy lies to his wife about his love; Maggie lies about her pregnancy; Brick lies about the nature of his relationship to his college chum Skipper. Everybody is lying to somebody about something. What was Tennessee Williams trying to tell us?

Perhaps that it is so easy to lie. We tell lies all the time, considering most of them to be insignificant. (We call those *white* lies.) We convince ourselves that we lie to protect another person or not to hurt his or her feelings, but most of the time it is ourselves we are protecting. Often it is easier to make up a false excuse rather than to tell the truth. We compliment people when we don't really mean it. We tell callers we are not at home when we really are. We assure creditors the check is in the mail while it sits in our checkbooks. We fudge line items on our income tax forms, convinced that "everyone does that." We say that Martha Stewart wasn't so bad after all. Yes, mendacity is alive and well.

Evidence suggests that lying is not limited to our personal lives. In 2003 the Nike Corporation brought a lawsuit to the California Supreme Court that argued corporations should enjoy the same "free speech right" to deceive that individual citizens possess. Nike suggested it should be able to say whatever it wants in its PR campaigns, even if the claims were untrue. Nike lost in the California Supreme Court but appealed to the

U.S. Supreme Court, where, although the case was dismissed, three justices dissented, indicating sympathy for Nike's appeal.

And who can forget the Enron scandal a few years ago where a major corporation was involved in a bold money scam in which it lied about its profits and concealed its debts? The name "Enron" has become synonymous with lies and liars. While Enron happened to get caught, other corporations may be just as duplicitous and conniving but get away with it. Dishonesty and lying is expected, even assumed. Honesty, when it makes an appearance, is what is shocking to many.

> *Truth is so obscure in these times, and*
> *falsehood so established, that, unless we love*
> *the truth, we cannot know it.*
> —BLAISE PASCAL

John Climacus writes: "No sensible man imagines that lying is a minor failing. Indeed the All-Holy Spirit pronounced the most dreadful sentence on this sin above all others; and if, as David says to God, 'You destroy all who speak falsely' (Ps. 5:7), what will happen to those who swear to their lies on oath?" (Step 12). Like Climacus, most religious traditions don't have a cavalier attitude toward lying. They think that it is serious and has far-reaching implications. In the Hebrew Scriptures, aside from the prohibition in the Ten Commandments against bearing false witness, the Book of Proverbs says:

> *There are six things the LORD hates,*
> *yes, seven are an abomination to him;*
> *Haughty eyes, a lying tongue*
> *and hands that shed innocent blood;*
> *A heart that plots wicked schemes,*

> *feet that run swiftly to evil,*
> The false witness who utters lies
> *and he who sows dischord among brothers.*
> (PROVERBS 6:16–19; EMPHASIS ADDED)

Two of the abominations to the Lord involve lying.

Likewise, Christianity prohibits lying. "The truth will set you free" (John 8:32) is one of the most-quoted utterances of Jesus. Jesus' whole mission revolves around trying to get people to give up the lies they live and to move into the light of truth instead: "For this I was born and for this I came into the world, to testify to the truth. Everyone who belongs to the truth listens to my voice" (John 18:37). In fact, much of the Gospel of John is concerned with the Spirit of truth prevailing in the midst of lies that threaten to extinguish that truth.

> *A lie gets halfway around the world before the*
> *truth has a chance to get its pants on.*
> —SIR WINSTON CHURCHILL

The truth spoken of in the Gospel goes deeper than merely not telling lies. It concerns living one's life in truth. It is not a one-time act, but rather a disposition toward life and relationships. Rather than *tell* a lie, some people *live* a lie. Sometimes their lives are based on deception or untruths, but more often they are based on denial or an inability to walk in the light of truth. This kind of falsehood is perhaps even more debilitating than the falsehood of lying because it affects one's stance toward life. An encounter with a revered religious writer and teacher brought this point home to me.

It happened in a bathtub. I've never liked baths, preferring the efficiency of a shower with a wide head that breaks all water conservation laws. However, when checking into a retreat center to lead a women's retreat, I couldn't have very well asked for a room with a shower. After all, nuns—whom I've been told prefer baths, though I generalize here—ran the place, and I didn't want them to think I was picky from the start.

"Welcome, Father," an elderly sister greeted me in the reception area. She smiled, causing an already well-trafficked face to double in creases. "I'm so glad you could be with us for the weekend. Now let me see what room they've put you in." She shuffled through some cards at a desk overshadowed by a black cross that looked as big as the one Jesus must have carried. "Ah, here you are. Oh dear. Did they tell you that you'd be sharing a bathroom?"

"Um . . . no, no, they didn't." *Geez. I hate that. Give me a simple bed, a hard chair, nothing on the walls. All okay. But give me my own bathroom . . . please.* "That's fine though, Sister. It's only for a weekend. Do you happen to know who I'm sharing it with?" *Please don't say one of the women who's making the retreat.*

"Yes, let me see." She shuffled through another set of cards, crinkling her nose, as if trying to reposition her bifocals. "It's with the other priest. He's leading the group from Bristol and you have the Hartford women. You're on slightly different schedules, though, so it should work out just fine." *Famous last words.*

"That's great. Thank you."

My room was typical for a retreat house, with the emphasis on simple and without a lot of taste. I checked out the bathroom first thing. Bathtub only, just as I had feared—and an old claw-foot one at that. I looked at the door to the other connecting bedroom. It had an old knob, slightly rusted, with one of the nails hanging halfway out. No lock. Not even an eyelet.

I changed and went to the conference room where I was scheduled to give an opening talk, which seemed to go fine, despite my tiredness from traveling. I returned to my room after the presentation and some obligatory chitchat by the refreshment table. Feeling sweaty, I longed for a shower and then remembered that I didn't have one. As I turned on the faucet in the tub, orange water laden with rust particles hit the porcelain and splattered against the side like aquatic fireworks. When the water finally cleared, I put the rubber stopper in and added the Calgon Bath Beads that sat on the shelf by the sink. Bubbles formed as the water rose.

I sat in the tub with a *Newsweek* magazine, doing my best to keep the pages dry. I must have fallen asleep because I awoke to the sound of rustling in the adjacent room and saw the magazine—waterlogged, half floating—nearly consumed by the clouds of foam. Someone coughed. Then it occurred to me that the bathroom door was unlocked and that the person on the other side had no idea that I was bathing. So I coughed back, loudly. A few times. I then started humming a few bars of something. Surely he'd get the hint.

I fished the magazine out of the water and was about to stand up to dry off, when the doorknob turned and a balding man with glasses walked in. I froze in the tub.

"Oh, I didn't know anyone was in here," he said, unfazed, in accented English. He wore an open-collar white shirt and gray pants.

"Yep, just me," I responded uneasily, while trying to be as blasé as he about the intrusion.

He stared at me, seemingly waiting for me to explain what I was doing in *his* bathtub.

"Didn't they tell you that we'd be sharing a bathroom?" I asked.

"No, I'm afraid they didn't, but that's fine. It's certainly a big enough bathroom for both of us." I couldn't place the accent. "My name is Henri Nouwen. Pleasure to meet you."

He extended his hand. I wanted to reciprocate but my hand was soapy and wet.

"I'm afraid I'll just wave," I said, raising a white mitt of suds into the air. "I'm Edward. Edward Beck." He moved toward me. Then what he had said hit me. *Henri Nouwen.* The *Henri Nouwen? I* knew *the face looked familiar.*

"You mean Henri Nouwen, the author?" I said.

"Yes, you've read my books?"

"Oh yes, well, some of them. Great stuff. Pleasure to meet you."

"Ah, mutual. You are a priest as well then?"

"Yes, Passionist."

"Ah, yes, Passionist. I've met some of your men along the way." He looked around, searching for something. I couldn't imagine what. His eyes landed on a wooden stool in the corner. "Mind if I sit?"

"Um, well, I was just about to get out of the tub. Perhaps you need to use the bathroom?"

"Oh, no, not really. Relax yourself. You look quite comfortable there." Obviously not the best reader of human emotions, he got the stool from the corner, carried it to the side of the bathtub, and sat down. As I attempted to reposition the quickly disappearing suds, he crossed his legs, put his elbow on his knee, and cupped his chin in his large hand. "Now, tell me about yourself."

Henri Nouwen is a celebrity in Catholic spiritual circles. Born in the Netherlands in 1932 and ordained a priest for the diocese of Utrecht in 1957, Nouwen wasted no time capitalizing on his intellectual acumen. After getting a degree in psychology and teaching at Notre Dame University for a few years, he realized that his deeper interest was pastoral theology. He accepted an invitation to teach in that program at Yale Divinity in 1971 and remained there for ten years. During that time he began writing some of his classic best-sellers in pastoral theology and spirituality, some of which I had read and liked, though I thought he sometimes beat a theme to death, as if he needed to convince himself.

"Well, not too much to tell," I said from my quickly cooling tub. "It's you who has all the stories. I've read some of them in your books. You've led quite an interesting life."

"I suppose so, yes," he said, "but interesting isn't always fulfilling. Now, isn't that true?" He looked somehow sad to me, troubled.

"I guess so," I said, not really sure what he was getting at. "I would think that you've had a very fulfilling life though. It sure sounds that way in your books."

"Yes, but you can't put everything in books." He paused and looked away. "Have you ever been in love?" he said finally, his eyes turning back to me.

"In *love?*" I said. He nodded. "Well, sure, I think so." *Talk about quickly getting to the heart of the matter.*

"Me, too. But I'm only now at this late stage of my life coming to see what that means. I've certainly written about it, but I'm not sure I've known it. My mother tried to teach me it a long time ago. I'm only now beginning to learn it."

"Oh," I said, not sure where to go from there.

"When you get rejected by someone, it's hard to remember you're beloved," he said. "Isn't that right?"

"Well, I know you've written a lot about being beloved," I responded, skipping right over his question—and the "rejected" part.

"Yes, now if only I could feel it. But I don't want to go into all that and make you do more work. Now that you are finished with the ladies, you want to go to bed. Your blue eyes are getting sleepy."

"No, it's just the warm water." I realized that Henri Nouwen wanted to share something with me but wasn't comfortable doing so yet. I attributed his awkwardness to the fact that we had just met. Or maybe it was my quickly vanishing suds, which were surely making *me* feel awkward. "Please, continue," I said halfheartedly.

"It's just that I've been hurt by a friend and I'm feeling a bit wounded." I remembered at that moment that I had read his book, *The Wounded Healer*, in college. Strange that he would use that word. "I bared my soul to him, and he couldn't take it. Maybe I was wrong to do so."

"I'm not sure we can ever be wrong when we share ourselves honestly with someone," I said, perhaps sounding a bit too much like Deepak Chopra.

"Some people can't take honesty. For a long time *I* couldn't take honesty. I lived in fear, worrying what people would say about the good priest, the famous Catholic writer. I still have fear, but less. That's a good thing, I suppose."

"What is it that you were afraid of?"

"Many things. Being known fully, for one. Do you find celibacy hard?"

"Yes, sometimes," I said, again caught offguard by the non sequitur. "It can get lonely."

"Yes, the loneliness. That is the toughest part. But then married people are lonely, too, are they not?"

"I guess so," I said.

"But it's a different kind of loneliness, no?"

"I really don't know. I've never been there."

"Sometimes I just need to be held, that's all. But I think he thought I wanted more."

"The person you bared your soul to?"

"Yes. Not only my soul, but my dreams, hopes, fears. Too much for him, I think. I used to be so reserved, and now I overwhelm people. How ironic, huh?"

"Intensity *can* have its drawbacks," I said.

"And its deep rewards," he said, almost defensively.

"Yes, of course."

"You know, I once met Thomas Merton, and we talked about some of this," he said. *Geez. And he* died *in a bathtub*, I thought. "I was at Gethsemani Abbey, and we arranged to have a private meeting together in his hermitage. 'Bring a six-pack with you,' he said to me. So, I did, and we talked late into the night. He struggled with love, too, you know. Love with a woman. Actually, more than one. I realized then, though, that his deep humanity is what made him such a wonderful monk. He was a real person, not afraid to live life. I've been afraid sometimes. Now my fear is that it may be too late."

"It's never too late. You're still here. You're still alive."

"Yes, but for how long?" Nouwen stood up abruptly and moved the stool back to its place beneath the window. "Well, my dear Father Edward, enough for one night. I've said too much, and you've said hardly anything. Next time, you talk more."

But there never was a next time. I saw him only briefly during the remaining day and a half of the weekend retreat, and there was no time for any conversation. The next night I half wished that he would walk in on me again while I was tak-ing a bath, but he did not.

In 1995, while traveling to Russia to film a TV documen-tary about Rembrandt's painting of the Prodigal Son from

Luke's Gospel, Nouwen suffered a heart attack in the Netherlands, his homeland. His ninety-three-year-old father and siblings cared for him in the hospital, but a week later, on September 21, 1996, the feast of Saint Matthew, Nouwen suffered a second, fatal attack. He was sixty-four years old.

In 1999 Michael Ford published *The Wounded Prophet,* the most revealing biography of Nouwen to date. In it Ford writes about Nouwen's consuming need for affection, intimacy, and friendship amid his struggle with his celibate priesthood. He suggests that Nouwen only started coming to terms with being gay in his final years, regarding it as his own "disability," a cross to bear. He expressed remorse at having been hard on gay students he had taught, of telling them that homosexuality was an evil state of being.

I don't know many of the intimate details of Henri Nouwen's life. I don't know the identity of the man who had rejected him; nor do I know if Nouwen ever found elusive peace before his untimely death. I do know, however, the *fear* that enabled falsehood to gain the upper hand in his life. It's not an intentional lying or a premeditated falsehood, but it can be just as insidious and destructive.

Maybe no one lives a totally authentic life. Mendacity is indeed all-pervasive. And while we may need some protective barrier to guard our so easily wounded hearts, truth seems to require a stripping-away of those protective barriers, revealing more authenticity, more freedom, more love. We do only go around once, and yes, this is not a dress rehearsal, and bravo to carpe diem and to every other overused and trite expression we have heard. Perhaps we utter them so frequently because they are true. Now if only their *truth* could permeate our lives.

While we all struggle with our own falsehoods and untruths, Nouwen's life highlights that the ultimate goal is to continually come more into the light of truth. In the same Gospel of John where Jesus says, "The truth shall set you free," he also says, "I came so that they might have life and have it more abundantly" (10:10). Yes, more truth, more life.

Questions for the Climb

1. When is it most difficult for you *not* to lie?
2. Do you feel guilty when you lie? Or has it become a way of life?
3. How do you feel when you have been lied to?
4. Do you ever feel as though you are *living* a lie?

Step 13

*

Despondency (Tedium) / Such a Bore

The cure for boredom is curiosity.
There is no cure for curiosity.
—DOROTHY PARKER

When I was a child, there was nothing worse I could say than "I'm bored." My mother would peer at me with disdain and say something like: "How can you say that? There are so *many* things that you could be doing if you used the brain that God gave you. Don't say that again, or I'll show you boring."

I am not sure why my being bored struck such a nerve with her. Maybe she viewed it as ingratitude for the blessings that being bored seemed to deny. I wasn't alone, however, in my ingratitude. Boredom is no stranger to adolescents. Whether it is lack of imagination, or laziness, or a developmental inability to see what really is, boredom is a plague of the young. Drugs, sexual experimentation, and even unlawful activity can be the result and create an even more destructive ennui.

That is not to say that only the young are bored. On the

second page of Georges Bernanos's 1936 novel, *The Diary of a Country Priest*, the priest talks about his not-so-young congregation this way:

> My parish is bored stiff; no other word for it. . . . the world is eaten up by boredom. . . . you can't see it all at once. It is like dust. You go about and never notice, you breathe it in, you eat and drink it. It is sifted so fine it doesn't even grit on your teeth. But stand still for an instant and there it is, coating your face and hands. To shake off this drizzle of ashes you must be forever on the *go*. And so people are always "on the go." . . . the world has long been familiar with boredom . . . but I wonder if man has ever before experienced this contagion, this leprosy of boredom: . . . a shameful form of despair in some way like the fermentation of a Christianity in decay.

The priest here suggests that boredom is all-pervasive in our society, "coating" us with a stifling malaise. And although the word *boredom* didn't enter the English language until well into the eighteenth century, its antecedents are recognized even in ancient texts. Evagrius of Pontus (345–399) lists *acedia* (often translated as "sloth") as the "most troublesome" of the Seven Deadly Sins. This same sin is the "noonday demon that threatens the monastic," a demon the hermits in ancient Egypt battled daily. ("A doctor calls on the sick in the morning, but tedium visits the hermit at noon," says Saint John Climacus.) In his hailed book *The Noonday Demon: An Atlas of Depression*, Andrew Solomon equates this "noonday demon" with debilitating depression, suggesting that boredom can be evidence of a serious medical condition.

The secret of being boring is to say everything.

—VOLTAIRE

Saint Thomas Aquinas also suggests that boredom (*acedia*) is related to depression, albeit not in the clinical sense: "On the other hand, the fact that a man deems an arduous good impossible to obtain, either by himself or by another, is due to his being over downcast, because when this state of mind dominates his affections, it seems to him that he will never be able to rise to any good. And since sloth is a sadness that casts down the spirit, in this way despair is born of sloth" (*Summa Theologica,* II–II, 20, 4).

For Aquinas, aspirations toward "the good" are everything. An inability to delight in the beauty of all that is good and holy suggests the absence of love or, at least, the nonrecognition of love. Boredom limits the possibilities of our lives because we fail to see the choices; Aquinas suggests that love makes those possibilities and choices endless, naming the difficulty in finding a bored person who is connected to love in a conscious and active way. Boredom usually indicates that the love available is not visible or has been taken for granted. The key is to get reconnected with the love.

One frequently sees this in marriages. The seven-year-itch syndrome kicks in when the love has become routine. In order not to be bored, the ennui-shrouded spouse begins to look elsewhere for excitement and revitalization, rather than reinvesting in a love that may hold promise even after the initial luster has dulled.

I once counseled a couple that had reached this seemingly impenetrable stage of boredom in their marriage. (Actually, I've counseled a number of couples in this stage.) Married for ten years, they believed that perhaps they should no longer stay together because there was nothing new to discover in the relationship. The husband was a shipbuilder in New Jersey and the wife a part-time office worker and mother of two children.

We sat in my office as the wife complained about the listlessness of her marriage.

"There's only so much I can hear about his working on boats," she said. "He has no other life or interests. When he comes home he wants to sleep or watch television. This isn't the marriage I expected."

The husband sat expressionless, staring straight ahead.

"And your life is so exciting, right?" he finally said. "You work in an office, for God's sake and you clean up after kids. Wow. Why is that any more exciting than my working on ships?"

"I never said it was more exciting," the wife said. "But I want more. I'm not content with just that. I'm bored as hell with my life."

"Well, I'm bored with you sometimes, too," he said. "But that's just the way it is. You get used to it."

"I don't want to get used to it," she screamed back. "I shouldn't have to. This is no life."

Despite my attempts to get the couple to rediscover the attraction that first brought them together, neither of them seemed interested. The boredom of their lives had damaged the bond they had shared. Surely, however, it wasn't simply about their chosen professions. The wife was right in saying "This is no life," but she didn't seem to know what to do to create more of one. Both had lost the passion for life that keeps relationships healthy and thriving. They divorced a year later.

Someone's boring me. I think it's me.
—DYLAN THOMAS

We talk about blue Mondays. Why are they so blue? Is it because we must once again go to work or school and begin the routines that bore us even more than staying home? Are we so disenchanted with our lives that we shrink from the resumption of our life patterns because we find them tedious and meaningless? Then why do we continue in them?

In his famous 1978 Harvard commencement address, Aleksandr Solzhenitsyn warned of the West's "spiritual exhaustion": "In the United States the difficulties are not a Minotaur or a dragon—not imprisonment, hard labor, death, government harassment and censorship—but cupidity, boredom, sloppiness, indifference. Not the acts of a mighty all-pervading repressive government but the failure of a listless public to make use of the freedom that is its birthright." If we are indeed a listless public, what has made us so, and what can we do to infuse our lives with new vigor?

We can do a few things. The authors I have just quoted suggest that boredom is an evil to be conquered if it leads to despondency, hopelessness, and ingratitude. Sloth is clearly the result of a refusal to celebrate the gift and potential of life. But there is another way to look at it. We can embrace boredom, hoping to transform it into something not boring at all. We have been convinced that we always need to be doing something to be happy, usually something *other* than what we are doing. So if we are driving, we can't simply be driving. We must also be listening to the radio or talking on the cell phone or doing both. Perhaps we are even listening to our 10,000-song iPod, the contents of which could last us our lifetime. What about simply listening to nothing instead?

The "art of doing nothing" has long been extolled by religious traditions. Nothing becomes something when nothing produces results that something cannot. The power of meditation is rooted in the power of nothingness. While doctors now recognize that nothingness can reduce stress, bring down blood pressure, and even reverse cardiac disease, those salutary effects are not necessarily the primary reason for the path of stillness. They are simply a happy by-product. The reason for stillness in the midst of chaos is so that the chaos does not consume us. Stillness gives us distance from what we cannot see when trapped in the never-ending swirl of diversion. It is the opportunity to see what matters most about our lives. Resisting the diversions is difficult, however, because we're convinced that activity is sexier than stillness.

> *The man who lets himself be bored is even*
> *more contemptible than the bore.*
> —SAMUEL BUTLER

The disciples of Jesus were no different from us. In one of the more dramatic scenes in the Gospels, Jesus is transfigured on the mountaintop in view of the disciples: "After six days Jesus took Peter, James, and John his brother, and led them up a high mountain by themselves. And he was transfigured before them; his face shone like the sun and his clothes became white as light. And behold, Moses and Elijah appeared to them, conversing with him" (Matthew 17:1–3).

This was heady stuff for the disciples. It sure beat listening to Jesus preach on the plain. If the disciples had become at all bored with their mission, this event certainly roused them from their inertia. Peter responds with the words of the quintessential thrill-seeker: " 'Lord, it is good that we are here; if you wish, I will make three tents here, one for you, one for Moses, and one for Elijah' " (17:4). Peter wants to set up camp and revel in the glitz for a while. Having made his way past the red velvet rope separating him from the glitterati, he doesn't want to go back to less luminous turf anytime soon.

But Jesus has another plan. Life is lived on the plain, not on the mountaintop. "Jesus came and touched them, saying 'Rise, and do not be afraid.' And when the disciples raised their eyes, they saw no one else but Jesus alone. As they were coming down from the mountain, Jesus charged them, 'Do not tell the vision to anyone until the Son of Man has been raised from the dead' " (17:7–9). Not only are the disciples not permitted to linger in the afterglow of the mountaintop, but they are also reminded that this mission is about suffering and death. This foretaste of glory may help to get them through that travail, but grandeur is not to be their normal state in life.

Who of us cannot identify with the desire to linger in the bright lights of glory, when compared with the alternative of trudging through the shadows of ordinariness? And yet ordinariness is where we find ourselves most of the time. The secret is to find the beauty and wonder in ordinariness. In Alice Walker's famed novel *The Color Purple,* the character Shug says to Celie, "I think it pisses God off if you walk by the color purple in a field somewhere and don't notice it." It's a great line because it heightens the beauty of ordinariness. We walk past the color purple all of the time, on our way to something or someone else, and we don't notice it. Maybe we fail to notice it because we think it would be boring simply to gaze at the color purple. Shug seems to suggest that we need to get past the illusion of ordinariness and boredom to see what is extraordinary and stirring right in front of our eyes. Boredom is a matter of perspective. What is boring to one person is exciting to another. What may be lackluster to us one day may appear scintillating the next . . . if our vision changes.

I can't remember being bored,
not once in my whole life.

—HARRY TRUMAN

My parents moved to Florida when they were still quite young. My father retired early (at fifty-four), and they had had enough of their changing neighborhood in Brooklyn.

"But what will you do everyday?" I remember asking.

"Nothing," my father said.

"Nothing?" I repeated back.

"Yeah. What's wrong with that?" he said.

"But won't you get bored?" I said.

"I don't think so. There's golf and swimming. How bored could I get?"

Now, almost twenty years later, I think that my father *is* bored. With the recent death of my mother I see that boredom only increasing. When my mother was alive my parents found themselves in paradise with little to do besides play golf and lounge by the pool. Each day's rhythm was exactly as the day's before. Not a bad life, you may think. But how much can one swing a golf club or lie by a pool or watch afternoon television before the activity becomes unbearable? With little to divert them, my parents seemed to me to be waiting until time ran out. (Is this why some people call Florida "God's waiting room?")

Of course, this is my perspective, not theirs. Once my mother's time *had* run out, I wondered if indeed she had been as content as she had seemed to be. Perhaps she was, requiring less external stimulation to feel fulfilled than I do. But in a rare unguarded moment shortly after my mother's death, my father admitted that he is, in fact, a little bored. "The evenings are long. And the days that I don't play golf are endless. I'm not sure what to do with myself sometimes. I never realized how much having your mother around made a world of difference, even if we didn't speak much. I guess I'm just bored without her."

What I want to say to my father is this: Use the boredom as an opportunity to go deeper. What about sitting with the boredom and seeing what it has to teach you? Allow the boredom to lead you to a place where you might find meaning. And then, when boredom is too consuming, what about volunteering somewhere in need? What about a continuing education class? But, of course, being the son, I can't say any of those things. Aside from my filial status, I'd also have to pretend that I am never bored or that, when I am, I always fill it with meaningful pursuits of contemplation and self-actualization. My father knows me too well to let me get away with that.

Saint John Climacus says, "Tedium is a paralysis of the soul, a slackness of the mind, a neglect of religious exercises, a hostility to vows taken. It is an approval of worldly things." While it may be all of those, tedium is also an opportunity. It is a step on the ladder that may lead to a greater appreciation of what is. We may even notice the color purple in places that we never have before.

Questions for the Climb
1. What causes you to be bored?
2. What do you do when you get bored?
3. Do you think boredom is always bad?
4. Have you ever tried to let boredom be a gateway to deeper fulfillment?

Gluttony / Super-Size Nation

Gluttony is not a secret vice.

—ORSON WELLES

What images do you conjure up when you consider the word "glutton"? Is it Henry VIII with a mutton chop dangling from his greasy mouth? Or perhaps some grotesque ancient Romans who would throw up after a hearty meal just so that they could eat more? That is surely one aspect of gluttony—and not an insignificant one. Food is an obvious partner in crime for the glutton, not only because we can witness the eating, but also the eventual results of an expanding girth and neck. Gluttony, one of the Seven Deadly Sins, can kill us not only physically but spiritually, as well. Saint John Climacus says: "Gluttony is hypocrisy of the stomach. Filled, it moans about scarcity; stuffed and crammed, it wails about hunger. Gluttony thinks up seasonings, creates sweet recipes. Stop one urge and another bursts out; stop that one and you unleash yet another. Gluttony has a deceptive appearance: it eats moderately but wants to gobble everything at the same time."

While we will return to the gluttony evidenced by overconsuming food, gluttony, as Climacus suggests, is about more than food. Saint Thomas Aquinas proposes, "Gluttony denotes, not any desire of eating or drinking, but an *inordinate desire* . . . leaving the order of reason, wherein the good of moral virtue exists" (*Summa Theologica* 2,148). Gluttony is about inordinate desire—not just for food but for anything. The virtues of temperance and self-control regulate gluttony. For Aquinas, heeding reason is the key to moderation, the antithesis of gluttony.

We live in a "more is better" society and have adopted this consumerist message. Overconsumption is a problem environmentalists and scientists long have been warning us about. As we continue to deplete our natural resources and energy sources, predictions about our future are increasingly more dire if we fail to change our unbridled consumerist behavior.

National and global gluttony suggests that, in depleting our natural resources, many are "eating up" more than their share. Globalization spotlights our apparent disregard for our environment. While the effects of global warming continue to be debated, it is undeniable that weather and environmental changes are occurring because of excessive human consumption. More important for our consideration are the reasons for this unchecked consumption. What are we filling? And why does it take so much to fill it?

> *Anyone who has watched gluttons shoveling*
> *down the most exquisite foods as if they did not*
> *know what they were eating will admit that we*
> *can ignore even pleasure.*
> —C. S. LEWIS

I remember hearing someone say to an unsuccessful dieter, "It's not about the pizza, it's about the pain." Her point was that the person was eating not because she really wanted the pizza but because she didn't want the pain of her unhappy life. The food was a cover for an inability to deal with emotional wounds, in her case abuse as a child. I think there is some truth to this. We overeat because we don't want to feel the emptiness that emotional baggage can bring. We buy and consume, seeking diversion from that emptiness. Related to our previous discussion on tedium and boredom, we attempt to fill and stuff our emptiness because we are afraid to confront the boredom that emptiness might produce.

I have a friend who fits the above description well. An African American who has always struggled in life, his family was poor and his home life far from ideal. An alcoholic father and an often-absent mother did little to shore up his sense of security. The victim of racial epithets hurled by insensitive classmates, my friend grew up wondering why life was so much easier for white folks with money. In fact, he longed to be white and have money. Half of that dream came true. A fortuitous job on Wall Street soon provided him with more money than he had ever dreamed possible. The good life came knocking, and he swung the door open wide.

My friend soon began gaining weight at an alarming rate—almost ninety pounds in a little over two years. He ate constantly. When I gently asked why he seemed to be eating everything in sight, he responded simply, "Because I can." Although he never went hungry as a child, once he could eat with no restraints, he did just that. He also began buying clothes and shoes with a startling abandon. While he needed some clothing changes due to his expanding waistline, most purchases were extravagant. His compulsive buying soon made it impossible for him to pass a high-end clothing store without purchasing something—a hundred-dollar tie, two-hundred-dollar cuff links, what have you. Buying them made him feel good, at least momentarily.

This external transformation did not seem to produce happiness, however. On the contrary, he seemed sadder than when he had had less. Rather than attribute his unhappiness to the hackneyed conclusion that simplicity enhances while riches produce discontent, I think my friend was unhappy because he expected more of the external gratification than was ever possible. It wasn't about the pizza. It was about the pain—pain with which he had never dealt adequately. I once heard gluttony described as demanding more pleasure from something than it was made for. My friend expected food and his endless array of purchases to fill the void of his deprived childhood. What he found out, however, was that one does not negate the other. Food and clothes simply cannot provide the kind of pleasure and satisfaction that he was seeking.

> *Gluttony is an emotional escape, a sign*
> *something is eating us.*
>
> —PETER DEVRIES

Aware of the truth that fulfillment comes from elsewhere, nearly all religious traditions have injunctions against gluttony and overindulgence. Buddhism is clear that one must avoid sensory excess, including sexual excess. "You should lose your involvement with yourself and then eat and drink naturally, according to the needs of your body." In saying this, the Buddha seems to understand that self-involvement leads to a preoccupation with sensory pleasures. One should eat and drink according to the *needs* of one's body, not according to the wants.

While Judaism doesn't have a lot to say about the excesses of gluttony, some interpret the laws of kasruth (keeping kosher) as discouraging excess. In the Old Testament the Book of Proverbs says, "Put a knife to your throat if you have a ravenous appetite" (Proverbs 23:2). And a few verses later: "Consort not with winebibbers, nor with those who eat meat to excess; for the drunkard and the glutton come to poverty, and torpor clothes a man in rags" (Proverbs 23:20–21). The moderate eater and drinker find favor with God; the glutton does not.

Fasting has always been extolled in the Christian tradition as a means of purification and sacrifice. Any kind of excess is frowned on. In his letter to the Corinthians, Paul writes, "Do you not know that your body is a temple of the Holy Spirit within you, whom you have from God, and that you are not your own?" (1 Cor. 6:19–20). That temple of the Holy Spirit must be kept pure through vigilance and moderation. The fourth-century Saint John Cassian sums it up well: "Stop eating while you are still hungry and don't allow your stomach to be filled to satisfaction" (*The Philokalia,* "On the Eight Vices").

Islam puts this lesson into practice with a whole month of fasting called Ramadan. Devout Muslims fast from sunrise to sunset during this holy time: no eating, drinking, smoking, or sex. They thus practice self-restraint and in doing so believe that they are courting Allah's favor.

> *Gluttony is a lust of the mind.*
> —THOMAS HOBBES

Religious traditions remind us to allow ourselves to be filled by that which can satiate, namely, the presence and power of God. But, of course, we don't always believe that, and we attempt to fill ourselves with other things. For example: How many televisions do you have? How many magazines do you subscribe to? How much gas does your car (or cars) consume? How much food do you throw away? How many CDs do you own? How many? How much? And . . . why?

My point is that we often fill ourselves in ways that may border on excessive. The Centers for Disease Control reports that more than six in ten American adults are overweight or obese and that most adults are about twenty-five pounds heavier than people were in the 1960s. Whether it is the food we eat, the clothes we have, the cars we drive, the movies we see, the stocks in our portfolio, or the amount of wine in our temperature-controlled cellars, we like to consume. Spiritual teachers encourage us to recognize what we are attempting to fill and attempt to show us another way to fill it.

Addictions cannot be overlooked when we consider gluttony. Although briefly alluded to earlier, addictions are in a gluttony category all their own. Addiction to alcohol, drugs, shopping, gambling, sex, or whatever else signifies an inability to partake in moderation. Addictions are rooted in compulsive, obsessive overconsumption. Aside from the physiological components of some addictions, many health professionals suggest that addictions are the result of compensating for some deep loss or insecurity. Addictions attempt to fill a deep void by numbing the pain we experience in our lives. From a spiritual perspective, we need to discern the underlying reason for our overconsumption if we are to be healed of it. What are we missing in our lives? What is the pain we are numbing? Do we believe it is in our power alone to end our misery?

Spirituality suggests that we cannot address what we are missing, our pain, or our misery alone. That is why the first step in successful twelve-step programs is to admit one's powerlessness. For an addiction to become manageable, one must acknowledge a "higher power" and turn one's will over to that higher power. "God is able; I am not," goes the familiar adage.

It is the natural station of the creature to be less than the Creator. But often we delude ourselves into thinking we are on equal footing. That is the original mistake (sin) of Adam and Eve in the Garden of Eden. They wanted to partake of that which they were told they could not, symbolized by the Tree of the Knowledge of Good and Evil. They had everything, but they wanted more. They were the original gluttons.

Like Adam and Eve, we consume because we can. We over-consume because we think we have a right. Our distorted worldview places us in the center of the universe with all else revolving around our needs. The glutton would have it no other way. I take more than my share because, for me, all exists to satisfy my appetites. Adam and Eve learned the hard way that such behavior leads to ruin. Unfortunately, many of us have not yet learned that lesson of our biblical ancestors. Until we do, we will continue to consume with an abandon that threatens our waistlines, our wallets, our health, and indeed our very existence. "You should remember that frequently a demon can take up residence in your belly and keep a man from being satisfied, even after having devoured the whole of Egypt and after having drunk the whole of the Nile" (Climacus, Step 14).

Questions for the Climb

1. What do you consume in a disproportionate way? Why?
2. Can you give an example from your life when you've covered the pain with the pizza?
3. Can you give one suggestion of how you would begin to address global gluttony?
4. How does your spirituality or sense of God help you resist gluttony?

Step 15

*

Lust / Sex in the Country

The difference between love and lust is like the
difference between strolling and skiing.

—LEO ROSTEN

Climacus might hate me for saying this, but lust doesn't seem that bad—at least not all of the time. While it may sound strange to reach the half-point of our climb by defending one of the Seven Deadly Sins, a fresh look at an old peccadillo may be, well, refreshing. After all, would any of us be around without lust? Reason enough to begin with the positives before considering the traditional and well-founded negatives.

When we think of lust, sex soon follows. But the Oxford English Dictionary doesn't make that connection initially. It defines "lust" this way: *1. Pleasure, delight; also, a source of pleasure. 2. Desire, appetite, relish or inclination for something. One's desire or wish.* While the definition goes on to enumerate some of the shadier aspects of lust, the dictionary leads with the positive. Lust is about appetites and pleasures, but not all appetites and pleasures are bad, despite our puritanical instincts that suggest they are.

When we say that someone has a "lust for life," it connotes the desire to live fully, intentionally, and wholeheartedly; it is about consuming life in all of its wonder and draining it dry of its richness. Often we hear of people who discover this lust for life only once they are presented with the alternative.

I recently visited a man in Sloane-Kettering Hospital in New York who is dying of a rare cancer. Once his wife and mother left the room, he began to cry uncontrollably. "What am I going to do?" he said, holding on to his chemotherapy IV pole. "I'm not ready to die yet. I was at the top of my game. I'm forty years old, for God's sake, with a great wife and kids. This makes no sense. I want to live." He spoke with passion, with lust in his heart. A good lust—a lust for life. Perhaps it might enable the miracle necessary to carry him through.

Lust can be the passion we need to advance our lives. The contrary abounds: People seemingly disinterested and, as suggested earlier, bored with life. A healthy lust can enable us to appreciate what normally we take for granted or fail to see. Insatiability for life reveals the multilayered dimensions we miss when not plumbing the depths.

Of all the worldly passions, lust is the most intense. All other worldly passions seem to follow in its train.
—BUDDHA

Lust is rooted in desire. And although desire has long been suspect in the Christian tradition, there is also precedent for seeing desire as a good. Saint Gregory Nazianzus, the fourth-century "Doctor of Theologians," said that God accepts our desires as though they were a great value and that the desire for God is a precious jewel that fascinates God as if it were the only thing in the world. Desire is, after all, the beginning of discipleship. One doesn't go in search of religious truth, meaning, or a deeper reality until an awareness of a void emerges. Desire for "the more" propels the search for it. For many people, that exploration leads to a deepening spirituality, wherein emptiness is no longer tolerable. The quest for "the more" begins.

When I was a freshman in college and working on Wall Street, I had my future well mapped out. With the firm promising me a lucrative career if I continued in its employ, I plotted my rise in the financial world and the acquisitions that would accompany it. Externally, my life was on the fast track toward realizing the American dream of success and material comfort. Internally, I was feeling restless and unfulfilled, as I couldn't imagine a life comprised simply of making trades and money. On a deeper level I wanted something more for my life. Desiring that my life have meaning and hoping to share that meaning, I left Wall Street and began pursuing a religious vocation.

While I didn't consciously "lust" for more, the *Oxford English Dictionary* suggests that perhaps I did. I "strongly desired" something and was willing to make radical choices to realize that desire. There was a lust in my heart. Awareness of an insatiable longing sometimes becomes apparent only when we find that which quells the yearning, if only temporarily. An intriguing story from the Jewish Talmud exemplifies another kind of lust:

> Rav Kahana lay under the bed of Rav, his illustrious teacher, who was carousing and speaking frivolously with his wife of sexual matters; afterward the teacher

had intercourse with her. Kahana made his presence
known and said to his teacher: "You appear to me to be
like a hungry man who has never had sex before, for
you act with great fervor in your lust." The teacher said
to Kahana, "Are you here? Get out! It is improper for
you to lie under my bed." Kahana said to him, "This is
a matter of Torah and I must study."

Rav Kahana wants to learn the art of lovemaking from his
master. What he discovers is that sexual lust for one's spouse
is permissible. Lust can draw two people closer together,
strengthening a bond that exists on less carnal levels, as well.
But Climacus's concern in his chapter on lust is that sexual desire can take us outside of the marriage or consume those who
lack the sustaining commitment of marriage. He therefore devotes much of Step 15 to the virtue of chastity as that which
keeps the body and soul pure, saying: "To be chaste is to put
on the nature of an incorporeal being. Chastity is a supernatu-
ral denial of what one is by nature, so that a mortal and cor-
ruptible body is competing in a truly marvelous way with
incorporeal spirits. A chaste man is someone who has driven
out bodily love by means of divine love, who has used heavenly
fire to quench the fires of the flesh."

> *Lust is the craving for salt of a*
> *man who is dying of thirst.*
> —FREDERICK BUECHNER

The Christian tradition teaches that all people, married and
unmarried, are called to chastity. Chastity within marriage is fidelity to one's spouse, while outside of marriage chastity is sex-

ual abstinence and the transformation of sexual desire into creative pursuits such as work, art, and service. That is the theory. In practice it is not always so easy, as many celibates can attest. Consciously channeling sexual energy into other outlets is an intellectual decision that may not always convince a hormone-flooded body. That is why religious traditions have long maintained that we cannot succeed in this task without a strong spirituality and what amounts to Divine intervention.

The Catholic Catechism teaches that lust is "a disordered desire for or inordinate enjoyment of sexual pleasure. Sexual pleasure is morally disordered when sought for itself, isolated from its procreative and unitive purposes." Thus, the Catholic teaching on human sexuality is always linked to procreation within the marital relationship.

In his 2006 encyclical, *Deus Caritas Est* (God Is Love), the first of his papacy, Pope Benedict XVI warned believers not to confuse lust with love or to degrade love "to mere sex." But in discussing the relationship between "eros" and "agape," Benedict is surprisingly positive about "eros," if in the proper context of marital love. He maintains that human physical love between spouses is connected to Divine love. It is only here that the full flowering of love is possible.

It was reported that two days before releasing the encyclical, Benedict spoke of the debt he owed to Dante's *Divine Comedy.* Peter Steinfels of the *New York Times* wrote, "Benedict's encyclical is a theological affirmation of the closing image of [Dante's] work: *'l'amor che move il sole e l'altre stele'*— 'the love that moves the sun and the other stars.' " Benedict said that for both him and Dante, love is "the primordial creative power that moves the universe." God is a lover with all of the passion of a true love. Eros can be part of the human pursuit of that true love, but must be viewed in context of the greater love of agape. In that way human love is modeled on Divine love.

While love that "moves the sun and the other stars" is a wonderfully positive notion for both Dante and Benedict, it is not equivalent to lust. In Dante's *Inferno,* the first part of *The Divine Comedy,* he explores the relationship between lust and love, and presents lust as the destructive force of possessive sexual desire that sends those who succumb to hell. They are "carnal sinners who subordinate reason to desire" (5:38–9). When one acts on misguided desire, one ultimately destroys others and sins in the process. The love that moves the sun and the stars is nowhere to be found in a love reduced to irresponsible physical gratification.

It is not only Dante who warns against the pitfalls of lust. The Book of Proverbs says "Can a man take fire to his bosom, and his garments not be burned?" (6:27). In Matthew 5:28 Jesus says, "Everyone who looks at a woman lustfully has already committed adultery with her in his heart." The implication is that if you give yourself over to lust, it will lead you into sin.

Ambition is the ecclesiastical lust.
—DANIEL NOONAN

Lust consumes one if it is not checked by the virtues of temperance and reason. Witness the testimony of those burdened by sexual addiction. Patrick Carnes, Ph.D., a 1970s pioneer in the study of sexual addiction, showed how some individuals become addicted to neurochemical changes in the body during sexual arousal and fantasy, not unlike a drug addict hooked on the pleasure sensation of narcotics. For the sex addict, sex is not a means to foster a loving relationship of intimacy but rather a means to escape pain or relieve stress. Lives have been destroyed by people's inability to temper sexual urges and desires and channel them into more loving and relational avenues. Unbridled lust can lead to disassociating the sex act from love, which is why religious traditions wisely warn against lust.

Despite such warnings, however, lust remains problematic even for those not sexually addicted, because it is rooted in our very nature and physiology. We have an instinct to procreate. We have hormones that activate our libidos and propel us toward sexual intimacy. We lust, plain and simple. What we do with that lust is crucial. While animals act on sexual urges whenever and wherever they can, religious traditions maintain that here we are separate from other primates. Through reason and temperance we can choose not to act on those instinctual desires for the sake of another good. Lust can be sublimated and its energy diverted into other life-giving channels.

The importance of using reason to avoid the pitfalls of lust is exemplified in a well-known humorous parable:

> One day the Lord came to Adam to pass on some news. "I've got some good news and some bad news," the Lord said. Adam looked at the Lord and said, "Well, give me the good news first." Smiling, the Lord explained, "I've got two new organs for you. One is called a brain. It will allow you to create new things, solve problems, and have intelligent conversations with Eve. The other organ I have for you is called a penis. It will give you great physical pleasure and allow you to reproduce your now-intelligent life-form and populate the planet. Eve will be very happy that you now have this organ to give her children." Adam, very excited, ex-

claimed, "These are two great gifts you have given me. What could possibly be bad news after such great tidings?" The Lord looked at Adam and said with great sorrow, "You will never be able to use the two gifts at the same time."

The plea of religious traditions is that we do learn to use both gifts at the same time. That is the only way to keep the gift from becoming a curse, a curse experienced not only in the sexual realm. If lusting is wanting and desiring, then the object of that desire can expand beyond the sexual. One can lust for power, possessions, control, or anything else, for that matter. Almost every category of human experience can be overtaken by lust if not kept in check by reason and temperance and a bow to religious wisdom. The sociopolitical realities of our world highlight the destructive power of lust when we witness the unjust acquisition of land, property, and resources (such as oil). Colonialism in all of its forms, including the economic colonialism of multinational and transnational companies, is a lust that destroys lives. Lust can therefore give life or take life. Connection with our spiritual natures encourages the former.

> *Society drives people crazy with lust*
> *and calls it advertising.*
> —JOHN LAHR

"I say, then: live by the Spirit and you will certainly not gratify the desire of the flesh. For the flesh has desires against the Spirit, and the Spirit against the flesh; these are opposed to each other, so that you may not do what you want" (Saint Paul's Letter to the Galatians 5:16–18). Despite the dualism apparent in the admonition of Paul, there is also a truth to be heeded. Lust can keep us from doing the things we wish. We can become subject to the whims of lust rather than to our higher instincts toward noble action based in reason and responsibility. Walking in the Spirit means that we recognize a loftier calling and acknowledge a power that trumps the allure of lust.

Granted, the allure of lust is not easily vanquished. Television, billboard ads, films, novels, and the Internet bombard us with sensual images that heighten lust. Easy accessibility to pornography that degrades and dehumanizes prompts an unhealthy disassociation between love and lust. We begin to view others as objects for our gratification rather than as persons worthy of our respect and nurturance. Constant vigilance is needed not to be consumed by Madison Avenue and Hollywood sex that offers no connection to spiritual values. In a culture where sex sells, we must be on guard not to be unwitting participants in that trading. When we participate in commerce with human beings as the commodity, we have begun a dangerous slide into the inexorable clutches of lust.

How do we guard against that slide? Climacus says through vigilance and prayer, and by "submit[ting] the desires of the body to the demands of the soul." In other words, we must acknowledge that physical pleasure is not the only purpose of the sexual relationship. Sex is not an end but a means to an end. We must concentrate on the relationship of love rather than on the sexual relationship. A partner is a person, not merely a body. It is only in this integrative pursuit of love that we can hope to tame the beast lust that threatens to devour our spiritual placidness.

Before lifting our heels in ascent from this step, I must acknowledge that the above is easier to write than to practice. Perhaps that is true of all of the steps, but lust in a particular way because of its all-consuming nature. The desire for sexual and sensual pleasure is strong. It literally propels us into the arms of one another. From an evolutionary and scientific standpoint, that is a good thing if the species is to continue. Human touch, intimacy, sexual expression, and orgasm are all goods. But inherent in those goods is the potential for bad. If we allow ourselves to be ruled by our base instincts, as lower animals do, we suffer the danger of denying what makes us unique as bodies with souls and spirits. We have the ability to be ruled by reason and charity rather than by our passions. Climacus says, "The chaste man is not someone with a body undefiled, but rather a person whose members are in complete subjection to the soul." May we readily bow before that worthy master, the soul.

Questions for the Climb

1. Do you think lust is unhealthy or healthy?
2. When has lust been destructive in your life?
3. Has lust ever been good in your life?
4. Are you aware of lusting after more than sex? What?

Step 16

✦

Avarice / Worshipping the God of Money

*The lust of avarice has so totally seized upon
mankind that their wealth seems rather to
possess them than they possess their wealth.*

—PLINY

"Money, money, money, money . . . Money makes the world
go round." So sings the master of ceremonies in Kander and
Ebbs's famed musical *Cabaret.* The song contains some truth.
Our world economy is built on money—who has it and who
doesn't. Paper commerce, based on real or imagined concrete
assets, determines the quality of life for billions around the
globe. But do we actually believe that the money in our wallets
represents gold held somewhere in reserve? Do gold bars give
the green paper value, or is it rather our assignation of meaning that gives money value? Do you think that a visit to Fort
Knox would allow you to finger the bullion representing the
greenback in your wallet? Try it. The only reason money is
valuable is because we decide to agree that it is. And even if you
do believe that your paper money is backed up by glistening

bars in some hidden Federal Reserve, what makes gold so valuable anyway—because it's shiny and pretty? You can't eat it. It won't keep you alive. So, who decides that gold is precious? Is it possibly all a ruse to perpetuate an unjust global economic system and, in the process, to present monumental challenges to our spiritual development?

Granted, I realize that we need money or some equivalent medium of exchange. Even before money was developed, goods were bartered in exchange for services or for other goods. Our capitalist system wouldn't have it any other way. And yet I wonder if there *is* another way. Can we retain both our capitalist system and our souls? To do so our disposition toward currency may need to change.

Climacus suggests that money sometimes leads to avarice, thus thwarting our spiritual advancement. "Avarice is a worship of idols and is the offspring of unbelief . . . Waves never leave the sea. Anger and gloom never leave the miserly." In writing that anger and gloom are the result of avarice, Climacus is suggesting that the inordinate desire to acquire and hoard wealth leads to unhappiness. While intellectually we may agree, how many of us learn the sobering lessons of that truism?

My grandmother used to tell my mother, "Marry rich. When bills come in the door, love goes out the window." Although my mother did not heed my grandmother's advice, my mother's anthem was not too dissimilar: "I've been rich, and I've been poor. And rich is better." While perhaps just her attempt at humor, I think she halfheartedly believed the words. Perhaps *all* of us believe them. Yet at the same time we espouse that "Money can't buy happiness." Well, which is it? We can't have it both ways. While we may say that lack of money sometimes contributes to unhappiness, I've met more unhappy rich people than poor ones.

The avarice of the old: it's absurd to increase
one's luggage as one nears the journey's end.

—CICERO

"Whoever loves money never has money enough; whoever loves wealth is never satisfied with his income," says the writer of the Book of Ecclesiastes (5:8, NIV), suggesting that avarice can sneak up on you. The money bar rises without us realizing it. A rich friend of mine is constantly moving that bar. Due to his prodigious talent, he has acquired great wealth. He travels first class, lives in luxury homes, has a staff of people attending to his every need, and drops $300 on a glass of wine without batting an eyelid. And yet he is continually lamenting his lack of money, insinuating that many conspire to fleece him of his well-earned booty. He said recently, "I have to be very conservative with my investments and with how much I give to charity. My talent won't last into my old age. I have to make enough money while I can to last me the rest of my life." My response was "You could stop working now and live on the *interest* of your money for the rest of your life." He felt chided and responded that I was not qualified to comment on his finances. While correct in his assumption that I'm no expert in high finance, nonetheless he cannot deny that 98 percent of people in the world will not see in a lifetime what he makes in six months. Now, that is *real* cause for lamentation.

The same gentleman once said to me, "I really want to simplify my life. Get rid of my big houses and my extra stuff. It's all too complicated. What I really want is just one room. I think I could be content living in just that." With no small dose of skepticism I said, "Well then, do it." He nodded with a determination that was almost convincing. The next month he acquired yet one more house—this time in the desert—to complement his urban and seaside dwellings. He seemed almost helpless to do otherwise.

It is no mistake that the word "miser" comes from the same root as *misery*—the Latin *miser*. Hoarding something that in itself has no real value or ability to satisfy can only make one miserable. Possessions are fine if they remain so, but when they begin to possess us, we are consumed by that which is not worthy of us.

Avarice is a vice that has a consuming life of its own. Just when we think we have enough, we feel we need more—we fall in love not with our possessions but with the process of possessing. The accumulation of additional stuff increases our perceived self-importance. But if today our self-importance is built on that which fire can consume tomorrow, it is hardly foolproof.

The world of spirit knows this to be true. In the Christian tradition Gospel stories and parables abound about the deleterious effects of avarice.

Someone in the crowd said to Jesus, "Teacher, tell my brother to divide the inheritance with me."

Jesus replied, "Man, who appointed me a judge or an arbiter between you?" Then he said to them, "Watch out! Be on your guard against all kinds of greed; a man's life does not consist in the abundance of his possessions."

And Jesus told them this parable: "The ground of a certain rich man produced a good crop. He thought to himself, 'What shall I do? I have no place to store my crops.'"

Then he said, "This is what I'll do. I will tear down my barns and build bigger ones, and there I will store all my grain and my goods. And I'll say to myself, 'You have plenty of good things laid up for many years. Take life easy; eat, drink and be merry.'"

But God said to him, "You fool! This very night your life will be demanded from you. Then who will get what you have prepared for yourself?"

This is how it will be with anyone who stores up things for himself but is not rich toward God.

(LUKE 12:13–21, NIV)

While the man's desire for security is understandable, the parable demonstrates that such security is fleeting. Jesus begins his teaching by warning against greed and a reliance on the abundance of possessions and concludes by disposing of the rich guy's barns with that great leveler: death. In desiring to increase and secure his wealth, the rich man mistakenly relies on his own resources for his future merriment. No small error, for that very night he will die. That is the fate of those who store up things for themselves instead of being rich in God. Their anxious striving puts them in their grave. As avarice dupes us into believing that we control our destinies by how much we possess and how secure we are, one cancer cell or wrong turn of the steering wheel puts that belief to rest—literally.

In another Gospel Jesus continues to make his point:

Do not store up for yourselves treasures on earth, where moth and rust destroy, and where thieves break in and steal. But store up for yourselves treasures in heaven, where moth and rust do not destroy, and where thieves do not break in and steal. For where your treasure is, there your heart will be also . . .

No one can serve two masters. Either he will hate the one and love the other, or he will be devoted to the one and despise the other. You cannot serve both God and money.

Therefore I tell you, do not worry about your life, what you will eat or drink; or about your body, what you will wear. Is not life more important than food, and the body more important than clothes? Look at the birds of the air; they do not sow or reap or store away in barns, and yet your heavenly Father feeds them. Are you not much more valuable than they? Who of you by worrying can add a single hour to his life? . . .

Therefore do not worry about tomorrow, for tomorrow will worry about itself. Each day has enough trouble of its own.

(MATTHEW 6:19–21, 24–27, 34, NIV)

These words are not a treatise against money and security. They are, however, an admonition against allowing money and security to become your god. Money and God can coexist, but you cannot serve both. A divided heart remains divided. We tend to let the physical world dominate our concerns because it appears most real and present to us. After all, it is natural, and not always bad, that we have anxieties over food and shelter. If we don't clothe and feed ourselves, who will? Spirituality teaches us, however, that we are more than the food we eat or the roof over our heads. Excessive worry about them will lead nowhere except to a place of anxious striving and unhappiness. Even if temporarily we feel secure, we will soon discover we are not. If there is a drought or the roof is blown away, who are we then? When security or money becomes the master, we are indeed enslaved.

Avarice is the sphincter of the heart.
—MATTHEW GREEN

Jesus attempts to teach us a way out of that dead end with a simple lesson: See your life as a gift from God rather than something *you* make happen. Resist hubris. If you seek first God's kingdom and righteousness, all that you need will be provided, as well. Rather than encouraging irresponsibility about our physical needs, Jesus' teaching is simply an articulation of truth. The person consumed by avarice lives the lie of self-sufficiency.

One final story from Luke's Gospel brings the point home.

> A certain ruler asked him [Jesus], "Good teacher, what must I do to inherit eternal life?"
>
> "Why do you call me good?" Jesus answered. "No one is good—except God alone. You know the commandments: 'Do not commit adultery, do not murder, do not steal, do not give false testimony, honor your father and mother.'"
>
> "All these I have kept since I was a boy," he said.
>
> When Jesus heard this, he said to him, "You still lack one thing. Sell everything you have and give to the poor, and you will have treasure in heaven. Then come, follow me."
>
> When he heard this, he became very sad, because he was a man of great wealth. Jesus looked at him and said, "How hard it is for the rich to enter the kingdom of God! Indeed, it is easier for a camel to go through the eye of a needle than for a rich man to enter the kingdom of God."
>
> (LUKE 18:18–25, NIV)

The predicament of the man of great wealth is clear. He is attempting to serve God and money, but he cannot do both.

While the wealthy person can serve God by being generous with his wealth, attachment to his wealth will produce only unhappiness. The interesting twist in the passage is that this is a righteous, commandment-abiding man who has kept all the rules since he was a boy. But he tips his hand by suggesting that he may be able to buy his way into Heaven the way he buys everything else. He wants to *inherit* eternal life, putting the realm of spirit on the same level as his daily commerce. This will not do. Jesus intuits the delusion and goes for the jugular. "Sell everything you have and give it to the poor." The rich man cannot recover from this rabbinic assault. In his eyes, if he gives away what he thinks gives him value, he is nothing. He fails to realize that Jesus is attempting to uncover his *true* value. Until the man can embrace that, he will have to join the camels at the divine impasse.

> *Poverty wants some, luxury many,*
> *and avarice all things.*
>
> —SENECA

In the [nineteenth] century a tourist from the States visited the famous Polish rabbi Hafez Hayyim. He was astonished to see that the rabbi's home was only a simple room filled with books. The furniture was a table and a bench.

"Rabbi, where is your furniture?" asked the tourist.

"Where is yours?" replied Hafez.

"Mine? But I'm only a visitor here."

"So am I," said the rabbi.

—ANTHONY DE MELLO, *THE SONG OF THE BIRD*

(GARDEN CITY, NY: IMAGE BOOKS, 1984, P. 137)

Finbar, my missionary friend in Pakistan, wrote this to me about a dream he had:

It was Lent and I was missing friends in Ireland. I remember wanting to hold these people, to have them with me, but they were so far away. With a restless ache in my spirit, I was feeling a bit clingy at the time. Then one night I had an illuminating dream. In the dream I was barefoot in a green fertile field, and I turned around to see a magnificent Easter lily tree, in full bloom, in the middle of a fenced-off part of the field. It was so stunningly beautiful that I was transfixed by it. Wanting some of its flowers, I climbed over the fence and ran to the tree. The leaves were a deep waxy green and the bell-like flowers were full and creamy white, adorned by yellow stamens particular to large calla lilies. I started to jump up to break off some of the Easter lilies so that I could have them all for myself, but each time I almost grabbed one, it eluded my grasp. I could *feel* the waxy texture of the leaves and stems, but they kept slipping out of my fingers. But I so wanted them! I thought, "If only I had a chair, I could stand on it and then break off some of the flowers." I looked around and saw a wooden house and decided to go inside to get a chair.

In the next scene of the dream I came out of the house carrying a wooden chair onto the wooden veranda surrounding the house. When I came onto the veranda I was stunned to see the field and the area surrounding the house crowded with people I knew from various times and places in my life. They were all there, each recognizable. I then had a sudden insight into the

Easter lily tree—while I was still in my dream! The insight was that I don't have to possess the tree or the flowers (or the people they represented). I don't have to break off any of the flowers because they are already mine. The tree is simply there, its beauty free to behold. I don't have to *own* it. Likewise (and this was the deeper insight within the dream), I don't have to—and indeed cannot—possess and cling to the friends in my life whom I wish could be close by. There was, I discovered, another way of meeting them, from the vast distance of Pakistan to the other places where they lived—in Spirit.

When I awoke from the dream I thought about it for a long time. I realized that I can't hoard. It's simply not good for me. I may respectfully and lovingly *hold,* but not own or possess. This more gentle way of holding allows for greater growth and love to dwell there.

If only we could live the wisdom of Finbar's dream. The implications could radically affect not only our personal lives but our communal life, as well. What would the world be like if we didn't hoard? There are more than 200 billionaires in the United States, while 5 percent of American households have assets over $1 million. In these same United States 37 million people live below the poverty line, including 21 percent of all children (15 million). The average allocation for families needing food stamps is $83 per month. That, while the baseball player Alex Rodriguez has a $252 million, ten-year baseball contract that pays him $170,000 per game. Something is wrong with these figures, and it's not the math.

Am I proposing a utopian socialist state where we have equal distribution of goods? While a more equal distribution and fairer tax laws would be a start, the problem goes deeper than that. It goes to our very soul, as individuals and as a nation. We have been convinced that it's okay to worry simply about ourselves and our families. This is America, after all, where we pull ourselves up by our bootstraps and make our own way. The 2005 hurricane Katrina taught a different lesson. Suddenly it was revealed to the world that some Americans had no bootstraps. In the richest nation in the world, many were barely getting by, their lives deemed less valuable than those with more substantial means. We were horrified by the television images, embarrassed that the world, too, suddenly saw our dirty little secret. But soon we forget and those who are left behind go faceless and nameless until the next cataclysmic event reminds us. The alternative is to release our grip now. It won't happen as a nation until it begins to happen in each one of us. And it won't happen in each one of us until we really do believe that *it's only money.*

> A generous man met a miser, and the miser said the other man was without discernment.... The collector of money may be stirred by charity, but, when the money is in, the grip tightens.
>
> (CLIMACUS, STEP 16)

Questions for the Climb

1. How much do you value money?
2. How is that demonstrated in your life?
3. If it was all taken away tomorrow, would you still be *you*?
4. Does God provide or do you provide? Or both?

Step 17

*

Poverty / Blessed Are the Poor in Spirit

Poverty is the schoolmaster of character.

—ANTIPHANES

I remember when my parents first found out that, unlike diocesan parish priests, as a member of a religious community I would have to take vows *before* my ordination.

"I'll have to take a vow of poverty," I said to my parents in their living room.

"Poverty?" my father responded. "You mean to help people who are poor?"

"No," I said. "A vow that *I* will remain poor."

"That one's not going to work for you," my mother said from the couch as she blew smoke into the air.

"What do you mean?" I said.

"You like nice things too much. Those priests and brothers won't know what hit them when *you* walk through the door."

"To say nothing of the fact that we've worked our whole

lives *not* to be poor," my father added, "and you want to go back there?"

In 1981 I did, in fact, take a vow of poverty while my parents sat in the chapel witnessing my spiritual leap. I didn't understand the full implications of that vow at the time, and I still don't. Nor have I lived the vow as ideally as I then imagined I might. And yet the detachment it has afforded from material things (bankbooks, personal ownership, and taxes) has been its own master class in the value of detachment from the material.

That Climacus chooses to introduce poverty as a spiritual step in this section of the "struggle against the passions" may be a bit confusing, or even deceptive, because he groups this classical spiritual virtue with passions to be overcome. While poverty is surely a social disease that affects millions around the globe, Climacus is not writing about poverty as a societal ill. Rather, he introduces voluntary poverty in relation to the preceding step, avarice, echoing Matthew's Gospel, where Jesus says, "Blessed are the poor in spirit, for the Kingdom of heaven shall be theirs." Climacus's poverty is a beatitude—blessing—to be celebrated rather than disdained. He includes it in this section in direct contrast to avarice.

> Poverty... is a resignation from care. It is life without
> anxiety and travels light, far from sorrow and faithful to
> the commandments. The poor monk is lord of the world.
>
> (CLIMACUS, STEP 17)

This was a hard notion for my parents to get their minds around and an even harder one for me to live. The value of poverty in the Christian tradition has its roots in the life and teaching of Jesus, who became poor that we might all be richer and see the godliness of simplicity and detachment. Jesus' peripatetic lifestyle, his reliance on the care of strangers, and the naked poverty of his ignominious death are testimony to a life not bound by worldly concerns. Jesus' detachment from possessions was a lesson he both taught and lived, to advance his notion that the kingdom of God is not rooted in earthly wealth but rather in spiritual abundance.

> Then a scribe came and said to Jesus, "Teacher, I will follow you wherever you go." Jesus said to him, "The foxes have holes and the birds of the air have nests, but the Son of Man has nowhere to lay His head."
>
> (MATTHEW 8:19–20, NIV)

Jesus *chooses* to have nowhere to lay his head because the urgency of his mission demands that he preach in town after town as unencumbered as a minstrel with only his instrument. He instructed his disciples to move about with the same abandon.

> And He summoned the twelve and began to send them out in pairs, and gave them authority over the unclean spirits; and He instructed them that they should take nothing for their journey, except a mere staff—no bread, no bag, no money in their belt—but to wear sandals; and He added, "Do not put on two tunics."
> And He said to them, "Wherever you enter a house, stay there until you leave town. Any place that does not receive you or listen to you, as you go out from there, shake the dust off the soles of your feet for a testimony

against them." They went out and preached that men should repent. And they were casting out many demons and were anointing with oil many sick people and healing them.

(MARK 6:7–13, NASB)

If you let the fear of poverty govern your life,
your reward will be that you will eat,
but you will not live.
—GEORGE BERNARD SHAW

Henri Nouwen once referred to Jesus' voluntary poverty as the "downward mobility" of Jesus. That may give us some indication of why it is not a popular cultural notion. We aspire to be *upwardly* mobile. The downwardly mobile are on a slide we want to avoid. Jesus invites us to ride that slide with our arms flung high in the air, like the children he invites us to emulate.

This is not an easy ride to take, especially in the face of the countercultural message it flaunts. Voluntary poverty as a spiritual discipline ignites the ire of some who see it as promoting a welfare state where others need to be supported so that they can pursue their spiritual quest. ("Yeah, I have to work so that you can sit and pray" is a comment I once heard.) While religious communities such as my own are self-sufficient (not depending on a diocese for their funding) so that their members can pursue a life of financial detachment, we no doubt depend on the generosity of others to enable that pursuit. But *poverty* is not the best word to describe the way in which we live. *Detachment* (one of the steps already considered) and *simplicity* are probably better words to describe the spiritual virtue to which we aspire. Not connected or bound to any one person, thing, or salary, so that we might be freer to respond to all.

There are, of course, examples in our Christian tradition of those who embraced poverty more literally, such as Saint Francis of Assisi. The son of a wealthy merchant, Francis rejected all of his possessions, stripping himself naked in the town square, as a testimony to the Jesus of the Gospels whom he sought to follow. He founded a community that lived in poverty and served the poor. For Francis poverty was not a deprivation but a positive passion. To live as Jesus lived was his goal.

Religious poverty may be fine for those who are supported by organized religious communities, but what about the normal working person? How does he or she aspire to this spiritual virtue? The answer is to be found in the steps on detachment and avarice, already examined in our climb. It is not the money that is bad. The attachment to it is bad. It is not the possessions that corrupt. It is the inability to do without them that corrupts. Voluntary poverty suggests that to do without may enable an emptying that can only be filled by a more spiritual reality, namely God.

> *The honest poor can sometimes forget poverty.*
> *The honest rich never can.*
> —G. K. CHESTERTON

"Blessed are you who are poor, for the kingdom of God is yours" (Luke 6:20). Here Jesus seems to be indicating that the poor manifest a deep trust and hope in God. Aware of their dependence and need, they are more open to receive the wisdom of Jesus' proclamation. By contrast, the rich, lying on their beds of ivory, are deluded in their self-sufficiency. Their possessions remain an obstacle to their spiritual growth. Granted, while lack of possessions does not guarantee an open and receptive heart, it may enable one. If possessions *are* abundant, they must be used in the service of others.

Some of these same values are extolled in other religious traditions, as well. While in Buddhism poverty is bad because it involves *dukkha* (suffering, frustration, ill-being), and the buddhists want to end *dukkha,* Buddhism does encourage nonattachment toward material goods. Buddhists are encouraged to do with less while leading a good life free of hunger and disease. The higher Buddhists (or more noble ones) renounce more. Buddhist priests vow poverty and live by the generosity of others. Similarly, spiritual poverty is extolled in Islam and is also a cornerstone of classical Sufi practice.

Such teaching may seem problematic or, at the very least, naive to our modern sensibilities. After all, we know that poverty also produces all sorts of social ills. Much crime is the direct result of people living in poverty. Perhaps there is no country in our western hemisphere where this is more evident than in Haiti, the poorest nation in the West. One of our Passionist priests, Father Rick Frechette, who is also a medical doctor, has labored among the poor in Haiti for many years. He more than anyone knows the deleterious effects of poverty. And yet even amid the hardship, he sees the spirit of a people shine through. He wrote the following reflection to me in an e-mail after a particularly difficult day laboring in the vineyard of despair that Haiti sometimes is:

> Yesterday, I sat on a hot rock on a road in the hot sun in a slum for nearly an hour, trying to get my senses back. I don't remember ever being so sad and tired, so sick of it all, so overcome with feelings of hopelessness and futility. That rock was in the middle of the infamous Cité Soleil, not exactly a tropical paradise. I

was there to answer a simple question: Can I trust the basic goodness of human beings? I had always believed I could, but now I doubted. A red truck—and my vocation—hung in the balance.

It all had started on Sunday, when we were bitten by the ancient serpent of evil—and it was a nasty bite. As a group from our orphanage set out to bury a small child who had died in our hospital, they were kidnapped from the cemetery at Drouillard; even the small body was taken by a band of thugs.

The grieving mother was pulled violently from the red truck that serves as our hearse. She was harassed, threatened and robbed, and then told to run for her life, with bullets ringing out after her. She ran like a terrorized dog, not even knowing where to go, and not having any idea if and where her precious child would be laid to rest.

Eric, one of the workers, and the dead child were taken in the red truck deep into the slums at Drouillard. It seems that one of the gang suddenly had a touch of humanity and said to their leader, "Boss, he was going to bury this child. Why don't you let him go and we can just keep the truck?"

Eric was dismissed with a grunt, and, after being robbed, started walking the few kilometers back to the cemetery in the hot sun, coffin on his head, throbbing with its precious load, fearing another attack. Somewhere along that abandoned roadway the serpent evil bit again. Eric, himself being an ex-orphan (from our own orphanage) and an ex-con, suddenly thought that I would never believe that he was kidnapped and that the red truck had been stolen. He thought that surely I would think the story was a cover-up for him stealing the truck himself. Tormented by these thoughts, his mind became twisted and distorted. When I finally met him for the first time since his ordeal, he launched into a full-scale verbal rage at me, accusing me of not caring about his situation and of doing nothing to help him.

I was baffled and had no idea where this was coming from or what he was thinking. In fact, as I was starting Sunday mass at our orphanage in the mountains, I had gotten a call that Eric had been kidnapped. By cell phone, I had already organized an army of people to help him and had been assured by the gang leaders that Eric would be released. But none of this seemed to matter to him. I had to take some action.

When I arrived at Cité Soleil to get to the bottom of the gang incident, I chose that hot rock in the middle of the street as my throne of protest. Two different gang leaders came to talk to me. They wanted to know why I was on the rock.

"Please go home. We will send the truck to you before the end of the day," they said. "Okay, so you refuse to go without the truck. At least move to the shade until we get it. We will buy you a Coke."

But it wasn't just the truck. I was protesting what was done to a dead child, to a grieving mother, to Eric, to my whole team, to the whole country. It wasn't just a truck.

When I wouldn't budge, the leader called Bazo finally said to me, "Mon Père, have you gone crazy?"

"Am *I* crazy? Are you sure your question is for *me*? Your friends kidnap the dead, and *I* am the crazy one? Why are you crushing these people? Why? This poor woman, already weighed down by poverty and sorrow, had this one small chance to bury her child with tenderness. And you smashed that chance. You heap terror on top of her poverty and sadness and send her running in fear and despair. And you have the gall to ask me if *I* am crazy?"

They rolled the red truck up to me complete with battery and jack, radio and papers.

"Here now. Please get out of the sun," the leader said. "They didn't know it was one of your trucks. Why don't you mark all your trucks a certain way so that everyone will know them?"

"Oh, really? Do we need to mark even a hearse now?" I said. "Are even the dead not spared this nightmare?"

When I finally got home, I stopped in the chapel for a quiet minute. Eric was in the corner, sobbing. I sat next to him, and he flooded with tears. He had heard that I went myself to Cité Soleil for the truck. He now knew that I believed him, and he apologized for doubting my faith in him. He sobbed even more deeply.

"Eric, you are keeping yourself in prison now," I finally said. "This kind of thinking isn't good for you. I love you, and I believe in you. That's what is good for you. And you are good for me. For God's sake, be free of this twisted thinking."

I took off the simple, carved, cow-horn cross that I have worn around my neck for many years and placed it around his neck. No great catch as far as jewelry goes, but I needed to give him a deep sign, something to stay with him. Then he said that the worse part of the whole ordeal for him was standing by helplessly as a poor grieving mother ran off in confusion and anguish. How he wishes he could find her and tell her that he saw the funeral all the way to the end, and that he had tenderly buried her little child.

As I watched his face and listened to his words, my energy returned to me with a surge. Yes, human beings are basically good, I thought. Even in this poor, sometimes hellish place, goodness shines through. Having had enough for one day, I left the chapel to go to bed, but not before reading the words of a favorite hymn: *"We will run, and not grow weary, for our God will be our strength. And we will fly like the eagle; we will rise again."*

Questions for the Climb

1. Do you ever see poverty as being valuable?
2. What is the hardest thing for you about living simply?
3. How can you help to address the ill effects of poverty?
4. What is the one thing that you could never give up?

Step 18

*

Insensitivity / Deaf, Dumb, and Blind

*The leadership of the Church blighted the hopes
of my generation of priests, a small fact
doubtless from their viewpoint. What right did
we have to hope anyway? But in their rigidity,
they created the climate of insensitivity. . . .
God forgive them for losing their nerve.*

—ANDREW GREELEY

"Insensitivity is deadened feeling in body and spirit. . . . Lack of awareness is negligence that has become habit" (Climacus, Step 18). Many a spouse has complained about this disposition in his or her partner. Sometimes we hear of a wife who complains that her husband is "insensitive and clueless." A friend of mine recently complained that her husband doesn't notice anything—when she gets a new haircut, when she takes a lot of time cooking a meal, or even when she's not there. "It would take him a week to realize that I was gone."

Etymologically, the word "insensitive" means to be disconnected from one's senses. For our purposes this includes not only disconnected from the five senses, but from that sixth sense we call intuition, or "spiritual knowing." From Climacus's perspective, disconnection from the latter may be the most detrimental because it keeps you from seeing the movement of the Spirit in your life. You become blind to the deeper realities of life that Climacus sees as paramount.

This failure to *see* is a detriment that Jesus harps on in the Gospels. In the fourth chapter of the Gospel of John, Jesus meets a Samaritan woman at a well whom he senses is thirsty not only physically but spiritually, as well. He knows that he embodies what she needs to slake her deeper thirst. After asking her for a drink (a literary irony, since *she* is the one who is thirsty), he says to the woman from Samaria: "If you knew the gift of God and who is saying to you, 'Give me a drink,' you would have asked him and he would have given you living water" (4:10). Jesus is, of course, referring to himself, but the woman is blinded from seeing that. She is insensitive to the power of the one who stands before her. She tries to exert her dominance by questioning the authority of Jesus.

"Sir, you do not even have a bucket and the cistern is deep; where then can you get this living water? Are you greater than our father Jacob, who gave us this well and drank from it himself with his children and his flocks?" (4:11).

By the end of the Gospel passage, however, she becomes more sensitive and begins to *see,* as she proclaims to her neighbors, "Come see a man who told me everything I have ever done. Could he possibly be the Messiah?" (4:29).

The implication is that the senses that connect us to life can also connect us to God, the creator and sustainer of our lives. The five senses work in accord with that deeper sixth sense, spiritual knowing.

The movement from being insensitive to more sensitive is

sometimes slow. It is a process we need to cultivate in our lives. Some people seem never to get there. They are blind to an obvious disconnect between what they say and who they are.

> *It is . . . axiomatic that we should all think of*
> *ourselves as being more sensitive than other*
> *people because, when we are insensitive in our*
> *dealings with others, we cannot be aware of*
> *it at the time: conscious insensitivity is a*
> *self-contradiction.*
>
> —W. H. AUDEN

A few years ago I had to interview a famous author about her spirituality for a local television show. It was an encounter with an extreme example of this insensitive disposition toward life. While I had no previous evidence of the woman's spirituality, I had been told that she was a lifelong Catholic who took that commitment seriously.

When I mentioned to some people that I was going to be doing the interview, I got some interesting reactions. "Watch your back with that one," one savvy publicist warned. "Good luck, better you than me," said a seasoned interviewer while audibly exhaling.

I attributed her reputation to her advanced age and her grande dame status. But how bad could she be? I wondered. And after all, a committed Catholic would surely cut a priest interviewer some slack. Talk about being blind.

A few days before the interview she called and said, "Father Beck, we never discussed my hair and makeup for this interview."

"Oh, that's not a problem," I said. "We have a fine hair and makeup person."

"Father Beck, don't insult me," she spat into the phone. "I have my own hair and makeup person. My reason for calling you is to confirm that you will indeed cover the cost of both of them."

I hesitated. It was a proposal that I hadn't anticipated, especially with our limited not-for-profit production budget.

"Hellooo?" she said.

"Um, yes, I'm here," I said, "Well, I suppose we could take care of that, but I hadn't anticipated it."

"Father Beck, this interview cannot *cost* me money."

"No, no, of course not. Well, how much would it be to cover your hair and makeup?"

"Usually, it's $1,200, but I'll make an exception and take only $1,000 from you."

I lost my voice again.

"Hellooo?" she moaned into the phone.

"Yes, I'm here. Well, I have to check about that," I said. I had expected her to say $250. What could they possibly do to her for $1,200 . . . a face-lift before the interview?

"Well, it's the only way I can do the interview," she said.

Luckily, a generous benefactor came through and put up the money. "This isn't for *her* makeup," she said to me as she wrote the check. "It's for *your* television show."

The crew and I were to arrive at the television studio at 4 p.m. for the setup, and the author was to make her appearance at 5 p.m. The first part of that equation went smoothly. Everyone on the crew was on time, and we had finished adjusting camera and lights by 5. We awaited the arrival of the famed author.

By 5:15 I was getting nervous. Had she forgotten? Was this just the fashionably late thing for celebrities to do? At 5:20 the phone in the studio rang.

"Let me speak to Father Beck," a gravelly voice barked into the phone.

"Speaking," I replied sheepishly, knowing it was she.

"Where the hell are you?" she barked even louder.

"I'm here in the studio waiting for you," I said.

"That's bullshit!" she screamed. "You're supposed to call me to come in when you're ready. I've been sitting here in the greenroom cooling my heels for twenty minutes. Now I'm going to be late for my appointment this evening."

"Well, I'm sorry, but that wasn't my understanding. I thought you were just going to come up at—"

"That's bullshit!" she screamed again. "You are to inform me when you're ready for me."

"Okay, well, I'm ready," I said, though now I wasn't sure that I was. The phone clicked dead.

I went in to inform the crew that we were off to a shaky start. Saying that I didn't know what to expect when she came through the door, I suggested that we placate her and just get through it. They nodded in agreement.

I decided that I would wait in the hallway for her and try to smooth things over before we began—to get rid of this bad karma that had crept in before I had even asked my first question. As I waited outside the door, my stomach was in knots; I was already intimidated. A door opened and in walked an assistant followed by the author who was dressed in a beige cashmere sweater, matching wool pants, and a white silk shirt and tie. Her hair and makeup were perfect, as well they should have been. I opened my arms to embrace her, my initial attempt at rapprochement.

"Don't touch me," she said in her smoky voice as she extended her arm to make sure that I kept my distance. "Don't you know you don't kiss somebody who has just had hair and makeup done? This isn't even my business and I know that."

"Oh, sorry," I said, stepping back. "Well, welcome anyway. And I'm sorry for the misunderstanding. I just thought . . ."

"Yes, well, you thought wrongly. Now let's get crackin' and get this thing over with. I have a book signing later to get to." That was the first I had heard about that.

She breezed past me into a small room off the studio to do some last-minute primping in front of a mirror. I informed her that the audio man would mike her for the interview. She nodded. The audio man approached as she stood with one hand on her hip.

"What are you going to do with that?" she said.

"It's a wireless microphone," the audio guy said. "I'm going to clip it on your pants in the back and then weave the wire up under your sweater so that we can clip the mike in front."

"Uh-huh. Fine. Well, then do it."

He had no sooner clipped the microphone on her and began routing the wire when she thrust her arms in the air like Evita singing "Don't Cry for Me Argentina" and screamed, "What the hell are you doing back there? You idiot! You're hurting me!"

"I'm sorry, but I only—"

"Give me that. I'll do it," she said, and grabbed the microphone cord, ripping it from the power pack on her back. "Get out."

The audio guy looked at me with a pained expression, shook his head, and walked into the studio.

I wondered how to handle this. I knew that I shouldn't allow her abusive behavior, but I knew also that we needed this interview and that I had to be careful not to have her walk out.

"Please. You are going to have to calm down," I finally said. "We can't go into an interview like this."

She spun from the mirror and said, "Father, please don't tell me what I can and cannot do. My assistant will help me put this thing on, and then let's begin this damn thing. We are wasting time. Let's get crackin'." She smacked her hands together.

Because we needed to sit close to each other for the proper camera angles on the set, our chairs had hardly any space between them. She stared at the floor while the cameraman counted us in.

"We're rolling," he said.

Suddenly a different person sat in front of me, one who was charming, engaging, and even somewhat deferential to my priestly status. She talked about her Catholicism, her praying, especially to Mary, and how we have to be conscious of giving to the poor. "If we have two pennies, we should give one away," she said dramatically as she clutched her chest. (I wondered if that meant I could expect a $500 rebate in the mail for hair and makeup.)

When one of the cameras malfunctioned during the interview, she became irate again, chastising the cameraman for not cuing her properly once we had begun again. "You have to tell me when we're rolling again! Don't you know you're supposed to say something?" "Dr. Jekyll and Mrs. Hyde" does not even begin to describe it.

As she was leaving, she said that she enjoyed the experience more than she thought she would, but that she had been nervous when she had arrived and was suffering from nagging back pain.

"I don't apologize, though," she said. "I'm just a tough dame sometimes. It's just the way it is." Hardly news to any of us by then.

As a much younger gentleman, who had arrived during the interview, escorted her out, I overheard her tell him that they were not going to be late for the party after all. So much for the book signing. I learned later that we had paid her for her hair and makeup for a party that she was attending that evening.

"She is one of the most insensitive people that I've ever met," one of the crew said as we were breaking down the lights and striking the set. He had no argument from any of us.

I thought a lot about it afterward. Couldn't she *see* the inconsistency of treating people like dispensable minions and then waxing eloquent about spirituality and faith? Was she so unaware that faith and actions need to be inextricably linked? Then I started to make excuses for her. She had had a difficult life and had experienced some personal losses. Perhaps her tough exterior was a shield for a more vulnerable interior. Come out swinging before you get hit first. She needed to exert her control from the beginning; otherwise, she couldn't function without having the upper hand.

And yet it made me sad. She had reached the autumn of her life and was still fighting demons of insecurity and fear. She had not yet seen that her only peace would come in letting go of the control she so insensitively exerted. And her faith seemingly had been of no help in getting her to that place.

> But while ignorance can make you insensitive,
> familiarity can also numb.
> —ANNA QUINDLEN

A few chapters after encountering the Samaritan woman in the Gospel of John, Jesus meets another person who fails to see, the man born blind. "[Jesus] spat on the ground and made clay with the saliva, and smeared the clay on his [the man's] eyes, and said to him, 'Go wash in the Pool of Siloam.' So he went and washed, and came back able to see" (John 9:6–7).

After his encounter with Jesus, the man born blind begins to become a new creation, not unlike the creation that occurs—also with clay—in the second Book of Genesis, "the LORD formed man out of the clay of the ground and blew into his nostrils the breath of life, and so man became a living being" (2:7).

That is the goal: to become a living being. The man born blind becomes a living being, a new creation, when he *sees* not only physically but spiritually as well. It takes some forty verses in this Gospel text for him to get there, until his final declaration of faith:

> When Jesus heard that they had thrown him [the blind man] out, he found him and said, "Do you believe in the Son of Man?" He answered and said, "Who is he, sir, that I may believe in him?" Jesus said to him, "You have seen him and the one speaking with you is he." He said, "I do believe, Lord," and he worshiped him. Then Jesus said, "I came into this world for judgment, so that those who do not see might, and those who do see might become blind."
>
> Some of the Pharisees who were with him heard this and said to him, "Surely we are not also blind, are we?" Jesus said to them, "If you were blind, you would have no sin; but now you are saying, 'We see,' so your sin remains."
>
> (JOHN 9:35–41)

Insensitivity is an important step on our climb. While we might not sense such a radical insensitivity in our lives as my author friend demonstrated, there are surely ways in which we fail to see what is most vital about our lives, and there are times when we think we see clearly but are truly blind; times when we don't (or can't) hear words of praise, encouragement, and challenge; times when we resist the touch of intimacy because we fear vulnerability; times when we don't taste the sweetness of life because we wallow in some of its bitterness; times when we fail to smell the sweet aroma of a luxuriant spring because we hold fast to the death of winter. Times when all of our senses shut down, making us truly insensitive. But perhaps there is no greater insensitivity than a disconnection from that sixth sense of spiritual knowing. For when we lose that connection, all of the other senses suffer, as well.

Questions for the Climb
1. Do you consider yourself insensitive at times?
2. What causes that disposition in you?
3. How has your blindness been healed?
4. Are you sensitive to "spiritual knowing" in your life?

*

Staying Awake and Staying Alert / Spiritual Starbucks

Awake, my soul, awake, lyre and harp.
I will awake the dawn!

—PSALM 57:9

At this juncture in our climb we are ready to take a larger leap. Perhaps John Climacus knew that when he decided to put two similar steps so close together on his spiritual ladder. While "Staying Awake" and "Staying Alert" differ in nuance, they are alike enough to consider together in one larger step upward. "Staying Awake" is an exhortation to come out of sleep or not to fall asleep, while "Staying Alert" is what we are encouraged to do while we are awake. Whatever our perspectives on these two steps, both connote spiritual virtues crucial to our living more fulfilled lives. So load up on some spiritual caffeine, and let's continue climbing.

When I was a younger priest (my second year ordained), I decided one Holy Saturday night that I would keep vigil the whole night until Easter Sunday morning. After all, I reasoned, that is the real intent of the Holy Saturday vigil, to watch in joyous expectation for the one we know emerges from the tomb of death on Easter morning. Members of the early Church did keep vigil all night. While our present-day, extended Holy Saturday night Catholic liturgy surely tests the endurance of some unsuspecting churchgoers who may have thought they were slipping in for a normal one-hour Saturday evening Mass, the current Easter vigil does not take all night. Even though we proclaim nine Scripture readings, light fires, renew vows, and liberally sprinkle freshly blessed water, we are usually home for the late-evening news.

But this one particular Holy Saturday I thought it would be spiritually enriching to return to the ancient tradition of keeping vigil all night. Just the day before, on Good Friday, we had heard Jesus remonstrate with his disciples about their failure to stay awake for even one hour while he was sweating blood in the Garden of Gethsemane as he prayed about his impending death. "Could you not stay awake with me for even one hour?" "Yes" was my answer this Holy Saturday night—and not just one hour, but all night.

Although we had just celebrated the Easter mystery at the vigil this night before Easter morning, once everyone had left the Church, something still seemed incomplete. The scent of newly placed Easter lilies punctuated the sanctuary, and white cloths streamed down a cross that just hours before had loomed stark and unadorned, but the daylight of Easter morning had not yet come. We were still in the tomb, still waiting for something to happen. So I wanted to wait there and stay awake, praying about the mystery of death and life that we were commemorating.

I couldn't have stayed awake long because I remember hardly anything about that night. I awoke Easter morning lying down in the church pew with the first hints of dawn bleeding through the stained glass windows. I chuckled as I lay there. *Just like the disciples,* I thought, though I probably didn't even stay awake as long as they had managed in the garden.

I was about to get up and go into the rectory to shower when a stream of pure sunlight shone through a broken part of the stained glass window that had been replaced with transparent glass. Seemingly filtering through that pane alone, the sunlight flooded the pew on which I was lying. Not the pew in front of me, nor the pew in back of me; only my pew. It started on my legs and slowly crept up my body until my face was fully illumined by the new sun, which felt warm, caressing, and forgiving. I couldn't have set the scene better if I had taken hours to orchestrate it for the filming of a movie. Now awake fully, I set about preparing to celebrate Easter with the glow of a sun that I carried with me throughout that day and for many days afterward.

> *I cannot be awake for nothing looks to me as it did before, Or else I am awake for the first time, and all before has been a mean sleep.*
> —WALT WHITMAN

In his letter to the Romans, Saint Paul writes: "And do this because you know the time; it is the hour now for you to awake from sleep. For salvation is nearer now than when we first believed; the night is advanced, the day is at hand" (13:11–12a).

Wakefulness is a spiritual concept that we find in many religious traditions. It is sometimes spoken of as awareness or attentiveness, or "becoming more fully conscious." Spiritual masters teach that many of us go through life asleep to what is most significant about our lives. We miss what is most real because we trivialize our lives with superficialities that matter little.

A father knocks on his son's door. "Jaime," he says, "wake up!"

Jaime answers, "I don't want to get up, Papa."

The father shouts, "Get up, you have to go to school."

Jaime says, "I don't want to go to school."

"Why not?" asks the father.

"Three reasons," says Jaime. "First, because it's so dull; second, the kids tease me; and third, I hate school."

And the father says, "Well, I am going to give you three reasons why you must go to school. First, because it is your duty; second, because you're forty-five years old; and third, because you are the headmaster."

Anthony de Mello, a Jesuit priest from India, tells this story at the beginning of his book *Awareness*. De Mello writes about wakefulness and coming to awareness because he believes that most of us wander through life asleep to what is most important about our lives. He says we need to "wake up!" and see what is.

The question arises: Awake to *what?* Eyes of faith help answer this question. The consciousness to which spiritual writers refer is ultimately the awareness of the presence, activity, and call of God in our lives. We must believe there is a deeper level to reality if we are to attempt to access its ebb and flow. While not precluding mystical experiences that occur in a state of religious rapture, wakefulness encourages attentiveness to the God who also visits us in the mundane events of our everyday lives. "Seeing" and "noticing" are part of this dynamic, but wakefulness demands even more. Wakefulness asks that we see, notice, and act upon what has more fully come to consciousness.

To live without killing is a thought which
could electrify the world, if men were only
capable of staying awake long enough to
let the idea soak in.

—HENRY MILLER

A friend of mine tells a story about his grandmother's tutelage that prompted such wakefulness. He had attended Mass with her in a church in Dublin. Before leaving the church, his grandmother stopped at the bank of candles where there was an old painting that he had never liked. His grandmother lit some candles, said some quiet prayers, and then walked closer to touch the painting and to bless herself. The painting, a common one in churches, was an ornate Madonna and Child known as *Our Lady of Perpetual Succor.* But the painting in this church was a little different. There was something wrong with the Madonna's eyes.

"After Granny touched the picture and blessed herself," my friend said, "I told her that I didn't like the painting."

"Why not?" his grandmother asked.

"Because Mary's eyes are funny. They're crooked. The painter did them wrong."

His grandmother looked at the painting more closely and after a few moments said, "Oh, son, her eyes are not crooked. The artist painted them that way. One eye is looking out at you, and the other is looking down at the baby Jesus in her arms."

My friend was struck by his grandmother's spiritual acumen, "how she was really seeing, and how what she saw came from and pointed to the depth and strength of her faith. She was awake to all of it, awake to life and to God. I learned something from her awareness. And it caused me to want to act differently. I wanted to reach her level of attentiveness."

We can indeed learn something from the awareness of others who seem to be more awake than we are. That is why we have spiritual masters and teachers. As their students, we need to watch their approach to life and try to emulate it, to lean into their way of seeing so that our vision and wakefulness is expanded.

In the Song of Songs we read: "I charge you, daughters of Jerusalem, by the gazelles and hinds of the fields, not to stir my love, nor rouse it, until it please to awake" (2:7). This text suggests that there is a time for awakening that cannot be rushed. We wake up only when we are ready. How often have we had experiences that seem the same in objective circumstances but are different in the way in which we perceive them? We walk past the same tree everyday, but on this one day we notice its beauty. We have heard the same Scripture passage for years, but one day we hear it differently. Why do we suddenly see something that we have passed by for months or really hear something that we have heard for years? Sometimes we are stirred to wakefulness by people or things outside of ourselves who point the way. We need help to become aware.

Our truest life is when we are
in our dreams awake.
—HENRY DAVID THOREAU

The eleventh chapter of John's Gospel is about someone awaking from more than a deep sleep, with some help. Here Lazarus is awakened from death itself. Although Lazarus has died, Jesus says to his disciples: " 'Our friend Lazarus is asleep, but I am going to awaken him.' . . . Then [after the stone of the tomb had been rolled back] he cried out in a loud voice, 'Lazarus, come out!' The dead man came out, tied hand and foot with burial bands, and his face was wrapped in a cloth. So Jesus said to them, 'Untie him and let him go' " (11:11, 43–44).

Some interpretations of this famous text point to the symbolic themes it raises. Like Lazarus, many of us are asleep—no, more than asleep, *dead*. Parts of us die. Hopes and dreams die. Relationships die. Faith dies. Often they die because we have not been vigilant in keeping them alive. We take things for granted, or we fail to give the proper nourishment for life to thrive. We walk around in a daze, like mummies, asleep to that which needs tending in our lives. While we have no indication in the text whether this was the case for Lazarus, we learn something from his resuscitation. The call of love, as the Song of Songs suggests, roused Lazarus from his sleep, as it can us. People who care about us desire us to have fullness of life. Like Jesus with his friend Lazarus, the call of love can set us free. "Untie him, and let him go!" These words resonate not only for Lazarus but all of us who have fallen asleep to the pulsating potential of our lives. Called forth from the tombs of our lives that bind with bandages that blind us to the power of love that surrounds us, we abandon tombs of lost relationships, addictions, betrayals, financial ruin, and the loss of loved ones. Just when we think hope has been lost, that all is dead, we discover that we have only been asleep.

Being asleep is not without its danger. The sleep spoken of here is not restorative but restricting. We miss a lot, as the following parable of Jesus suggests:

> "At that time the kingdom of heaven will be like ten virgins who took their lamps and went out to meet the bridegroom. Five of them were foolish and five were wise. The foolish ones took their lamps but did not take

any oil with them. The wise, however, took oil in jars along with their lamps. The bridegroom was a long time in coming, and they all became drowsy and fell asleep. At midnight the cry rang out, 'Here's the bridegroom! Come out to meet him.' Then all those virgins rose and trimmed their lamps. The foolish ones said to the wise, 'Give us some of your oil; our lamps are going out.' 'No,' they replied, 'There may not be enough for both us and you. Instead go to those who sell oil and buy some for yourselves.' But while they were on their way to buy the oil, the bridegroom arrived. The virgins who were ready went in with him to the wedding banquet. And the door was shut. Later the others also came. 'Sir! Sir!' they said. 'Open the door for us.' But he replied, 'I tell you the truth, I don't know you.' Therefore keep watch, because you do not know the day or the hour."

(MATTHEW 25:1–13, NIV)

And the heart that is soonest awake
to the flowers is always the first to be
touch'd by the thorns.
—THOMAS MOORE

Vigilance is needed not to miss our visitation, which can come in many forms. Being spiritually rooted in life experience implores us to look for those visitations in unlikely places. As perhaps on an airplane.

I did not look forward to flying after September 11, 2001. I had been scheduled to go to London for a book event in early October to publicize the release of my first book, *God Underneath: Spiritual Memoirs of a Catholic Priest,* and all of the expenses had been paid. Despite my praying that the event would be canceled, it was not. If I wanted to live what I preached about love conquering fear, I had no choice but to board the plane.

As I was packing the night before the trip and listening to the radio, then Attorney General John Ashcroft encouraged vigilance in the face of a possible second terrorist attack. Perhaps a sign from God that I shouldn't go? No, simply my own fear haunting my tragic-scenario-ladened mind. *Go to London,* I told myself. I finished packing and went to bed with my stomach still dancing from the radio announcement.

I awoke the morning of the flight to pouring rain. But this was no ordinary rainstorm. Thunder, lightning, and howling gales of wind made for a violent display of nature. I wondered if perhaps it was a sign from God, but, again, I knew better. How self-centered to think that God was making it rain, simply so that I wouldn't go to London. I reluctantly gathered my bags and headed to Newark International Airport.

After passing through six security checkpoints, I arrived in the international departure lounge. Still nervous, I took out a book and attempted to read it. Instead, I found myself counting the number of men in turbans who were waiting with me in the departure lounge. Although I felt embarrassed by and ashamed of my racial profiling, nine did seem like an unusually high number.

I was only in my plane seat five minutes when a flight attendant approached me.

"Edward Beck?" she said.

"Yes," I answered somewhat hesitantly, wondering what was wrong.

"Follow me, please, and take your carry-on with you," she said curtly, turned on her heel, and made her way toward the front of the plane.

Great . . . what now? I wondered. *Don't tell me that they are taking me off of the plane.*

She passed by the exit door to the plane and motioned me forward into the first-class cabin.

Smiling, she turned and said, "Because you are a frequent flyer and the flight is so empty, we are upgrading you to first class. Have a wonderful flight." She pointed at the comfortable-looking leather seat on the aisle.

"Well, thank you," I said. The flight suddenly didn't look so bad after all.

"May I get you something to drink?" she said.

"Um . . . yes, a Bloody Mary . . . and make it a double," I said. She smiled knowingly.

Five minutes before they shut the door of the plane for our departure, a man in a turban, whom I had noticed in the departure lounge, made his way down the aisle of the first-class cabin. He stopped at my seat—of course—and looked at the numbers above my head.

"Excuse me, that's my seat by the window," he said in accented English.

Geez, great, I thought.

My stomach started doing somersaults again. The Bloody Mary didn't last long in my glass. My flying companion took out a medical journal and began reading, while I wondered if I was going to sleep at all during the transatlantic flight that now seemed as perilous as my imagings.

Astounded that we were taking off in such inclement weather, I gripped both sides of my seat as the plane raced down the runway and shook even more as its nose lifted into the formidable winds. The plane wasn't the only thing shaking. My turbaned companion looked at me and put his medical journal in the seat pocket in front of him. He smiled, extended his hand to my clenched one, and introduced himself. He said that he was a medical doctor who had been detained in this country after September 11 and now, finally, almost one month later, was being allowed to go home to his wife and children in London, whom he loved and missed so much.

I looked up and for the first time *really* saw him. Kind eyes and a gentle face, a human being. Suddenly the plane broke through all of the turbulence and was above the clouds, and there was that peace that comes with just the hum of the engine. And then the sunlight broke through the clouds and streamed through the plane window across this man's face. He glowed. I knew that it was God breaking through to me, breaking through my fear, prejudice, and ignorance, to teach me something about compassion, something about our common humanity, and something about waking up from my perilous sleep.

I think that's how it happens. It is in the ordinariness of our lives where suddenly God breaks through and we *see* differently, and because we do, we are called to *act* differently. To act like people awake and no longer asleep. And as I recall a church pew on Easter Sunday morning and a dreaded flight to London, I'm struck that it has often been real sunlight that has banished the darkness of the night for me. Perhaps subtlety doesn't work well with me.

Questions for the Climb

1. Do you feel asleep to what is most important about your life?
2. How have others helped you to "wake up"?
3. Are you sufficiently aware of the deeper currents of life?
4. Do you think prejudice is a type of sleep?

$Step$ 21

*

Fear / Space Mountain Syndrome

Do the thing you fear most and
the death of fear is certain.

—MARK TWAIN

I wrote about my fear of roller coasters in a previous book; how I was intimidated by a kiddies' roller coaster in Brooklyn and how my mother made it worse by telling stories of how in the winter she would swoop down the icy tracks of the huge L.A. Thompson Roller Coaster in Coney Island on her sled. No seat belts, no protective cart, nothing but a prayer to keep the blades of her sled in the frozen tracks. And imagine me afraid of a little kiddies' roller coaster.

What I didn't write about earlier was my adult encounter with a roller coaster. After having sworn them off after my maiden voyage at age six, I had managed to avoid roller coasters for my adolescent and adult life. Well . . . almost.

I had just completed a retreat in Orlando, Florida, and was spending a day off with a priest friend from high school. Although I had heard much about Disney World, I had never been there. My friend considered this an unpardonable lacuna in my pop-culture education.

"You've *never* been to Disney World or Disneyland?" he said. "That's practically un-American. We'll have to take care of that."

And that's what he did. He had gotten day passes from parishioners who worked at Disney, and we were enjoying the various theme parks one sunny spring day. Eating in the different "countries" of the Epcot Pavilions, strolling the back lots of the MGM Studios, and enjoying the lulling boat ride in Magic Kingdom's It's a Small World were just my speed. But before long we were standing beneath a giant monolith of steel and white aluminum called Space Mountain that looked like an outer-galaxy sports stadium. The ride itself was not visible from the outside, but the screams emanating from inside were audible.

"Now, this is the *best* ride in the whole park," my friend said with conviction. "We *must* go on this."

"I don't think so," I said, as I eyed the stories-high structure that cast an ominous shadow over us lowly peons below.

"Oh, yes, it's so great," he said. "You cannot come to Disney and not experience Space Mountain."

"But, Philip," I said, "you know I don't go on roller coasters. I'm afraid of roller coasters."

"But this isn't a roller coaster," he said.

"Well, then, why are they screaming like that?" I said.

"Because they're in the dark and a few space creatures jump out at you. It's kind of like an outer-space It's a Small World, but only more fun, and a bit more scary."

"But It's a Small World wasn't scary at all," I said.

"Exactly," he said. "It's kids in there screaming. Not adults like us. You'll be fine."

I'm not sure why I accepted such a lame explanation, but I did. And soon we were waiting for our turn to ride the celestial It's a Small World ride. When the carts rolled into the boarding station, I had queasy déjà vu.

"Philip, these look like roller coaster carts," I said.

"No, they don't. They look like little space rockets. All the carts on these rides look alike anyway. They're just like the Small World carts, only these don't go in water."

"Are you sure . . ." I started to say.

"Would you please just relax and get in," he said, as he motioned me into the cart being held by a ride-weary attendant.

I secured the seat belt and held on to the stationary bar in front of us.

"Seems like an awful lot of restraint for a gentle space ride," I said.

"Relax. Just close your eyes and have fun."

"Close my eyes?"

We pulled out of the holding station into inky blackness, and, before I knew it, we were pitched at a ninety-degree angle and slowly ascending straight up.

"What's going on?" I said, tightly squeezing his leg.

"We're going up," he said, laughing.

"I can feel that, but how are we getting back down?"

"By the tracks, of course," he said, laughing some more. "Ouch. You're hurting me."

"You haven't felt anything yet," I managed to say, before the cart careened over the top of the hill and rushed downward at a speed that was literally breathtaking.

By the time I had stumbled out of the cart and into the blinding sunlight, my head was spinning and I felt nauseous. Philip was surprised that my reaction to a "simple roller coaster" was so extreme.

"Haven't you ever been afraid of something?" I asked.

"Yeah, but not a ride," he said.

"Well, we don't choose what we are afraid of," I said.

"That's true, but you might as well pick something that can really harm you."

Later I realized that he didn't get what I was saying. Fear is not a choice. But riding a roller coaster is. I can choose not to ride a roller coaster and thereby avoid confronting that fear. A lot of other fears can't be avoided. John Climacus writes that "[fear] is a lapse from faith that comes from anticipating the unexpected. Fear is danger tasted in advance, a quiver as the heart takes fright before unnamed calamity. Fear is a loss of assurance." But we don't choose those lapses or dangers. And the effect they have on us can be debilitating.

> *To fear the worst oft cures the worse.*
> —WILLIAM SHAKESPEARE

A Spanish Jesuit, Carlos Valles, begins his book *Let Go of Fear* with a story about fear's paralyzing effects. He writes that when he was stationed at a difficult mission in India, he often needed to get away for some respite. He would ride his bicycle to a bucolic field about two miles from the mission. One beautiful, sunny day he was riding to the field. Birds were singing, flowers were flaunting their vibrant colors, and peace was permeating the air. As Carlos was enjoying the idyll, suddenly he noticed a shift in the landscape, and he sensed danger in the air.

He stopped his bicycle and, two feet in front of him, a cobra reared up, its hood outstretched. The snake, however, wasn't paying any mind to Carlos. Its gaze was fixed on the branch of a nearby tree where a small bird sat paralyzed by the cobra's gaze. While he had heard that snakes could have this kind of effect on birds, Carlos had never seen it before. The bird had a voice, but it couldn't sing. It had wings, but it couldn't fly. It sat paralyzed simply by the gaze of the cobra.

Carlos jumped off his bicycle and began to stomp his feet and to wave his arms. After a few moments the snake slithered off into the grass. As soon as it did, the bird began to sing, and a few moments later, it spread its wings and soared into the azure Indian sky.

Carlos begins *Let Go of Fear* with this story, because he says that this is what fear does to us in our lives: It paralyzes us; it keeps us from moving forward in our lives. Undeniably, we are a people of many fears. The number of psychologically classified phobias appears endless, everything from acousticophobia (fear of noise, usually loud noise) to xenophobia (fear of strangers, foreigners, or aliens). While there are medications and psychological therapies to deal with certain fears, Climacus includes fear as one of the steps on his ladder because it also has spiritual relevance. Fear limits our spiritual maturation because it denies the reality of the sustaining power and dominance of the love of God.

> *Fear defeats more people than any*
> *other one thing in the world.*
> —RALPH WALDO EMERSON

A friend of mine was at a Scripture conference where a scholar said that in the Bible God says "Do not be afraid" 366 times. This scholar said, "Once for each day of the year and once for leap year." He went on to suggest that perhaps God says "Do not be afraid" so many times because God knows that we are. What is even more perplexing than our seeming inability to embrace this injunction is the tendency of some to fear this very God who says "Do not be afraid" 366 times. Many were raised with a severe, judgmental God who stands ready to punish even the most minor infraction. So rather than rest in the Divine bosom of one who desires to shield us from that of which we are afraid, we run from that which we perceive poised to slap us down for our transgressions. Fear indeed, with no help from religion.

> When He got into the boat, His disciples followed Him. And behold, there arose a great storm on the sea, so that the boat was being covered with the waves; but Jesus Himself was asleep. And they came to Him and woke Him, saying "Save us, Lord; we are perishing!" He said to them, "Why are you afraid, you [people] of little faith?" Then He got up and rebuked the winds and the sea, and it became perfectly calm. The men were amazed, and said, "What kind of a man is this, that even the winds and the sea obey Him?"
>
> (MATTHEW 8:23–27, NASB)

Maybe that's the way it feels sometimes—like Jesus (or God) is asleep in the boat while we are perishing. *Don't you see that we are drowning?* becomes the cry of our hearts. *Don't you see that my husband is abusive? Don't you see that my son is drug addicted? Don't you see that my best friend is being sent to prison? Are you asleep?* We fear that we are being left to deal with these vagaries of life alone. But the words echo back, "Why are you afraid, you people of little faith?"

We are afraid because the succor we desire and need does not always appear self-evident. At times we *do* feel alone and vulnerable. The consolation of a God we cannot wrap our arms around, metaphorically or actually, seems like a distant promise. And yet that promise is sometimes all we have to hold on to.

> *We must build dikes of courage to hold back*
> *the flood of fear.*
> —MARTIN LUTHER KING JR.

Some spiritual writers have maintained that there are only two human emotions: love and fear. All other emotions are derivatives of these two. The positive ones—(joy, forgiveness, peacefulness, contentment, appreciation)—stem from love and the negative ones—(hate, prejudice, depression, anger, guilt)—stem from fear. They cannot exist at the same time because they are mutually exclusive. The joy that comes from love is no longer present once the sadness that comes from fear is present. Similarly, the light of love banishes the darkness of fear. The task, therefore, is to let love dominate our lives so that fear has no room to exist. The Bible seems to agree with that assessment:

> God is love, and the one who abides in love abides in God, and God abides in him. By this, love is perfected with us, so that we may have confidence in the day of judgment; because as He is, so also are we in this world. There is no fear in love; but perfect love casts out fear, because fear involves punishment, and the one who fears is not perfected in love.
>
> (1 JOHN 4:16–18, NASB)

It is not easy to let love dominate in a world that seems to promote fear and all of its negative offshoots. Even the news is intent on instilling more fear. "Lead with that which bleeds" seems to be the news producers' anthem: weapons of mass destruction, bird flu, high-fat food hazards, and incurable pandemics that threaten our future existence. When I visit my parents in Florida in the summertime, every newscast seems to warn of impending hurricanes, even when none is to be found on the meteorological map. The hint of a tropical depression in Africa is fodder enough for the fearmongers of Southwest Florida's news. They broadcast warning upon warning until they stir up a frenzy. Yet when we do actually have a natural disaster, like Hurricane Katrina in 2005, we are unprepared and not sufficiently warned. It makes no sense.

The disciples were not exempt from fear's deleterious effects:

Immediately He [Jesus] made the disciples get into the boat and go ahead of Him to the other side, while He sent the crowds away. After He had sent the crowds away, He went up on the mountain by Himself to pray; and when it was evening, He was there alone. But the boat was already a long distance from the land, battered by the waves; for the wind was contrary. And in the fourth watch of the night He came to them, walking on the sea. When the disciples saw Him walking on the sea, they were terrified, and said, "It is a ghost!" And they cried out in fear. But immediately Jesus spoke to them, saying, "Take courage, it is I; do not be afraid." Peter said to Him, "Lord, if it is You, command me to come to You on the water." And He said, "Come!" And Peter got out of the boat, and walked on the water and came toward Jesus. But seeing the wind, he became frightened, and beginning to sink, he cried out, "Lord, save me!" Immediately Jesus stretched out His hand and took hold of him, and said to him, "You of little faith, why did you doubt?" When they got into the boat, the wind stopped. And those who were in the boat worshiped Him, saying, "You are certainly God's Son!"

(MATTHEW 14:22–33, NASB)

In the Gospels there seems to be some correlation between water and fear, however unintended. If it's not a storm at sea, then it's a daredevil walk on water that goes bad. But Peter sinks only once he becomes frightened, once he loses faith. When fear is held at bay, even gravity can be defied. What the Gospel writers, John Climacus, and present-day spiritual writers seem to know is that fear limits us, while unfettered risk opens us up. In this step of our spiritual journey, we are called to examine the limiting and paralyzing fears of our life and to acknowledge how they are rooted in a lack of sufficient faith.

My biggest fear in life is to be forgotten.
—EVITA PERÓN

One of the joys of working in an African American parish on the south side of Chicago when I was a theology student was the wonderfully rich and diverse liturgical experiences at Saint Sabina Church. Because the church is well known and respected in the African American community, each year on the birthday of Dr. Martin Luther King Jr. someone from Dr. King's family would come to address the congregation. Once when I was there Yolanda King, Dr. King's daughter, was the guest speaker. She said that when she was a little girl, her father had this play ritual with her whereby he'd take her by her hand into the kitchen, put her on top of the refrigerator, step back, open his arms, and say, "Jump, Yokie, jump!" She was always frightened at being so high in the air and she'd cry, "No, Daddy, I'm afraid. Daddy, it's too high. Daddy, take me down."

She said this would happen time and time again, and her response was always the same: "Daddy, I'm afraid. Daddy, it's too high. Daddy, take me down."

One evening Dr. King returned home after having been away for about two weeks during a difficult campaign when an attempt on his life had been made. He came through the door looking tired and a bit disheveled and said nothing to anyone in the family. He looked at Yokie, took her by the hand into the kitchen, and set her on top of the refrigerator. Stepping back and with his voice breaking, he said, "Jump, Yokie, jump."

She said that she doesn't know whether it was that he had been away so long or looked so bad, but, for the first time, she jumped off the refrigerator with abandon. Her father caught her in his open arms, held her tight, and with tears in his eyes said, "Yokie, you've learned something very important tonight. You've learned what it means to trust someone other than yourself. You've learned what it means to jump."

I will always remember that story because it strikes me as the same lesson we all need to learn in life and in our relationship with God. Somehow we are all that little kid sitting on top of the refrigerator afraid—afraid of intimacy, afraid of risking, afraid of failure, afraid of whatever. The outstretched arms of the power of love that casts out all fear beckons us forward to make the leap, to trust those arms will be there to catch us and embrace us in the power that perfect love generates. How long do we sit on top of that refrigerator instead?

Questions for the Climb
1. What is your deepest fear?
2. How do you deal with fear?
3. Do you ever fear God?
4. Have you had the experience of love casting out fear?

Step 22

✳

Vanity / Botox Nation

*Even in a time of elephantine vanity and
greed, one never has to look far to see the
campfires of gentle people.*

—GARRISON KEILLOR

"Vanity of vanities, says Qoheleth, vanity of vanities. All things
are vanity" (Ecclesiastes 1:2). In one of the most recognizable
and quoted phrases in the Bible, the author of Ecclesiastes
gives a wake-up call for his listeners and for us. While some call
him a pessimist, others say he is a realist who warns against ex-
pending too much energy on what is here today and gone tomorrow. It all passes, so concentrate only on that which lasts.
After all, the word "vanity" comes from the Latin *vanitas,*
meaning "empty." Why invest in emptiness?

Legend has it that Alexander the Great (356–323 BCE)—
one not known for his modesty—commanded that, after his
death, his hands should not be bound and wrapped in burial
cloths, as was the custom, but rather should be left exposed for
all to see. The point? His hands were *empty.* While this thirty-

three-year-old conqueror had amassed a huge fortune and many empires, in death he held on to none of it. Not an iota of his possessions would travel with him to the eternal empire, giving credence to the proverb "There are no pockets in a shroud." (A friend amends that to say, "I've never seen a U-Haul following a hearse.") Emptiness of emptiness. All things are empty.

John Climacus approaches vanity from a different angle, referring to it as "vainglory" and often equating it with spiritual pride.

> Like the sun which shines on all alike, vainglory
> beams on every occupation. What I mean is this. I fast
> and I turn vainglorious. I stop fasting so that I will draw
> no attention to myself, and I become vainglorious over
> my prudence. I dress well or badly, and am vainglorious
> in either case. I talk or I hold my peace, and each time
> I am defeated. No matter how I shed this prickly thing,
> a spike remains to stand up against me.

Damned if you do, damned if you don't.

While vainglory may haunt our spiritual pursuits and the emptiness of vanity may expose our superficial concerns, for many the word "vanity" aligns itself with the primary dictionary definition: excessive pride in one's appearance or accomplishments; conceit. Writing this chapter in Los Angeles provided me an up-close look at "excessive pride in one's appearance"—observable on practically every street corner and behind many of the lightly tinted car windows on Rodeo Drive.

The knowledge of yourself will
preserve you from vanity.
—MIGUEL DE CERVANTES

Although I live in New York City, not exactly home to the un-self-conscious and humble, nothing prepared me for the sights of our western counterpart, called by some "La La Land." Virtually everyone seemed buffed and shined and pulled to perceived perfection. Granted, this trip required that I visit Beverly Hills and Hollywood—perhaps upping the elective surgery quotient—but, nonetheless, I wondered if cosmetic self-altering has become epidemic.

One night I was sitting in a restaurant popular with the Hollywood elite when one of my boyhood crushes from television walked into the dimly lit garden. I knew it was she, but only hints of her former self remained. Though still regal, with an erect posture and a dancer's gait, she looked painfully thin. Dressed in a skirt too short for her no longer toned legs, she sauntered to her table while three men trailed behind. When she passed me I saw that her once-expressive face was pulled preternaturally taut. I suddenly felt sad. It wasn't simply because she had had extensive cosmetic surgery (as had others in the small garden), but because I imagined she felt that she had to, pressured as so many women, especially celebrities, are to be eternally young and wrinkle-free. While attention to appearance is hardly new in a city where the infamous line of a deluded Norma Desmond in *Sunset Boulevard*, "Mr. DeMille, I'm ready for my close-up," still reverberates, cosmetic realtering has taken it to a new level. Why is it occurring?

The average age for having a face-lift in this country is forty-eight; the American Society of Plastic Surgeons reports that there was a 325 percent increase in cosmetic procedures between 1992 and 2000. While disappointed that my once-unerring television queen had succumbed to this trend and could no longer lift her forehead in surprise, I was also dismayed that I understood why she had caved. Even as a priest I feel the pressures to look young and attractive in a society that seems to value little else. My thinning hair and sagging chin cause me to wonder: If I no longer look acceptable on the outside, will anyone value the inside? External preening gets immediate attention while the interior plumage takes longer to unfurl and to be appreciated.

I am more susceptible to external concerns when plagued by other insecurities. Perhaps vanity is about more than excessive self-preoccupation or even growing older. Could vanity really be about dying or about fearing and denying death?

In a wonderful scene in the Academy Award–winning movie *Moonstruck*, Olympia Dukakis's character is trying to understand why men have affairs, especially with women much younger than they are. She finally tells a would-be gentleman caller that it's because men are afraid of death, suggesting that, by having affairs with younger women, men retain their youthfulness and, in their unconscious minds, ward off death. In words similar to these she says, "But it doesn't matter who they're sleeping with. They're going to die anyway. We're all going to die."

We *are* all going to die, but we don't live that way. Rather, we pretend we will live forever. In our vanity we can hardly imagine a world without us, for without us there is no world for us. It therefore becomes crucial for us to stoke the illusion that our lives will exist as long as we say they do. Youthfulness, vitality, grayless hair, tight skin, and toned muscles are the fuel for the illusion.

> *If boyhood and youth are but vanity, must it*
> *not be our ambition to become men?*
> —VINCENT VAN GOGH

In a Scripture passage already considered in a previous chapter, Jesus says, "Therefore I tell you, do not be anxious about your life, what you shall eat or what you shall drink, nor about your body, what you shall put on. Is not life more than food, and the body more than clothing? . . . And which of you by being anxious can add one cubit to his span of life?" (Matthew 6:25, 27, RSV).

Jesus is attempting to allay superficial concerns by pointing to weightier ones. Why worry about that which passes and over which you have little control anyway? Focus on perennial spiritual matters. Connect deeply with others and with God. Clothe your soul with a mantle of justice and peace. This is where true happiness is to be found.

We may agree with these truths intellectually, but it is hard to live them. While Jesus is talking more about fearing for one's life and sustenance than about the pressures to conform to standards of appearance, the constant pressure to measure up to Madison Avenue standards of beauty and acceptability can also be overwhelming. Fostering a relationship of prayer and connectivity with the source of life we know to be God can be our most effective weapon in fighting off the encroachment of the destructive forces of comparison and competition. Taking time each day to connect with God puts our trivial concerns into perspective. I come to see that my sagging chin means little when weighed against sagging world economies that create inhumane conditions for many of the world's peoples. While I may remain concerned about flabby skin, it seems less important when compared with more paramount issues of justice and peace. Time spent in quiet reflection and prayer helps me to gain that perspective. Aristotle said that "the unexamined life is not worth living." Do we take the necessary time to examine what is most important about our lives—and the lives of others? And does that examination take us to a higher plane?

> *Possibly, more people kill themselves and others*
> *out of hurt vanity than out of envy, jealousy,*
> *malice or desire for revenge.*
>
> —IRIS MURDOCH

Consider this interchange in which Jesus is invited to comment on revered Jewish texts.

> One of the teachers of the law came and heard them debating. Noticing that Jesus had given them a good answer, he asked Jesus, "Of all the commandments, which is the most important?"
>
> He said to him, "You shall love the Lord, your God, with all your heart, with all your soul, and with all your mind. This is the greatest and the first commandment. The second is like it: You shall love your neighbor *as yourself.* The whole law and the prophets depend on these two commandments."
>
> (MATTHEW 22:34–40; EMPHASIS ADDED)

Loving oneself is not a bad thing. Self-love teaches us that we are lovable and capable of loving others. Conversely, vanity is loving oneself in a destructive way, because it is a distorted self-love, superficial and skin deep. The Greek myth of Narcissus reveals the destructive quality of self-love rooted in vanity.

One day in the forest the young Narcissus meets the exiled nymph Echo who falls in love with him. Uninterested, Narcissus shouts at her to go away. Saddened and defeated, Echo leaves until all that is left of her is the distant sound of her re-verberating voice. The other angry nymphs ask Nemesis, the goddess of vengeance, to punish Narcissus for his cruel behav-ior. Nemesis causes Narcissus to fall in love with his own reflec-tion in a stream, and he becomes so self-absorbed in the adoration of his own image that he pines away and dies. The gods then turn him into the beautiful and fragrant flower by which he is known today.

The message is clear: Self-absorption destroys. One's view becomes so myopic and self-centered that the reality and meaning of life becomes distorted. We have all met people whose lives revolve only around themselves. How tiresome they are. We prefer not to be in their company because we sense that the only company they really enjoy is their own. Life turned inward in a selfish way becomes life soon extinguished. Perhaps this is why the myth of Narcissus has inspired a psy-chological disorder that bears his name: narcissistic personality disorder (NPD), described by the fourth edition of the *Diag-nostic and Statistical Manual of Mental Disorders* as "a pervasive pattern of grandiosity (in fantasy or behavior), need for admi-ration, and lack of empathy, beginning in early adulthood and present in a variety of contexts." Narcissism and vanity are *dis-*orders that cloud the true order of life and relationships.

The surest cure for vanity is loneliness.
—TOM WOLFE

In Oscar Wilde's novel *The Picture of Dorian Gray,* published in 1890, Dorian is described as "wonderfully handsome, with his finely-curved scarlet lips, his frank blue eyes and his crisp gold hair. . . . All the candour of youth was there, as well as all of youth's passionate purity." Dorian Gray is convinced by

Lord Henry Wotten that his own looks are his greatest virtue. He scandalizes his English upper-class peers by selling his soul for the sake of his beauty, thus ensuring that he will not grow old. "If it were I who was to be always young, and that picture [painting] that was to grow old . . . I would give my soul for that!"

Dorian's wish is granted. He remains youthful and leads a hedonistic life, while the painting ages and becomes uglier and more deformed. By the end of the novel Dorian realizes his terrible sins and attempts to destroy the portrait by stabbing it as his servants run to attend to his cries. "When they entered, they found hanging upon the wall a splendid portrait of their master as they had last seen him, in all the wonder of his exquisite youth and beauty. Lying on the floor was a dead man, in evening dress, with a knife in his heart. He was withered, wrinkled, and loathsome of visage. It was not till they had examined the rings that they recognized who it was."

Although the story may seem bizarre to our modern sensibilities, Wilde makes a statement about the emptiness he saw reflected in the Victorian culture and society of nineteenth-century England. He charges that the upper class attended to the superficialities of life while ignoring the wide chasm of wealth and poverty that created a society of haves and have-nots. The disparity between the rich and the poor was ignored while how one was perceived was exalted. Tragedy and death are always the result of such unreflective behavior.

Which brings us back to our friend Qoheleth. The Book of Ecclesiastes is concerned with the purpose and value of human life. Merit or toil does not yield happiness; riches and pleasures don't, either. Human wisdom is pure folly. Existence is empty and monotonous if one is preoccupied with that which cannot satisfy. All is emptiness unless one lives in proper relationship with the Creator and sustainer of all life. "Whatever is, was long ago given its name, and the nature of a [person] is known, and that he cannot contend in judgment with one who is stronger than he. For though there are many sayings that multiply vanity, what profit is there for a [person]?" (Ecclesiastes 6:10–11). Vanity of vanities. All things are vanity. Except, of course, the things rooted in God, which do not pass away.

Questions for the Climb
1. Do you consider yourself vain? Why or why not?
2. Do you think that vanity is related to a denial of death?
3. Is cosmetic surgery a moral issue or simply a personal choice?
4. How do you love yourself in a healthy way?

Pride / Can Prejudice Be Far Behind?

> *It was pride that changed angels into devils;*
> *it is humility that makes men angels.*
> —SAINT AUGUSTINE

You may be happy to read that this is the last of our steps that deals with passions to be overcome in the pursuit of spiritual and personal maturity. It has been a long climb through the negative to get to the positive. Bear with me in surmounting one more obstacle, and then it is smooth sailing to the higher virtues.

Once again we have a deadly sin with which to contend. In fact, pride is known as the "father of all sins" or the "first of the sins." Often referred to as hubris, excessive pride has been critiqued in the religious traditions as that which keeps us from acknowledging our proper status in the universe. The medieval theologian Thomas Aquinas wrote that "inordinate self-love is the cause of every sin . . . the root of pride is found to consist in man not being, in some way, subject to God and His rule" (*Summa Theologica* 1,77). Aquinas suggests that pride interferes with an individual's recognition of the power and superiority of God.

Pride is known as the "first of the sins" because it is the sin attributed to Adam and Eve in the Garden.

> The serpent asked the woman, "Did God really tell you not to eat from any of the trees in the garden?" The woman answered the serpent: "We may eat of the fruit of the trees in the garden; it is only about the fruit of the tree in the middle of the garden that God said, 'You shall not eat it or even touch it, lest you die.'" But the serpent said to the woman: "You certainly will not die! No, God knows well that the moment you eat of it your eyes will be opened and you will be like gods who know what is good and what is bad." The woman saw that the tree was good for food, pleasing to the eyes, and desirable for gaining wisdom. So she took some of its fruit and ate it; and she also gave some to her husband, who was with her, and he ate it.
>
> (GENESIS, 3:1b–6)

Pride or hubris is equated here with the desire to be like God. People are not content with their more lowly status of being human but desire to be equal with the Creator, having the same power and wisdom. It is easy to see how pride can lead to other sins and weaknesses; if left unchecked, it can affect almost every facet of life.

> *Generosity is giving more than you can, and*
> *pride is taking less than you need.*
> —KAHLIL GIBRAN

Some physicians have been accused of having excessive pride, behaving like God in their treatment of patients. Human genetic engineering and extreme manipulation of the human fertilization process are examples of medical science overstepping the boundaries of right relationship between creature and Creator. Some doctors are deluded into believing that they are creators, deigning to bestow life by their scientific expertise and, at times, capricious whim. Related to the encroachment of medical science into the sphere of the Divine is the dangerous participation of would-be parents in choosing the sex and genetic disposition of their hoped-for baby. Some parents have aborted fetuses if they were not of the desired gender. While positive advancements also have been made in helping couples to conceive a child, one must ask: When is the experimentation too much? At what point do we overstep the boundaries of what should be relegated to the Divine purview? Pride in our own capabilities can blind us from seeing this human/Divine line of demarcation.

It is not only Christianity that condemns overweening pride. In Hinduism, the deadly sin of pride is linked pejoratively to the ego (I), which ignores the more inclusive community (we). In Islam, Muhammad says, "He in whose heart there is as much as a grain of pride will not enter paradise . . . pride is disdaining what is true and despising people" (*Sayings of Muhammad,* Sir Abdullah Suhrawardy). In the Hebrew Scriptures we read: "Blessed is that man that makes the Lord his trust, and looks not to the proud, nor to those that turn aside to lies" (Psalm 40:5).

A friend looked perplexed when I noted the disdain of religious traditions for pride and that it was one of the Seven Deadly Sins.

"I thought pride was a good thing," he said. "Don't we try to instill pride in our children? Don't we take pride in our country?"

These are fair questions. Pride can have a positive side, as well. But Climacus is not warning us against the positive. He is admonishing us about the shadow side of excessive pride, and he is not restrained in his criticism: "Pride is a denial of God, an invention of the devil, contempt for men. . . . It is a flight from God's help, the harbinger of madness, the author of downfall. It is the cause of diabolical possession, the source of anger, the gateway of hypocrisy." Why such a strong reaction to a quality some see as positive?

> *If I had only one sermon to preach it would be*
> *a sermon against pride.*
> —G. K. CHESTERTON

My first assignment as a priest was to an inner-city parish in Union City, New Jersey. One of my ministries was to visit the local hospitals at least once a week to offer counseling and to administer the Sacraments to Catholic patients. Visiting hospitals is not my favorite part of being a priest. It was the mid-1980s, at the height of the AIDS epidemic, when most of those afflicted were dying. One Friday I was asked to see a young man who had been admitted with AIDS. Although I didn't know him, his parents were parishioners in my parish.

When I walked into the room, I was stunned by how bad this young man looked, achingly thin with large brown eyes that seemed the most alive part of a face that had begun wasting away. Those eyes turned away from me when I entered in my Roman collar.

"Hi, my name is Father Edward," I said. "Your parents are

parishioners at my parish. I wanted to visit you to see if there was anything you needed."

"Oh, my parents asked you to come?" he said, looking out the window. "My mother or my father? No, don't answer that." He turned to look at me. "I know for damn sure it wasn't my father. He thinks I'm going straight to Hell no matter what, so it's too late even for the priest to save me, I'm afraid."

"Actually, your parents didn't ask me to come," I said, taken aback. "You're on my list."

"Your list?" he said. "Oh, how nice. Do you want to condemn me to Hell, too, Father? Because I really don't want to hear any of your Catholic bullshit. So, if you'd please just leave me alone." He turned back to the window.

"I'm not here to condemn you," I said. "I'm here because I want to be. And I want to help in any way that I can."

So began my relationship with Jeff, one that would last a short month and a half. But during that time our conversation broke through superficialities to matters of his aching heart. His life as a gay man had not been easy, replete with being mocked and abused. And while he had been beaten up by teenagers more times than he could count, no beating was more detrimental than that which he received from his father. Although not physical, his father's emotional pummeling had left scars apparent every time Jeff attempted to speak about this man, who was absent in his son's dying days.

"Jeff, I want to go and talk to your father," I said, after I had been seeing Jeff for about three weeks. "You need to resolve some of this. I'm sure he does, too."

"Father Edward, what part of what I'm saying don't you understand? The man hates me. He feels as though I've ruined his life. The football coach wound up with a gay son who couldn't even throw a ball. Don't you see, he takes it as a personal embarrassment? It's always been that way. It's not going to change now."

"But you're dying," I said. It was the first time either of us had articulated what was so obvious.

"Yeah, I know," said Jeff, his eyes filling up. "And he couldn't give a shit."

I arrived at their house at 7:30 p.m. Jeff's mother had assured me that they would be finished with dinner by then. She greeted me warmly at the door and brought me into a paneled family room where the TV was playing loudly.

"John, please turn that off. Father Beck is here."

Jeff's father, a tall man with broad shoulders and a gray crew cut, stood and extended his calloused hand.

"Hi, Father, nice to see you. Please sit down. Wanna beer or something?"

I didn't waste any time in getting to why I was paying this pastoral visit.

"John, you know that I've been seeing your son the past couple of weeks."

"Yeah, my wife told me. Thanks for doing that. Must be hard for you."

"Hard for me?" I said.

"Yeah, given my son's lifestyle and all that."

"I can assure you, John, that it has been nothing but a privilege to get to know your fine son over these weeks."

"Well, that's nice of you to say, Father. But what can I do for you?"

"I'm here because your son is dying, and you've had no relationship with him for a number of years now. There's a lot of hurt there. And I'm sure that you want to try to remedy that before it's too late."

"There is nothing to remedy or talk about, Father. You of

all people know what the Church teaches, and you know that my son has an illness that he's refused to get help for. Case closed."

"Refused to get help for? There is no getting help for it. He's dying from it."

"I'm not talking about that. I'm talking about his lifestyle."

I was frustrated and saddened by what little headway I seemed to be making with Jeff's father. Something inside of him had turned cold. He saw his son as an unredeemed sinner, but more significantly, he saw him as an embarrassment. Jeff wasn't a son of whom John could be proud. And it was John's pride that kept him from loving the son he had been given.

"Do you know what it's like to be ashamed of your son when he walks down the street because you know that everyone is making fun of him?" he said to me at the door, as I was leaving.

"I think it's probably far worse to be the person that they're making fun of," I said, and turned and left.

Five days later I was called to the hospital at 3 a.m. Jeff was dying, and his family wanted him anointed with the Sacrament of the Sick. When I arrived at the hospital room, Jeff's mother and brother were at his bedside. His mother was stroking his hair as Jeff struggled to breathe. His brother was holding his hand. Jeff's father sat in a chair by the door. It was the first time he had been in the hospital room since his son had been admitted.

I moved to the bed to console Jeff's mother and brother and to begin praying some final prayers with Jeff.

"John, would you please join us here around the bed while we anoint Jeff and say some prayers?" I said, like a command.

He sat by the door with his arms wrapped around his stomach, his head down, never looking up. He shook his head no. I looked at his wife and son and could tell that they had already tried to break through with no success.

"Go ahead, Father," Jeff's mother said. "Pray with us for my son."

I prayed with them and anointed their son and brother. At one point Jeff moved—had he opened his eyes?—and I want to believe I even saw him smile. He died less than five minutes after we finished praying the Sacrament of the Sick. His mother and brother were crying profusely. It was not until then that John got up from the chair, came over to the bed, and put his arm around his wife's shoulder. She tightened at his touch. He looked at his dead son, and tears began to well up in his eyes. He reached his hand out and put it on Jeff's forehead. And to my utter amazement, he whispered: "Don't go, son. I love you."

It took everything inside of me not to say "It's too late."

> *Pride grows in the human heart*
> *like lard on a pig.*
> —ALEKSANDR SOLZHENITSYN

There are all kinds of pride. Unchecked, some can be deadly indeed. In Dante's *Divine Comedy,* the souls of the proud in Purgatory are weighed down by heavy rocks that they carry, preventing them from looking upward. The proud see only their feet and have no perspective on all that surrounds them. The myopia induced by pride prevents spiritual advancement. "An old man, experienced in these matters, once spiritually admonished a proud brother who said in his blindness, 'Forgive me, father, but I am not proud.' 'My son,' said the wise man, 'what better proof of your pride could you have given than to claim that you were not proud?' " (Climacus, Step 23).

Jane Austen titled one of her most famous books *Pride and Prejudice*. While the title aptly describes the attitudes of many of the characters of this nineteenth-century novel, perhaps there is another reason Austen chose to link the two. Both are forms of blindness. In the novel, Elizabeth Bennet and Mr. Darcy are unable to connect because of the way their pride and prejudice keep them from seeing the reality and possibilities of their relationship. In addition to the pride of the novel's protagonists, the pride of the gentry class causes them to look down on the lower classes as those not worthy of respect or even recognition. Pride's sister, prejudice, keeps the haughty from seeing the worth and dignity of every person regardless of social standing. Ultimately, this is Climacus's problem with pride: "It happens, I do not know how, that most of the proud never really discover their true selves. They think they have conquered their passions, and they find out how poor they really are only after they die."

Now, having conquered or at least acknowledged our passions by climbing Climacus's ladder together, let us move on to the higher virtues so that we might master them before we, too, die.

Questions for the Climb

1. Has pride ever been destructive in your life?
2. Has pride limited your capacity to love?
3. How do you feel when you are with a person full of pride?
4. What can you do to guard against unhealthy pride?

Step 24

✳

Simplicity / Coach Class

Simplicity in character, in manners, in style; in
all things the supreme excellence is simplicity.
—HENRY WADSWORTH LONGFELLOW

'Tis the gift to be simple, 'tis the gift to be free,
'Tis the gift to come down where you ought to be,
And when we find ourselves in the place just right,
'Twill be in the valley of love and delight.
When true simplicity is gain'd,
To bow and to bend we shan't be asham'd.
To turn, turn will be our delight,
Till by turning, turning we come round right.
—JOSEPH BRACKETT, "SIMPLE GIFTS," 1848

The words of this old Shaker tune still resonate in their simplicity. It is indeed a gift to be simple. The Shakers, a splinter
group from the Quaker community in England, arrived in the
United States in the eighteenth century and peaked in mem-
bership at around six thousand in the mid-nineteenth century.

Their name derives from their ecstatic worship, during which they would literally shake with the power of the Holy Spirit. What they perhaps are remembered for most, however, is their simplicity, not only in their strong work ethic and communal lifestyle but in, oddly enough, their furniture. Their simple, functional furniture designs with clean lines and little excess, a precursor to our modern, minimalist designs, remain popular.

Simplicity is, however, about more than furniture design. It is about creating space amid all of the complexities and distractions of life to savor what is most valuable and lasting. Other religious traditions also have latched on to this virtue as the bedrock of their beliefs. The Quakers espouse a Testimony of Simplicity as one of the tenets of their faith. This testimony exhorts Quakers to live simply, untethered to material possessions, because of their belief that the spiritual life and character of a person are more important than possessions. Their ideal is to be free of physical and spiritual clutter. Thus, even their worship spaces are unadorned and have plain wooden benches. In simplicity one creates a place for God to speak through the gathered community.

Another intriguing religious group is the Amish. Having their origins in the Anabaptist tradition and the Mennonite Church, the Amish remain an extreme witness of the call to simplicity. From their beginnings in the United States in the early eighteenth century until now, the Amish have remained staunch defenders of the value of simplicity in the face of the encroaching allure of technology and globalization. A visit to the Amish country of Pennsylvania still finds people in traditional dress (designed to encourage humility and separation from the world) who travel by horse and buggy—perhaps the best way to avoid high gas prices and dependence on oil. With an emphasis on local community reliance, Amish homes have no electricity or modern conveniences that most of us consider indispensable. Emphasizing peace and nonviolence, they do not join the military. (Nor do they draw Social Security.) Some see their lifestyle as foolish and reactionary, a refusal to acknowledge the positive advancements of science and technology. Others wonder if the Amish can help us recover what we have lost in our rapid "advancement."

> *The ordinary acts we practice every day at*
> *home are of more importance to the soul than*
> *their simplicity might suggest.*
> —THOMAS MOORE

In his *Summa Theologica,* Thomas Aquinas writes that "God is infinitely simple." If it is true that our lifelong task is to become more like God, simplicity is an undeniable calling. But it is a calling many of us would rather not hear.

I am writing these lines in the business class cabin of a plane flying from London to New York. I worked hard for this upgrade from the coach class in which I was booked. Due to an airline mixup too convoluted to relate, I felt I was entitled to compensation. After pleading my case to three supervisors who eyed me with suspicion, I was finally awarded a seat of cushy leather and access to endlessly flowing wine and food. I breathed a self-satisfied sigh of relief. Then I opened the computer to write and realized that I was working on this chapter, "Simplicity." *How ironic,* I thought. I wanted none of the simplicity of coach class and all of the excesses of business class. One might argue that there is nothing wrong with enjoying some extra comfort during a taxing transatlantic flight, and I would agree. But I began wondering: Do I *really* want to live simply? And what does it actually mean anyway?

Someone recently said to me, "The best things in life aren't things." I believe this to be true and try to live by the wisdom of that maxim. It's *not* always easy. We live in a complex society that requires complex skills. There is nothing simple about BlackBerrys, cell phones, computers, iPods, and the multitasking that such technological wizardry requires. Nor is there anything simple about navigating life in a culture where the unsophisticated is often shunned and the urbane is exalted. The challenge is to create simplicity even amid the mind-boggling complexity. While most of us do not desire to live in radical Amish simplicity, can we nonetheless learn something from it?

In his *Ladder of Divine Ascent* John Climacus uses three images to describe simplicity: childhood, Adam in the Garden, and Saint Paul the Simple. Considering these three might help us in our own quest for the simple amid the complex.

Climacus says: "Unadorned simplicity is the first characteristic of childhood" (Step 24). This claim is hard to dispute. Who has not marveled at the innocence and simplicity of a child? We are born into this world naked and dependent, needing the simplest things for life to flourish. When my nephew Jack was born, I was fascinated by his utter wonder at the simple realities of color and movement. A dancing mobile of bright reds and greens could keep him riveted for amazingly long periods of time. Granted, once he got older and was introduced to Game Boy and other video and technological entertainment, he wasn't entertained as simply; but before he was "corrupted" by the technological world, the simplicity of what induced pleasure was quite startling. What we don't know, we really don't miss.

The art of art, the glory of expression and the
sunshine of the light of letters, is simplicity.
—WALT WHITMAN

And people were bringing children to [Jesus] that he
might touch them, but the disciples rebuked them. When
Jesus saw this he became indignant and said to them, "Let
the children come to me; do not prevent them, for the
kingdom of God belongs to such as these. Amen, I say to
you, whoever does not accept the kingdom of God like a
child will not enter it." Then he embraced them and
blessed them, placing his hands on them.

(MARK 10:13–16)

Christians call the transcendent self the "child of God." When
we understand our relationship as creature to Creator, we are
most in touch with who we really are. When Jesus tells the disciples not to push the children away, he is also trying to tell
them to accept who they really are. Only then can they enter
the kingdom of God. Children are open and free—and simple.
They don't worry about what others think of them. Although
they may be transfixed by a video game, children also can
spend hours playing with a cardboard box. They rarely care
about what they look like or what they are wearing. In order
to receive the blessing of who we really are, Jesus exhorts us to
become more like children, blissful in their simplicity. As children of God, we come to know that what we actually need can
only be given from above and from within.

"As long as Adam had [simplicity], he saw neither the
nakedness of his soul nor the indecency of his flesh" (Climacus, Step 24). There is freedom in the simplicity of unselfcon-
scious nakedness. Aside from some possibly prurient reasons,
perhaps this is why nude beaches and clothing-optional resorts
remain popular and intriguing. When stripped down to the essentials, we are simply who we are. There is no more pretending, hiding, or fooling. What you see is what you get. When

Adam and Eve live in right relationship to their God and the creation that surrounds them, they are peaceful in their simplicity and their nakedness. Once they cloud the simplicity with the desire to be more than they are, they lose that gift. "Then the eyes of both of them were opened, and they realized that they were naked; so they sewed fig leaves together and made loincloths for themselves" (Genesis 3:7).

Saint Paul the Simple is an enigmatic figure from the third century. Although little is known of him, it is said that he went to join Saint Anthony of the Desert after catching his wife in the act of adultery. Saint Anthony thought that Paul was too old to become a monk, but after Paul passed the severest of tests with remarkable docility, Anthony was convinced that he was called to the eremitical life. "He was the measure and type of simplicity, and no one has ever seen or heard or could see so much progress in so short a time" (Climacus, Step 24).

Monks continue to be role models of simplicity to our modern culture. The members of the Order of Cistercians of the Strict Observance (commonly known as Trappists) follow a strict interpretation of the sixth-century Rule of Saint Benedict. Perhaps the best-known member of this group was Thomas Merton. Prayer, penance, and work define the lives of these monks, who abstain from meat, fish, and poultry and remain silent for most of the day. The simplicity of such austerity is designed to make them more accessible to God; in the distraction-free quiet they are more disposed to focus on the essentials of life.

It is simplicity that makes the uneducated more
effective than the educated when addressing
popular audiences.

—ARISTOTLE

Once I took my adult cousins Carol and Denise to visit the Trappist monastery in Spencer, Massachusetts, for the afternoon prayer hour. As we approached the stone chapel, my cousins stopped in the lush green grass surrounding the monastery.

"Listen," Denise said.

"I know," Carol replied.

"What?" I asked, as I turned to look at them. They were tilting their heads as if trying to hear more keenly.

"Do you hear that?" Denise asked.

"I don't hear anything," I said.

"That's the point," said Carol. "I've never heard quiet like that. There is not one sound except that gentle wind."

"It's unbelievable," said Denise. "I've never been so aware of the quiet before."

After the prayer service, as we were driving back to the retreat center where we were staying, Denise asked, "Why do you think they live that way? So austere."

"I think it's a very special vocation," I said. "They believe it's making them holier. And they're not only praying for themselves. They're praying for the world and witnessing to something that they think the world has forgotten."

"Consider ourselves reminded," said Carol.

Others also are attempting to remind us of the importance of simplicity. On a global scale, the ecological movement aims to alert us to how quickly overconsumption is destroying our planet. Automobiles are the second largest source of carbon dioxide pollution in the world (the chief culprit in global warming), exceeded only by coal-burning power plants. Producing and buying more fuel-efficient cars and cutting our electricity use through energy efficiency can make enormous strides in saving the environment. Energy conservation can become part of our everyday lives, but it may require living more simply. Giving up our SUVs and Hummers seems a small price to pay, yet we resist most encroachment on our consumerist "liberty."

According to the National Resources Defense Council, although the United States makes up just 4 percent of the world's population, we produce 25 percent of the dangerous carbon dioxide pollution from the burning of fossil fuels—more than China, India, and Japan combined. The council explains that "each time you choose a compact fluorescent light bulb over an incandescent bulb, you'll lower your energy bill and keep nearly 700 pounds of carbon dioxide out of the air over the bulb's lifetime. By opting for a refrigerator with the Energy Star label—indicating it uses at least 15 percent less energy than the federal requirement—over a less energy-efficient model, you can reduce carbon dioxide pollution by nearly a ton in total."

Simplicity doesn't necessarily mean doing without. Rather it points to a conscious awareness that one is not alone in the world. "Live simply so that others might simply live" might seem like a hackneyed phrase reserved for social justice enthusiasts, but there is truth in that simple statement. If I do with less, there *is* more for others. It's quite simple. When 2.8 billion people in the world live on less than two dollars a day, how much do we really need?

> *There is a certain majesty in simplicity which*
> *is far above all the quaintness of wit.*
> —ALEXANDER POPE

A fourteenth-century friar named William of Occam authored a scientific theory that still is used today. Known as Occam's

razor, it states simply that entities should not be multiplied beyond necessity. In other words, keep it simple. Recently a
friend of mine said that he realized he spent most of his life
dragging himself to a job he hated so that he could buy more
stuff he didn't really need. The more he spent, the more he
needed to work at a job he hated to cover the expenses. Then
it hit him: If he spent less, he could work less, and then he
could spend more time doing what he wanted to do. The impetus for this brainstorm was when a friend said, "Think of
five activities that you enjoy doing. Then think of the five activities that occupy most of your time. If they don't match up,
you're doing something wrong." Living more simply has
helped him to align those lists.

So here I am in the business class cabin, enjoying every
minute of it—from the warm nuts, to the French Sauvignon
Blanc, to the fully reclining seat that does everything but
scratch my back. While simplicity doesn't exclude comfort, I
feel a bit guilty because there is nothing simple about the excesses in this class of service. Is it simply Catholic guilt that I
feel, or is there something inherently askew about the disparity between classes of service? Does one deserve to be treated
better because he or she has more money—or a gripe worthy
enough of an upgrade? Can the rich be simple, too?

I took a walk to the coach cabin to stretch my legs and saw
the cramped people, including one exasperated father who had
a young child hanging off his neck. Would I want to be back
there for this trip? No. I accept this largesse with little regret.
Kind of.

But the next time I am in coach, which will undoubtedly
be the next time that I fly, I hope that I remember some
things—such as the fact that although the people in front may
be eating and resting better, it doesn't *make* them any better. In

fact, they may be at a disadvantage because, like me, one day they may miss what they can no longer have. Simplicity can keep us from getting too caught up in what is easily taken away.

Believe it or not, I thought seriously about offering that man with the child my seat for the second half of the flight, kind of like paying the toll for some unsuspecting driver who follows you through the booth—random acts of kindness and all that. Unfortunately, that thought never translated into action because I was too comfortable. I also made excuses: Why should I discriminate? After all, what about the old lady back there?

Perhaps when I learn to embrace voluntary simplicity more exuberantly, I'll care less about the hot fudge sundae in business class and more about the guy in coach whose squirming kid would have happily eaten it.

Questions for the Climb

1. Are you attracted to simplicity in others? Why or why not?
2. Do you wish your life was simpler?
3. Is it easier to be spiritual when we live more simply?
4. Do you contribute to our environment by your voluntary simplicity?

Step 25

✳

Humility / Earth Tones

*Humility is the foundation of all the other
virtues hence, in the soul in which this virtue
does not exist there cannot be any other virtue
except in mere appearance.*

—SAINT AUGUSTINE

An old Jewish anecdote explains humility this way: In the village synagogue, during the High Holy Days, the rabbi prostrates himself on the floor, saying "God, before You I am nothing." Immediately the richest man in town prostrates himself on the floor, saying "God, before You I am nothing." Right after that the town beggar prostrates himself on the floor, saying "God, before You I am nothing." The rich man whispers to the rabbi, "Look who thinks he's nothing."

Years ago I was giving a parish retreat in Augusta, Maine. Each evening of the retreat a woman usually dressed in yellow chiffon (though one night she wore light blue) and a large hat sat in the front row of the church. She had a dramatic flair. Aside from her chi-chi clothing, she stood out because of her exaggerated gestures and broad responses to my preaching. She nodded, lifted her waving hand in affirmation, and "amened" a few times. She even blessed herself with the sign of the cross in a baroque manner, like an abbess.

The last night of the retreat I was having dinner in the rectory with the parish priests. It was a well-appointed dining room with dark wood panels and an ornate chandelier. Waterford crystal sat on a high-gloss wood table with the pastor at one end, his associate at the other, and me in the middle, to the pastor's left. The pastor did not look as relaxed as he had on previous evenings.

"We're in trouble," he said to his rotund associate, who was already digging into his four-greens salad.

"What do you mean?" said the associate, garbling the words because of his full mouth.

"Lillian withdrew a lot of money from the credit union today. They're not even sure they can open the doors tomorrow."

I didn't know much about credit unions, but apparently the parish had a credit union that served as the primary bank for many of the parishioners. The parish ran the credit union and thus benefited from the money that was deposited there.

"How much money?" the associate asked.

"Thirty-five thousand dollars," the pastor said, looking over the top of his glasses to make sure the figure had registered with his fellow priest. It was as if I weren't even at the table.

"In cash, all at one time?" the associate said, no longer chewing.

"Yep. They tried to discourage her. Even asked her if they could transfer the money in a few installments, but she'd hear none of it. She said she needed her money today and could not wait for it. It cleaned them out."

"Wow, I wonder what she needed it for."

"I don't know, but she's so wacky, I'm sure it's for something bizarre. Let's hope she doesn't pull something like this again any time soon. Her money practically keeps that credit union afloat."

After dinner I was in the church early to set up for the final retreat service. Although the retreat had been well attended, the people had been reserved, in a New England sort of way. The woman in the front row was like a welcome dash of spice in an otherwise lackluster meal. By the time we started the evening service, however, she wasn't in her usual front seat. I imagined that she had bailed on me for the last night to attend some Ya-Ya Sisterhood–like meeting where they *all* wore lavish hats.

But I was wrong. Ten minutes after we had started she made her way down the center aisle with a flourish, her hand fluffing her crinoline dress. Decked out in gold for this final night, she swept into the pew, as if it had been reserved for her, discreetly waved her fingers at me, and smiled broadly through crimson red lips. I tried to continue with my sermon, pretending that I hadn't noticed the display, but you couldn't miss it. Some men smiled at her while the women sitting next to them scowled. This was a woman who drew hot or cold responses, but seldom lukewarm.

I was standing at the back of the church saying good night to people when I noticed her waiting for me by a statue of Mary. When most of the retreatants had departed, she sashayed up to me.

"Father, at last we get to speak face to face," she said breathlessly.

"Hi, how are you," I said. This was indeed the first time we had spoken. "I'm Father Edward." I extended my hand.

"Oh, I know exactly who you are. How could I not? You are marvelous. Simply marvelous."

"Well, I don't know about that, but thank you."

"Now, don't be modest, Father. I haven't heard anything like you since Fulton Sheen."

"Well, then you need to get out more," I said, and chuckled.

"You humble man, you," she said, and grinned. "In any event, Lillian is my name, and I want to make a confession." She leaned in toward me and lowered her voice. "I didn't put anything in the collection basket tonight. I'm making a different kind of offering to you."

"Oh?" I said. *So this is Lillian,* I thought. No doubt she was the woman the priests had been speaking about at dinner. How could I not have guessed?

"And here it is," she said, and pressed a gold envelope with a slight bulge into my hand.

"Oh, well, thank you. I'll just drop this into the collection basket with the other envelopes."

"Oh, no, you can't," she said with a little girl's lilt, as she waved her index finger back and forth like a metronome. "There is not money in there. It's something else. Please open it."

"Now?" I asked, a bit embarrassed in front of the few lingering people. She nodded. I opened the envelope and found a large key inside. I took it out and looked at it.

"What's this?" I asked.

"Come this way, my dear man," she said as she walked out the church doors with her fingers beckoning me to follow.

When I and the intrigued parishioners followed her outside, she was standing at the top of the church steps with her arms crossed and a large grin on her face.

"Well, what do you think?" she said.

"About what?" I said, growing more confused by the moment.

"That," she said, and pointed to a sparkling gold Cadillac. Adorned with the largest red bow I had ever seen, the behemoth car sat glowing under the streetlights in front of the church.

"What's that?" I said, my heart starting to pound faster.

"That, my dear father, is your new car. Isn't it lovely?"

"My new car?" I said. "Oh, I don't think so."

"Oh, yes it is," she said in a singsongy girl's voice. "You mentioned how much traveling you have to do going from church to church with your wonderful ministry. Well, now you can travel in comfort and style. It's the least I could do to make sure that you arrive at other lucky churches well rested. I saw that little tin box you're driving. It simply won't do."

"But you don't understand. I can't accept anything like this. I take a vow of poverty. I can't drive around in a Cadillac. To say nothing of the fact that I don't deserve such an extravagant gift."

"Of course you deserve it. Don't be so humble."

"It's not about being humble. It's about . . . well, I'm not sure what it's about. But I know that I cannot accept it."

"You simply must. It's already paid for. I've driven it off the lot. I can't return it."

"Well then, I'm afraid you've bought yourself a new gold Cadillac. Please don't misunderstand me. I really do appreciate the gesture. But I just can't accept it."

"Father, that car is more than a gesture. It is a token of my love and appreciation. You might as well have spit on it for how you're responding. You've hurt me deeply."

"Not as much as I'd be hurt if I ever pulled up in front of the monastery in that," I said.

The pastor, arms folded, glared at me from the side door of the church.

As I was driving south on Route 95 in my tin box I wondered what she would do with the car. Perhaps they would let her return it after all. But I wondered more about why I felt so embarrassed by such a lavish gift (aside from the fact that it would have conveyed a flashier image than my vow of poverty could sustain). The word "humility" comes from the Latin word humus, meaning "ground or soil." But not just any soil. It is the compost, the richest soil, the soil that helps things to grow. Humility is spiritual dirt that allows internal growth because it gets to the truth of who we are. It is not that false modesty we sometimes see displayed, where a person willingly makes him- or herself the footstool of the "more worthy." Rather, humility is the simple acknowledgment that in the greater scheme of things, we exist in proportionate importance to everything and everyone else. As we have seen already, pride can distort that proportion, deluding us to think that the world revolves around us. Humility keeps us balanced in truth. Truth is that the gift of the Cadillac was way out of proportion for what I had done and would have presented an image not true to who I am and what I do. Whatever hint of humility I may possess allowed me to see that.

> *If I only had a little humility, I'd be perfect.*
> —TED TURNER

Hasidic Jewish Midrash says: "To be fully human in the best sense of that word, each of us should walk around with two pockets. In each of those pockets is a slip of paper. One of the slips of paper says, *For my sake this whole magnificent, amazing universe was created.* The other slip of paper says, *I am but dust and ashes."* While the author's precise point can be debated, humility helps us locate the appropriate balance between these two extremes. Both hold truth, but the totality of truth is not found in either one. Our lives fall somewhere in between.

The Book of Job is a classic on humility. When Job first begins to be tested by calamity in his life, he says, "Naked I came forth from my mother's womb, and naked I shall go back again. The Lord gave and the Lord has taken away; blessed be the name of the Lord" (1:21). But that resignation does not last long as the tribulations continue. By the end of the book a beseiged Job is questioning God, demanding answers for the innocent suffering he has endured. God's response from the whirlwind of the storm is a simple one: I am God, and you are not. "Where were you when I founded the earth?" . . . "Have you ever in your lifetime commanded the morning and shown the dawn its place?" (38:4, 12).

God's long and showy response, by which He firmly establishes His Divine status as creator and sustainer of the universe, is sufficient to convince Job to embrace his rightful place in the cosmic panoply. Job's final response to God's spectacular verbal display is a classic speech on humility: "I know that you can do all things, and that no purpose of yours can be hindered. I have dealt with great things that I do not understand; things too wonderful for me, which I cannot know. I had heard of you by word of mouth, but now my eye has seen you. Therefore I disown what I have said, and repent in dust and ashes" (42:2–6).

A reverential awe before the inscrutable transcendence of God is rooted in the virtue of humility. Most religious traditions agree. Taoism even claims that humility is one of the three treasures that one must possess in order to be in harmony with the universe (the tao). When one is not in harmony with the universe, the dissonance is obvious.

For some people, Donald Trump may epitomize the antithesis of humility. Whether his braggadocio is a trumped-up performance designed to attract ever more publicity or not, Trump appears to revel in his claims of self-importance and indispensability. As he builds skyscrapers in New York and elsewhere, Trump's concrete empire potentially distorts the reality of his ultimate insignificance.

> *What the world needs is more geniuses with*
> *humility; there are so few of us left.*
> —OSCAR LEVANT

Some years ago I read an article in the *New York Times* reporting that Trump was building an unsightly row of luxury apartment buildings along the Hudson River that were blocking the views of buildings behind them. A woman whose view of the river and sky had been robbed said, "Can you imagine what this man is taking away? Can you imagine somebody taking away the moon, the sun, and the stars?"

While Trump's building mania may rob the celestial sphere in a limited way, Job's realization is that only God possesses the ultimate power to move the sun and the stars. Sometimes in our foolishness and lack of humility we think that we do, too. The psalmist, like Job, reminds us otherwise: "When I see your heavens, the work of your fingers, the moon and stars that you set in place—What are humans that you are mindful of them, mere mortals that you care for them?" (Psalm 8:4–5). On his deathbed, the Jewish theologian Abraham Heschel said to his friend, "Sam, never once in my life did I ask God for success or wisdom or power or fame. I asked for wonder, and he gave it to me."

In peace there's nothing so becomes a man as
modest stillness and humility.
—WILLIAM SHAKESPEARE

A friend of mine who is in Alcoholics Anonymous reminded me that the twelve-step program is based on humility. "The very first step," he said, "requires that you admit your own powerlessness. You cannot advance until you do that. If that's not humility, I don't know what is."

The seventh step is even more explicit: "Humbly ask God to remove our shortcomings." Those in AA realize that reliance on a higher power is the only way to overcome a disease that renders them powerless. They admit that they cannot get well on their own. They need help from God and others. This acknowledgment seems to be the reason for the success of the twelve-step programs. The spirituality of humility helps one to accept one's mortality in all of its fragility and tentativeness. God can then work, often through the beneficence of other wounded healers.

Jesus told a parable to those who had been invited to a banquet at a Pharisees' house, noticing that they were choosing the places of honor at the table. "Rather, when you are invited, go and take the lowest place so that when the host comes to you he may say, 'My friend, move up to a higher position.' Then you will enjoy the esteem of your companions at the table. For everyone who exalts himself with be humbled, but the one who humbles himself will be exalted" (Luke 14:10–11).

Jesus is in touch with the danger of running after honor and esteem. Attachment to them is like a drug that makes our souls sick. We can get addicted at a young age, trying to please our parents with good grades, our coaches with good performances, or our friends with our newest toys. We get attached to the recognition such things bring because we mistake it for the affirmation that we desire on deeper levels. Thirst for recognition and honor confounds humility because we no longer see the truth of what really matters. Instead we become swept up in being "better than" in order to get noticed more.

Ambition depends on being seen by others. Vying for the place of honor at the table is a metaphor for how we conduct ourselves at work, in school, on a team, or in our family. As we nudge our way to the more honored positions, we enter the competitive arena that ultimately enslaves us to the opinions and attitudes of others. For example, a pop singer friend of mine loses self-worth when people don't buy her albums. She wallows in self-pity and dejection, forgetting that dependence on fickle consumers for one's value is a sure way to unhappiness. Jesus suggests that we be humble enough not to worry about the top position. Only then may we be exalted.

Humility doesn't ask us to be a doormat; it invites us to become a threshold. The truth about who we are in our finiteness and fragility can be a doorway to happiness as we grow older and change. "The appearance of this sacred vine [humility] is one thing during the winter of passions, another in the springtime of flowering, and still another in the harvest time of all the virtues" (Climacus, Step 25). Gratitude is the ultimate result of humility because we realize that most of who we are and what we possess has little or nothing to do with us. Talents, intelligence, privilege, friendship, compassion, and love are all gifts. We receive them in humility when we hold them gently and with open hands.

It ain't the heat, it's the humility.
—YOGI BERRA

We began by recalling that the word "humility" comes from the Latin *humus*: dirt, compost, fertilizer. One Ash Wednesday I was dutifully administering the ashes of remembrance, repentance, and humility on parishioners' heads. One by one they came forward reverently as I dipped my thumb into the glass bowl of the ground ashes and then imposed the ashes on their foreheads, making the sign of the cross. "Remember that you are dust and to dust you shall return. Remember that you are dust and to dust you shall return . . ."

I was about halfway through the people in line when I looked down to see a blond, blue-eyed boy about six years old standing in front of me. I had just marked his mother with a formidable cross, and he eyed me with suspicion. He winced as I reached down to smudge his forehead with my blessed dirt, as if I were giving him a needle between his eyes.

"Remember that you are dust and to dust you shall return," I said solemnly.

"Speak for yourself," he said, and scampered to his blushing mother.

Sign and symbol are sometimes lost on the young. May it not be so for us.

Questions for the Climb
1. Do you view humility as a positive virtue that you possess? Why or why not?

2. What prevents you from acknowledging your limited status in the greater order of Creation?
3. Do you think that God's answer to Job is satisfactory? Why or why not?
4. Do you see "powerlessness" as a positive or negative?

$Step$ 26

✳

Discernment / Show Me the Way

God never gives us discernment in order that
we may criticize, but that we may intercede.
—OSWALD CHAMBERS

In *The Ladder of Divine Ascent* John Climacus devotes many
pages to the discernment step. Nine centuries later, in his
Spiritual Exercises, Saint Ignatius of Loyola, the founder of the
Jesuits, devised what is considered the classical schema for
spiritual discernment. Perhaps if Ignatius's brilliant treatise
had been available to Climacus, he would have written fewer
pages. That he does not, however, signals the importance of
this step in his spiritual climb. Ignatius's *Rules for Discernment*
and Climacus's insights are the foundation for our considering the necessity of discernment in seriously approaching the
spiritual life.

Discernment is more than simple decision making; we
need not *discern* straightforward decisions. A cursory consideration of positives and negatives may suffice for deciding. *What*

color should I paint the bedroom? Which restaurant shall we eat in on Saturday? What kind of car should I buy? While some of these may be significant decisions, they do not require spiritual discernment. We need simply to decide and to act.

Spiritual discerning is weightier and more involved. It is reserved for life-direction choices or grave decisions that have lasting effects. *What should I do with my life? Should I marry this person? Should I make a career change? Should I do a year of volunteer service?* These are questions requiring discernment.

In Step 26 Climacus writes:

> Among beginners, discernment is real self-knowledge; among those midway along the road of perfection, it is a spiritual capacity to distinguish unfailingly between what is truly good and what in nature is opposed to the good; among the perfect, it is a knowledge resulting from divine illumination, which with its lamp can light up what is dark in others. To put the matter generally, discernment is—and is recognized to be—a solid understanding of the will of God in all times, in all places, in all things; and it is found only among those who are pure in heart, in body, and in speech.

One can see why Climacus places this discernment step near the top of his ladder. Only the spiritually mature can discern well. The primary questions are: *What does God want of me? Where is the Spirit leading me? How do I listen for the voice of God in my life?* Such questions presume an active, prayerful relationship with God that allows me to discern the Divine will in my life. Without that relationship, spiritual discernment is not possible.

I saw the error to be, that men think that it
will be something seen by the natural eye;
but 'tis spiritual discernment that is needed,
the eye of God in his people.

—MARGARET MACDONALD

Anne Lamott says that a minister friend of hers compares discernment to stepping into a spotlight that God shines along the way. When you step into the light, there is just enough illumination for that round circle of lighted space until the next spotlight appears, and then you step into that one. It is the way God leads, and if you follow, you wind up exactly where you're supposed to be. The task, of course, is to see the spotlights.

Vocational discernment is one of the most crucial types because of its lifelong implications. While important for marriage and other career choices, good discernment is especially vital in the selection of religious life or priesthood because those vocations are explicitly predicated on a perceived call of God. I know something about this.

When I first felt called to religious life and priesthood, I was not aware of the prolonged spiritual discernment necessary. At that point I was going to college full time and working full time in a brokerage firm on Wall Street. My schedule left little time for contemplation. Yet I could not quiet the incessant call to consider a different path. As I walked to the office building on Water Street in downtown Manhattan, my spirits would droop. The thought of another day crunching numbers to profit a company for which I felt little attraction or allegiance was disheartening. There had to be more to life, and I needed to discover that *more*.

Ignatius of Loyola advised that we pay attention to our affect in discernment. While I discern with my heart and head, experiences of consolation and desolation are key in Ignatian discernment. *What are the joyful and sorrowful feelings and experiences in my life, and why are they so? As I contemplate a decision, do I feel joy or sorrow (consolation or desolation)?* Paying attention to "moods" and "spirits" as we contemplate life choices is indispensable to good discernment.

When I considered embarking on a religious vocation, my spirits would lift—indeed, soar. I had met a group of men during a high school retreat whose lives seemed centered on what mattered. They appeared happy and fulfilled in what they were doing. The priests and brothers of the Congregation of the Passion were devoted to a mission to which I thought I could give my life and find fulfillment. When I imagined myself doing what they were doing, I felt happy.

Peacefulness of spirit while contemplating a life choice is an important positive indicator. Once a choice has been discerned, it is important to note the continuance or not of that serenity of spirit. This can be an indication of whether one's will is in harmony with God's will for the person; or, perhaps more poetically, whether one's dream is in accord with God's larger dream for the person.

Feelings, however, are not the only criterion in discernment. Ignatius recognized that feelings could be fickle. We must also use our intellect to discern. It is helpful to make a list of the positives and negatives of the choice. What are the practical implications? In weighing the pluses and minuses, we must also consider how our decision will affect others.

Once I joined the formation program of the Passionists and began my studies, discerning became more complex. I saw up close what living a communal religious life entailed, and it wasn't all feel-good. I missed my family and my former life in New York City. Being young and single in New York now seemed more appealing than when I had been there. The menial tasks I was charged to perform in religious life seemed to bear no relevance to becoming a priest. Some of the people in the formation program with whom I was forced to live didn't thrill me, either. Yet even though my positive feelings weren't as consistent as before I had joined, a profound peacefulness of spirit continued. Whether I was feeling happy or sad, content or restless, underneath a deep current of tranquility and rightness perdured. I was also aware that I was giving myself to a life that could make a difference for others. That realization of a higher good made the emotional fluctuations tolerable.

Good discernment requires that we never make an important decision when feeling low or high. Ignatius counseled that extreme consolation or desolation is not a good space in which to discern. We must wait for a time of equilibrium and then discern the meaning of feelings of consolation or desolation. Also, after having made a decision through a process of discernment, we should revisit the choice later to seek confirmation. Discernment need not be carved in stone; it is ever evolving.

The long formation process of religious life and priesthood respects the rule for discernment. On average, people spend nine years in formation before making a final commitment to religious life. In that time I had many highs and lows and feelings of consolation and desolation.

The emotional vacillations of an experience of falling in love nearly derailed my religious pursuit. I had not gone looking for a relationship that threatened my religious vocation, yet there it was, seemingly a gift. Suddenly confused, I wondered, how could God be offering me two goods that required opposite life paths? Amid the confusion, I was also giddy about the possibilities this new relationship offered—until I realized that

I wasn't free to pursue them without altering my life direction. That is the rub of discernment. It usually isn't a choice between a good and a bad, but between various goods, thus making discernment a thorny undertaking. Discernment presumes that we don't simply do what we want to do. Sometimes it leads us to choose not our will, but rather that which we perceive to be God's will.

> *I always imagined when I was a kid that*
> *adults had some kind of inner toolbox, full of*
> *shiny tools: the saw of discernment, the*
> *hammer of wisdom, the sandpaper of patience.*
> —ANNE LAMOTT

One of the most helpful components in my spiritual discernment has been the assistance of a spiritual director. Climacus and Ignatius both suggest that we not navigate the sometimes treacherous waters of spiritual discernment alone. A spiritual guide and companion can help us gain objectivity and balance in our spiritual charting. When I was confused about being in love while still desiring a religious vocation, my spiritual director asked me to pray about the goodness of both choices and then to consider what I felt God wanted me to do. This was no easy task. How could I be sure? My feelings while praying varied from day to day. How could I presume to know what God felt?

Spiritual discernment implies that we can indeed know God's will for us. While at the time I felt that God would approve of whichever path I chose, eventually there was a clear indication that religious life and priesthood was God's desired path for me. I had been given the gifts and talents necessary to pursue this life, while the prerequisites required for a committed relationship to one person weren't as available to me. Service to many people energized me; attentiveness to one person in a romantic sense did not. Also, I had a palpable sense that life as a religious would satisfy me in a way that nothing else would, not even a relationship. I have no rational explanation for that deep intuition, other than it was God-given.

An added consideration in my spiritual discernment is how my decision affects the community and the wider Church, as I believe that God speaks through the broader faith community, too. In discernment I must incorporate others' perceptions and views about my decision. Everyone I consulted during my discernment perceived me as better equipped for a religious vocation than for a relational one. One elderly woman in the parish where I was working said, "Sweetheart, I know someone would be lucky to have you, but not as lucky as we all are to have you." My mother put it another way: "What girl could stand you?" I found wisdom in the thoughts and feelings of those whom I trusted, even if, at times, they seem rooted in self-interest, or a little too much honesty. In Step 26 Climacus writes, "God, after all, is not unjust. He will not lead astray the souls who, trusting and guileless, yield in lowliness to the advice and decision of their neighbor. Even if those consulted are stupid, God immaterially and invisibly speaks through them and anyone who faithfully submits to this norm will be filled with humility."

> *Her great merit is finding out mine—there is*
> *nothing so amiable as discernment.*
>
> —LORD BYRON

Of course, not everyone discerns a religious vocation or has nine years to make a good discernment. Most discernment is less involved, yet no less directed by the hand of God, if one pays attention. People who discern well have remarkable capacity for doing great things. Historical figures who used spiritual discernment have left lasting marks on society—people like Martin Luther King Jr., whose grounding in religious beliefs and principles caused him to discern choices rooted in justice, even when it jeopardized his life. From a Birmingham jail he wrote, "Just as the prophets of the eighth century BC left their villages and carried their 'thus saith the Lord' far beyond the boundaries of their home towns, and just as the Apostle Paul left his village of Tarsus and carried the gospel of Jesus Christ to the far corners of the Greco-Roman world, so am I compelled to carry the gospel of freedom beyond my own home town. Like Paul, I must constantly respond to the Macedonian call for aid." King discerned that call deep in his spirit.

Similarly, Mahatma Gandhi's struggle against British imperialism was grounded in spiritual discernment that demanded he act on his convictions once they were revealed. No different for Desmond Tutu who in his struggle against apartheid in South Africa said, "Faith is a risk, but it is a risk I cannot risk living without." These men are models of spiritual discernment that called them to actions that perhaps they wouldn't have chosen if left to their own predilections.

Of course, there are historical figures and religious leaders who claim good discernment and seem to make choices not based in the goodness and love of God. Witness the radical fundamentalism sweeping religious groups and the sometimes horrific results. The mass suicide at Jonestown and the destruction of the World Trade Center are but two examples. "By their fruits you will know them" (Matthew 7:20) clearly resonates. Good discernment must be tested by the results—not only personal but communal, as well.

While our discernments may not lead us to do grand things in service of humankind, we are assured that good discernment begets goodness. When we attempt to make important choices in accord with God's desire for us, we can be confident that those choices will bear good fruit. When we step into that Divine spotlight one step at a time until more is revealed, our path will always be lighted. "Our eyes are a light to all the body. Discernment of the virtues is a light to all the mind" (Climacus, Step 26).

Questions for the Climb

1. Do you *discern* important decisions in your life, or do you simply *decide*?
2. Do the barometers of consolation and desolation reflect your own experience of good discernment?
3. How might you discern better?
4. Do you believe that God has a will for you that you can come to know?

Stillness / Beside Restful Waters

*Many writers who choose to be active in
the world lose not virtue but time, and
that stillness without which literature
cannot be made.*
—GORE VIDAL

I read somewhere that if you put a frog in a pot of cold water on a stove and gradually raise the heat, the frog will boil to death before it has the sense to jump out of the pot. The point of the story was that we are like the frog—no matter how much our lives heat up, we remain in the pot until it kills us. We lack the sense to jump out. Many of us know what it's like for our lives to heat up. Expanding technology demands that we multitask and produce more, often creating lives of frenetic activity. Amid struggles to retain normalcy, we find ourselves bombarded by noisy gadgetry and pulled in every direction. How do we cope?

One executive friend of mine recently told me about his

vacation. He, his wife, and their three children had gone to Nantucket for seven days.

"It was awful," he said as we were catching up in an Upper West Side Starbucks.

"Why?" I said. "You had perfect weather the week you were away."

"The cell phone service on that island was so spotty, it was maddening. I kept having to drive around just to have a conversation, and even then the calls kept getting dropped."

"What was so important that it couldn't wait?" I said. "After all, your family was with you."

"Work, my friend," he said, his tone implying *How could you even ask?*

"But you were on vacation," I said.

"I am never *totally* on vacation," he said. "I have to be always available by phone and e-mail. And that was the other thing. Try finding wireless hot spots for your laptop on that godforsaken island."

"I don't think I'd want to on vacation," I said.

"That just goes to show you the difference between your life and mine," he said. "I have to work all the time in order to stay competitive in my job. You get to drop out every now and again, and nobody misses you. . . . Well, you know what I mean."

I *did* know what he meant and appreciated our differences. My friend has little or no stillness in his life. It is like being on a merry-go-round that never shuts down for the night. Round and round at a dizzying pace until one day he just falls off. In Step 27 Climacus writes, "We are like purchased slaves, like servants under contract to the unholy passions." And they didn't even have electricity back then, never mind cell phones or laptops.

Climacus's seventh-century reflections illustrate that it is not only technology that disquiets our souls. Inner stillness is also thwarted by internal wars waged by some of the passions already discussed and by other interior conflicts. Climacus placed inner stillness near the top of his ladder because, without stillness in our lives, none of the other virtues is attainable. Taking time to be still may be our only hope in advancing higher on this ladder toward fulfillment.

I have written before about a thirty-day retreat that I made in a hermitage in the middle of the woods of Big Sur, California. What is most memorable about that retreat is the quiet and stillness I experienced. It took me about seven days to become comfortable with it, but once I settled into the stillness and it into me, my view of inner and outer realities changed.

With nothing to distract me from the stillness, simple things emerged in startling relief. Golden sunrises and fuchsia sunsets became anticipated moments for wonder and gratitude. The soaring of the eagles and condors over the verdant mountains lifted my soul in appreciation of the beauty I often miss. My curiosity was piqued by the sounds of the elephant seals calling to one another in the cobalt Pacific waters, as I wondered what they might be communicating. Walking in the woods became an occasion to marvel at the genius of an ecosphere inhabited by species I couldn't name, yet which I observed with childlike wonder.

The internal engagements were no less awe-producing. Once the noise in my head quieted, I gained remarkable clarity. Amorphous ideas I had been pondering for months took shape and led to clear action. I moved from wondering if I should remain in my ministry at the time, to deciding to request a transfer when my time in the woods had ended. Stillness brought this clarity.

Once I knew only darkness and stillness.

—HELEN KELLER

Pascal wrote, "I have concluded that the whole misfortune of men comes from a single thing, and that is their inability to remain at rest in a room." Being at rest in a room was a richer experience than I had imagined, revealing to me that, rather than escaping the world through stillness, one enters more deeply into it.

Yet we seemingly avoid the solitary experience, perhaps afraid of ennui that may ensue. We choose instead a frantic pace that prevents stillness from revealing its hidden potential. Why? Some say they keep the frenzied pace to earn more money; others are driven by fame, wanting to be the best or most recognized; still others are appeasing demanding parents (or even a severe God), whom they're convinced are never satisfied. While these motivators may not be bad in themselves, the results of anxious striving for money, fame, or the approval of others often disappoint. The aching we long to fill remains.

In his notebook that eventually became the classic *Walden,* Thoreau wrote: "The mass of men lead lives of quiet desperation." To counter that tendency, Thoreau embarked on a project "in undisturbed solitude and stillness" in his cabin. Ralph Waldo Emerson had offered him free use of his woodlot along the northern shore of Walden Pond, and there Thoreau built a ten-by-fifteen-foot cabin, the interior of which was furnished with a small desk and lamp, a bed, a table, and three chairs— "one for solitude, two for friendship, three for society."

"I went to the woods," he explained, "because I wished to live deliberately, to front only the essential facts of life, and see if I could not learn what it had to teach, and not, when I came to die, discover that I had not lived."

If water derives lucidity from stillness, how
much more the faculties of the mind.
—CHUANG TZU

I suggested earlier that fear of death causes us to try to remain
perpetually young. Could our inability to be still also be an attempt to stave off death? Do we perhaps believe the axiom that
it's harder to hit a moving target, so we don't sit still? Do we
fear that metaphoric vultures will hover if they perceive our inertia? If we slow down too much, are we confronted with the
mortality that our constant movement attempts to keep at bay?

One friend says that he'll have plenty of time in retirement
to take it easy. Until then he's going to work eighteen-hour
days and make as much money as he can. This friend's brother
died of a heart attack at age forty-five, pursuing the same
dream. His brother's death has done nothing to slow down my
driven friend.

If he opts off the dizzying merry-go-round at some point,
he may be surprised by the results. When people try to reclaim
their lives, new worlds can emerge. Yoga and meditation classes
are filled with people attempting to slow down and reconnect
with their bodies and spirits, thus cultivating their capacity for
inner listening. Religious traditions have long maintained
the need for stillness and quiet for centered and fulfilled lives.
The Judeo-Christian tradition of being still has its roots in the
Fourth Commandment extolling Sabbath rest:

Remember to keep holy the sabbath day. Six days you
may labor and do all your work, but the seventh day is
the sabbath of the Lord, your God. No work may be
done then either by you, or your son or daughter, or
your male or female slave, or your beast, or by the alien

who lives with you. In six days the Lord made the heavens and the earth, the sea and all that is in them; but on the seventh day he rested. That is why the Lord has blessed the sabbath day and made it holy.

(EXODUS 20:8–11)

Sabbath rest is time to stop, to notice, and to be thankful for the gifts from our Creator. And not only are *we* to rest and be still, but all of creation is, too: "For six years may you sow your land and gather in its produce. But the seventh year you shall let the land lie untilled and unharvested" (Exodus 23:10). Even the earth needs to be still and rest. Constant producing drains valuable resources; stillness allows them to be replenished. The reading goes on to say that, ultimately, the land is God's and we are but tenants and aliens. Good stewardship requires stillness in caring for the creation with which we have been entrusted.

It is noteworthy that even the animals should not work on the Sabbath because all of creation must rest. Studies have suggested that animals have highly developed intuitive sense, probably based in their acute physical senses. They seem to intuit when something ominous or dangerous is about to occur. It has been widely reported that in the devastating tsunami that struck off the Indonesian coast in December 2004, killing over 200,000 people, practically no animals died. Speculation is that they sensed the impending danger and fled to higher elevations. Part of their intuition comes from stillness that allows them to be connected to the elements (land, water, air) in a heightened way. While human beings have this capacity for intuitive knowing, it may be diminished due to our highly evolved cerebral and cognitive skills. We become less intuitive and more fact-based. The more detached we become from our bodies, the less at home we are in ourselves. Stillness can bring us back to ourselves and to more intuitive knowing.

> *If a man would travel far along the mystic*
> *road, he must learn to desire God*
> *intensely but in stillness.*
> —ALDOUS HUXLEY

Stillness is necessary to listen for the voice of God. The previous step, Discernment, suggests that often God speaks through people and experiences, not in dramatic ways but in quiet ones. When God asks Elijah to go outside and stand on the mountain to wait for Him, the result is surprising: "A strong and heavy wind was rending the mountains and crushing rocks before the Lord—but the Lord was not in the wind. After the wind there was an earthquake—but the Lord was not in the earthquake. After the earthquake there was fire—but the Lord was not in the fire. After the fire there was a tiny whispering sound. When he heard this, Elijah hid his face in his cloak and went and stood at the entrance of the cave" (1 Kings 19:11b–13a).

We miss the tiny whispering sounds if we do not spend time in the stillness of the cave. The hollowed-out places in our lives might not present themselves of their own accord; we may need to carve them out of the mountains of work, relationships, and distractions that fill our lives. A daily walk in nature, a monthly retreat day, ten minutes a day in a quiet place of prayer, riding in the car with no radio, a long swim, sitting and pondering a dazzling sunset—all are opportunities to savor the stillness and to pay attention. Without such occasions we live only on the surface of what is experienced; to get beneath takes reflection born of stillness.

Today many waiters begin their spiels in this way: "Can I bring you still, sparkling, or tap water?" Although in New York City I always order the good old tap water, considered to be some of the best in the nation, the other two waters offered present an interesting choice of opposites: still or sparkling. Maybe that encapsulates our struggle with stillness. Sparkling seems sexier. It bubbles; it effervesces; it moves. Still is, well, still. It just lays there. And yet all bubble and no stillness can wear us out. When we lean too much toward the sparkle, we risk being all surface with no depth—too much fizzle and not enough earthly grounding. Climacus suggests that the best way to sparkle is to take time to be still.

Questions for the Climb

1. Do you take time to be still?
2. How do you feel when you begin to slow down?
3. Does stillness frighten you?
4. Do you sense God more acutely in stillness?

Prayer / In the Still of the Night

*The continuance of your longing is the
continuance of your prayer.*
—SAINT AUGUSTINE

With so many books and articles written about prayer I fear
that I can contribute little new, but Climacus's words give me
hope: "Prayer is by nature a dialogue and a union of man with
God. Its effect is to hold the world together." Each of our
prayers is its own dialogue, our own unique experience of God
and the ineffable. So while others can attempt to teach us
about prayer and can relay their experience of God in prayer,
no one's experience is the same. I can learn from the mystics
and others who have traversed the landscape of prayer, but I
can know and write only about *my* experience of it. "You cannot learn to see just because someone tells you to do so. For
that, you require your own natural power of sight. In the same
way, you cannot discover from the teaching of others the
beauty of prayer" (Climacus, Step 28).

As is true of most people's relationship with God, mine has

gone through many stages and developments. The point at which my prayer became tangible and defined was during my novitiate year, my first year in the monastery after graduating from college. Up to that point I prayed in mostly superficial ways, if one can call *any* prayer superficial: asking for things I wanted or needed, requesting help or intercession for other people, and occasionally being moved to give thanks for the wonder and beauty that surrounded me. It was all good, but without any developed sense of communicating with the Divine. I did what I had been taught since I was a child and copied what I saw others doing—the basic ABCs of praying.

A major shift occurred during my year as a novice in the monastery. Suddenly I felt lured into praying, sometimes even against my will. Although the novitiate is intended to be an intensive prayer experience, one cannot make that happen; it either does or it doesn't. It began to happen for me about the third month after I had arrived. Up to that point, prayer had been an obligation but not a real desire. I did it because I knew it was the right thing to do and perhaps because I feared punishment from God if I didn't.

Suddenly, three months into my novitiate, I could not spend enough time praying. Sitting in the chapel for hours meditating, I was unaware of how much time had passed. I would also awaken in the middle of the night, rise from my bed, put on my religious habit, and go to the chapel to pray for an hour. I would have preferred to be sleeping, but something or someone else was calling me to pray.

I remember talking to the novice director, Father Raphael, about this during a spiritual direction session.

"I'm getting up in the middle of the night to pray," I said.

"Why are you doing that?" he said.

"I'm just feeling called to it. I wake up. There's something about praying in the stillness of the night that appeals to me. While everyone is sleeping, it's almost like keeping watch."

"Are you doing it for yourself or for God?" he said.

"What do you mean?"

"We have to be careful of pride when it comes to such matters," he said. "You may be praying at night because you think it makes you holier. So you can be better than everyone else who's sleeping. Prayer can't be about that."

"I don't think it's that," I said. "I didn't decide to do this. It just started happening. It's as if I'm being drawn to it."

"*It* or God?" he said.

"God," I said.

"Make sure. Because if you're doing it for any other reason, or if it's more about you than God, then I want you to stop."

"Okay."

My nightly encounters continued for about three months more because I was convinced that it really was more about God than me. I was being wooed. Although I didn't know it at the time, such periodic intense experiences of prayer are not uncommon. They are similar to the infatuation stage of a relationship. Time is not an object. You will do anything to be in the presence of the one you desire. It surprised me because previously that hadn't been my experience of prayer. Prayer had been more work than anything else. But during this time, it was truly heavenly—until once again, some months later it became work again.

> *In a world of prayer, we are all equal in*
> *the sense that each of us is a unique person,*
> *with a unique perspective on the world, a*
> *member of a class of one.*
>
> —W. H. AUDEN

In the Gospels, when the disciples ask Jesus to teach them to pray, he does not suggest a formal, distant way of communicating with God. Instead, he teaches them to address God as Father (*Abba,* literally "Daddy") (Luke 11:2). The *Our Father* is perhaps the most important prayer in Christianity because it is the prayer that Jesus himself teaches us. Most noteworthy is that we are taught to address God in the familiar. For so many people God can seem like a distant reality and someone we dare not approach with any familiarity. The Old Testament depictions of God often present a deity who must be revered from a distance. One cannot see the face of God and live. Jesus makes a theological leap by drawing God closer to us. While God will always be "other than," Jesus is suggesting that God can be known more intimately. In fact, God *wants* to be known more intimately. Christianity teaches that Jesus is the human face of God. Therefore, we have, in fact, seen God and lived.

In the beginning of most relationships, we talk a lot. It is the way we get to know one another. Uncomfortable with silence that may hang heavily in the air, we are likely to interrupt it with words, any words. As a relationship matures and an instinctual means of knowing develops, fewer words seem needed. If most communication truly is non-verbal, that is even more the case with one whom we know intimately. The same is true of our relationship with God. Instead of talking, we learn to listen, to hear the voice of God. Affective prayer, sometimes known as Prayer of the Heart, is where heart speaks to heart and listens for a response. Believing that God wishes to communicate with us, we find that intentional affective prayer becomes one of the primary means by which God does just that.

If the only prayer you said in your whole life
was "thank you," that would suffice.

—MEISTER ECKHART

There are many different forms and types of prayer. The various religious traditions have their own postures and approaches. Sufis whirl; Quakers sit; Jews sway; Native Americans dance; Christians kneel; Muslims bow. No matter what our bodies do to facilitate communication with the Divine, the intent is the same: to dispose ourselves to be in a conscious relationship with God. We communicate with God because we believe it is good for us, but also good for God.

The four Gospels in the New Testament all have variations of the following text from the Gospel of Matthew: "Ask and it will be given to you; seek and you will find; knock and the door will be opened to you. For everyone who asks, receives; and the one who seeks, finds; and to the one who knocks, the door will be opened" (Matthew 7:7–8; cf. Mark 11:24, Luke 11:9–10, John 16:24). The texts all refer to asking God for something in order to receive it. But this can be a tricky notion.

A parishioner once said to me, "I don't understand why we have to ask God for anything if He is all-knowing and all-powerful. Why doesn't He just give us what we need without our having to ask?" It is a good question. Is God simply playing hard to get with us—refusing to budge until we implore God to do so? Or rather, could it be that we need to articulate our desires in order to truly know them? Maybe we pray as much for ourselves as we do for God.

There is something in us that needs to call out to a power greater than we are. While some claim it is an irrational need to create meaning and direction in a world that can seem to be lacking both, others maintain it is something else: It is the result of God creating us to be in relationship, especially with the Divine. We are social by nature, and so is God. Catholic theology teaches that God is a community of three divine persons called the Trinity: Father, Son, and Spirit. If humankind is created in God's image, we are by our very nature communal, as well. The greatest expression of our communal nature is our communion with God, which is most fully realized in prayer. We reach out to a God who reaches back to us. Prayer is the lifeline by which we do that.

> *Prayer does not change God,*
> *but it changes him who prays.*
> —SØREN KIERKEGAARD

"O come, let us worship and bow down. Let us kneel before the Lord, our maker" (Psalm 95:6). The communal aspect of both ourselves and God reveals the need for and power of shared prayer. Liturgical prayer occurring in synagogues, churches, mosques, and temples signifies the desire to worship God in common. Prayer is not simply an individual activity. We lift our voices together in worship and praise as a communal act reflecting the truth of who we are as creatures of a Creator who desires relationship with us. In the Gospel of Matthew Jesus says, "Again, (amen,) I say to you, if two of you agree on earth about anything for which they are to pray, it shall be granted to them by my heavenly Father. For where two or three are gathered in my name, there am I in the midst of them" (Matthew 18:19–20). So we gather two and more, believing that God is a potent participant in that assembly. The power of prayer in numbers increases.

Thomas Merton once described God as "that circle whose

center is everywhere and whose circumference is nowhere." The all-encompassing reality of God presumes a God who has "got the whole world in His hands." Because of that image, many struggle with personal and global realities where God appears to have dropped the world from those protective hands. Personal tragedy, global warfare, and natural disasters all become reasons to question the efficacy of prayer. How could God allow this to happen? Why isn't God hearing my prayer? If God is all-powerful and all-knowing, why isn't He stopping this?

These are questions we hear often as people grapple with seemingly unanswered prayer. Sometimes the apparent unresponsiveness of God causes even pious people to lose faith. Since the time of Job (and probably before that), humankind has struggled with the notion of a God of love who seems to let bad things happen indiscriminately. Authors have gotten rich trying to explain this anomaly. Faith demands that we keep asking even if God's response seems contrary to our supplication. God's wisdom is not ours. "For my thoughts are not your thoughts, nor are your ways my ways, says the Lord. As high as the heavens are above the earth, so high are my ways above your ways and my thoughts above your thoughts" (Isaiah 55:8–9). Satisfying or not, these words seem to be our answer to unanswered prayer.

> *I believe in prayer. It's the best way we have to*
> *draw strength from heaven.*
> —JOSEPHINE BAKER

Even when we feel ignored by God, the very act of praying is formative. It changes us. A long time ago I was introduced to the Jesus Prayer, which has a complex history that dates back to the New Testament passage where the blind Bartimaeus calls out to Jesus, saying "Jesus, son of David, have mercy on me" (Mark 10:47b). My introduction to the prayer came from an unlikely source, the 1961 J. D. Salinger novel *Franny and Zooey*. In the novel Franny has been introduced to the classic work *The Way of a Pilgrim*, a nineteenth-century book by an anonymous Russian peasant whose life is changed by praying the Jesus Prayer. Franny is convinced that she, too, would like to learn to pray unceasingly and have her life changed.

After reading *Franny and Zooey*, I decided that I had to read *The Way of a Pilgrim*, as well. No book has been more influential in my spiritual development. The Russian peasant reads commentaries on the Jesus Prayer from the classic Eastern Orthodox work, the *Philokalia*, a compilation of texts of the masters of the Eastern Orthodox tradition from the fourth to fifteenth centuries. The commentaries, many of which extol the powers of the Jesus Prayer, convince the peasant that he must incorporate this prayer into his life. When he does, everything changes.

The prayer has two primary effects: First, it transforms his relationship to the material world around him: "When I prayed in my heart, everything around me seemed delightful and marvelous. The trees, the grass, the birds, the air, the light seemed to be telling me that they existed for man's sake, that they witnessed to the love of God for man, that all things prayed to God and sang his praise." Second, it transforms his relationship to his fellow human beings: "Again I started off on my wanderings. But now I did not walk along as before, filled with care. The invocation of the Name of Jesus gladdened my way. Everybody was kind to me. If anyone harms me I have only to think, 'How sweet is the Prayer of Jesus!' and the injury and the anger alike pass away and I forget it all."

When I read *The Way of a Pilgrim*, I wanted what the Russian peasant had. But the exhortation seemed far too easy: Simply pray the words "Jesus, Son of God, have mercy on me, a sinner" over and over again. Repeat the words in your mind until your heart begins to pray them. Inhale as you pray "Jesus, Son of God," and exhale with the words "have mercy on me, a sinner." Pray the words in accord with the beating of your heart. Pray the words repeatedly until you find yourself praying them with no intention of your will. Pray them until your heart is praying them unceasingly. That was all there was to it. How could such a simple prayer be transformative?

And yet it was just that. I found myself praying the prayer at the most unusual times: while taking a shower, driving, having a conversation with someone, and even while I was speaking. Unlike a song that you can't get out of your head, the prayer wasn't annoying or distracting. It was calming and helped to focus me. The point was not so much the meaning of the words as the calming repetition of the mantra. In Saint Paul's letter to the Thessalonians he counsels, "Pray without ceasing" (1 Thessalonians 5:17). The Jesus Prayer helped me to do that.

I began to notice myself becoming more patient. Little things like long lines at grocery stores and traffic jams didn't bother me as much. I recognized human need around me in a heightened way. The beggar on the corner had a face, one that I remembered. I was more aware of my own weaknesses, but not in a guilt-ridden way—more in a way that called for deeper compassion. Gratitude for the gift of life filled me in a way that made me feel giddy at times. I perceived more and criticized less. The mercy of Christ filled my heart in a new and abundant way.

Lest it appears that I was on a fast track to sainthood, the effects of this prayer have not been consistent, mostly because

I haven't been. Too often I have let the prayer slip from my heart, failing to call it to consciousness because I grew tired of its demands, inured to its power. However, when I have attempted to reconnect to it through conscious meditation and practiced repetition, its power returns once again. It is a gift that never fails.

Persistence in prayer may be the most important virtue of all. In his gospel Luke teaches the importance of this persistence. In the parable, a friend comes at midnight asking for a loaf of bread and is initially refused. Eventually, because of his perseverance, he is given the bread. "I tell you, if [his friend] does not get up to give him the loaves because of their friendship, he will get up to give him whatever he needs because of his persistence" (Luke 11:8). Likewise with the widow who, upon continually pestering a judge for a decision in her favor, is finally rewarded: "Because this widow keeps bothering me I shall deliver a just decision for her lest she finally come and strike me" (Luke 18:5). Scripture scholars have suggested that, in the parables, God is the sleeping friend who ultimately relents and God is the recalcitrant judge who finally yields. When we persist with God, ultimately we get our way. "Ask and you shall receive. Seek and you shall find. Knock and it shall be opened to you." Even now sometimes I wake up in the still of the night to do just that.

Questions for the Climb
1. With what prayer form are you the most comfortable?
2. Do you pray more for your sake or for God's?
3. Do you think that prayer changes anything? What about God's mind?
4. How would you like to pray differently?

*

Dispassion / Can't Touch This

It is easier to exclude harmful passions than to
rule them, and to deny them admittance than
to control them after they have been admitted.

—SENECA

I am surprised that Climacus chooses *dis*passion for the penul-timate step. I would have thought the opposite: that by the time we reach the top of the ladder, *passion* for life and God should take hold in a radical way and carry us to the pinnacle. And yet Climacus slows us down with dispassion. Why?

By dispassion I mean a heaven of the mind within the
heart.... A man is truly dispassionate—and is known to
be such—when he has cleansed his flesh of all corruption;
when he has lifted his mind above everything created, and
has made it master of all the senses; when he keeps his
soul continually in the presence of the Lord and reaches
out beyond the borderline of strength to Him.

(CLIMACUS, STEP 29)

After reading that, we may have to wait on this step for a while before proceeding. The ideal Climacus presents hardly seems attainable, yet should we strive for it anyway?

We have all heard the phrases: Don't let your emotions get the better of you. Don't lose your head. Control yourself! Underlying these exhortations is the realization that our passions sometimes can overcome us. When emotions rule, we can get in trouble. "Moderation in all things" seems to be a good edict when it comes to our passions and emotions. Climacus encourages a detachment that creates an inner and outer freedom. (Recall that detachment was our second step. Now detachment from our passions is the next to last step.) He is asking us to learn to control and direct the energy of our passions. We can be people of passions yet not be enslaved by them. Climacus is not suggesting we live in a zombielike passive indifference but rather that we be free from the tremendous sway of emotion so that we make healthy and wise choices that deepen our relationship with God and others. How do we attain such liberation?

Subdue your passion or it will subdue you.
—HORACE

Following is an example of how *not* to be liberated. It reveals the opposite of dispassion—and in an embarrassing way. Living in New York City presents unique challenges. Not least among them is securing a parking spot, should you be fortunate enough to have a car. Luckily for me, the Passionists provide a car for my ministry. Well, not always luckily, because then there is the problem of hunting for a parking space. The daily grind of that elusive search can wear on one. The simple sight of a blinking yellow light signaling that a car is leaving a coveted spot brings joy. What in any other city may not cause even a blip on the radar screen of happiness bounds off the charts in Manhattan.

One day I was late for a meeting on the Upper West Side of Manhattan. I had been circling the neighborhood for twenty minutes looking for a parking space to no avail. My patience was on a short leash. As I turned down West 81st Street, I spotted a Volkswagen Jetta pulling out of a spot halfway down the block. I gunned the engine and arrived in perfect time to pull alongside the car in front of the spot and begin my finely tuned parallel parking by backing into the space.

As I started to back up, a yellow Volkswagen Bug raced behind me and began to drive headfirst into the spot. I started beeping, but the woman driving the Bug continued to nose her way into the spot. I kept backing up slowly. Each of us was inching our way into the spot from opposite directions. She wasn't stopping, and neither was I. We came within a hair of hitting each other, and we stopped. I rolled down my window.

"What do you think you're doing?" I said, or rather *screamed*. "This is my spot."

She shook her head no and gripped her steering wheel with both hands like a spoiled child. I gripped mine right back. Two kids in the sandbox, heels dug in.

"Move your car," I shouted out my window. "This is my spot. I was here before you, and I signaled for it. Now move."

She shook her head again, this time more vehemently. She threw her car into park with a determined push of her arm and took out a magazine from her canvas handbag. She placed the magazine on her steering wheel and began to casually page through it. I felt my blood pressure in my ears. I shifted my car into park, got out, went over to her driver's window, and began banging on it.

"Move your car!" I shouted through the glass. She ignored me, paging through her magazine as if I weren't even there. I hit the side of her door with my hand. "I said move your car." Nothing. "If you don't move, I'm going to keep backing into this spot, and you're going to be sorry." I had become a raving lunatic in the middle of 81st Street, determined not to lose this battle with a woman who was just as determined as I. Where was the compassionate priest who sat and listened to other people confess to becoming overcome by their passions? Nowhere to be found. Now I was the one who would need to seek out the confessional and kneel on the penitent's side. (Luckily, I wasn't wearing my clerical collar for this embarrassing episode.)

I jumped back in my car and pulled forward a bit so that I could position myself better to begin my daring backup maneuver. As I did so, she quickly moved her car forward, scraping the side of both of our cars. I couldn't believe it. I was livid. I shot back out of the car, screaming "Look what you've done, you jerk! What, are you crazy? What are you trying to do!?" At that point, she held the steering wheel, put her head on it, and began to cry. Then she took out her cell phone and began punching buttons.

I felt terrible. Here I was in the middle of the street screaming uncontrollably at a woman over a parking space. We both now had damaged cars—and egos. I walked back to my car and sat in the driver's seat wondering what to do. I figured that I had to call the police and make an accident report, even though the damage was minuscule. As I was dialing my own cell phone, a police car pulled up beside us. One of the policemen came up to my window.

"License and registration, please." Two words I never like hearing a policeman say.

The policemen tried to convince me to give the woman a hundred dollars to cover any damages rather than to make a report and escalate the situation any further. I resisted, saying that this was as much her fault as mine.

"She should be paying for *my* damages," I said.

"Father, we can do it that way, if you want. But I wouldn't advise it. She's the hysterical woman. You're the ogre priest. You won't win. Give the woman a hundred bucks and say good-bye to this and to her."

Chagrined, yet grateful that I had gone to the ATM that day, I took two crisp fifty-dollar bills out of my wallet and walked over to the seemingly distraught woman who was standing next to the other policeman.

"Here," I said, and handed her the money. "Hope this covers *everything*." There was more than a hint of sarcasm in my voice.

She pocketed the money with a speed that was almost comical, said a chipper "Thanks," and then pulled her car fully into the still-vacant spot. She locked her Volkswagen with the push of a button and a definitive beep, then strolled down 81st Street with what I'm sure was an impish smile.

The policeman looked at me and said, "Father, it was a hundred well spent. Believe me. We deal with this stuff everyday. Good luck finding a spot." They pulled away and so did I, and found a spot on the very next block.

If passion drives you, let reason hold the reins.
—BENJAMIN FRANKLIN

Passion gets the better of us when we are too attached. The attachment can be to anything: another person, our possessions, our egos, the need to be right, or even a parking space. Dispassion means that you don't try to possess anything or anyone. In that way, passion has no room or reason to escalate. Although perhaps I had a right to the parking space, in my head I had acquired ownership before I had even parked. An indifference based on a nonpossessive stance would have defused the confrontation. Would the woman still have been wrong? From my perspective, yes. But being dispassionate would have prevented me from risking public humiliation or perhaps even worse.

Of course, we are encouraged to be dispassionate about more than parking spaces. For example, you can have and love a child, but you don't possess the child. Once you possess, or think that you do, passion can distort. The actions or fate of that child have a disproportionate effect on your life when ownership is presumed. The life of the child is not yours. Ownership of anything can be odious because it gives us an illusory sense of entitlement and control.

Married couples do not possess one another. When they attempt to do so, the passions of jealousy and anger can easily overcome what is good in a relationship that is better based on mutual freedom and respect. When we get attached to things in the world, we create a false reality that we own what we perceive. When that to which we are attached is taken away, we experience pain. If we remove the attachment, we remove the pain, as well. That is dispassion.

Money, too, can be an attachment. We fear losing it, or it being stolen. Our preoccupation with it grows until soon it dictates everything in our lives. Nonattachment to it produces the freedom that is the hallmark of dispassion.

There is something haunting in the light of the
moon; it has all the dispassionateness of a

*disembodied soul, and something of its
inconceivable mystery.*

—JOSEPH CONRAD

In the Gospels, Jesus epitomizes dispassion in his own Passion. In the Gospel of John, Pilate gives Jesus the opportunity to stop his crucifixion. When the authorities claim that Jesus professes to be the Son of God, Pilate is "afraid, and went back into the praetorium and said to Jesus, 'Where are you from?' Jesus did not answer him. So Pilate said to him, 'Do you not speak to me? Do you not know that I have power to release you and I have power to crucify you?' Jesus answered (him), 'You would have no power over me if it had not been given to you from above'" (John 19:8b–11a).

Jesus is convinced of the necessity of his mission. He will not hold on to his life under ignoble conditions because he knows that his life is given from above. He will die in truth and dignity rather than admit to lies and deceit. His abandonment to Divine will in his Passion is the embodiment of dispassion.

Being rooted in one's truth is the key to holy indifference. When we know who we are and what our true relationship to the world and to others is, passion cannot control us. The Jesuit Anthony de Mello says:

> An attachment destroys your capacity to love. What is love? Love is sensitivity, love is consciousness. To give you an example: I'm listening to a symphony, but if all I hear is the sound of the drums I don't hear the symphony. What is a loving heart? A loving heart is sensitive to the whole of life, to all persons; a loving heart doesn't harden itself to any person or thing. But the mo-

ment you become attached in my sense of the word, then you're blocking out many other things. You've got eyes only for the object of your attachment; you've got ears only for the drums. The heart has hardened. Moreover, it's blinded, because it no longer sees the object of its attachment objectively. Love entails clarity of perception, objectivity. There is nothing so clear-sighted as love.

(*AWARENESS*, IMAGE, 1990, P. 140)

Which leads us to our next and final step.

Questions for the Climb

1. Which is more important to you: your passion or controlling it?
2. When your passions get the better of you, how do you respond?
3. Does anything about dispassion make you uncomfortable?
4. Who or what do you wish you could be more dispassionate about?

Step 30

*

Love / Lovely Limitlessness

*For one human being to love another; that is
perhaps the most difficult of all our tasks, the
ultimate, the last test and proof, the work for
which all other work is but preparation.*

—RAINER MARIA RILKE

"All you need is love, all you need is love." So sang the Beatles
for the first time in 1967. Climacus thought the same fourteen
centuries earlier. At last, as we reach the top of the ladder on
this long and arduous climb, our reward is nothing less than
the most perfect of all virtues and human emotions: "Love, by
its nature, is a resemblance to God, insofar as this is humanly
possible. In its activity it is inebriation of the soul" (Climacus,
Step 30). Drunk with love, let us ponder this final step atop
the celestial ladder.

Love is indeed a many-splendored thing, meaning many
things to many people. It would be foolish to think that this
chapter could capture the essence of love in its totality. As we
perch on the final step toward lovely limitlessness, rather than

try to exhaust the topic, I will restrict myself to the kind of love Climacus would have us consider.

The New Testament was originally written in Koine (common) Greek. Unlike English, which uses one word for *love*, three words exist in Greek: *eros, philia,* and *agape.* Each has its nuance and specific meaning. *Eros* refers to erotic, romantic love; *philia* (or *phileo*), to friendship and brotherly love; and *agape,* to divine, unconditional, self-sacrificing love. Climacus is referring to the latter. *Agape* love most mirrors Divine love and is love without limits.

In the New Testament, *agape* is repeatedly referred to as that Christian love we are called to emulate in participating in the love of God: "You shall love [agape] the Lord, your God, with all your heart, with all your soul, and with all your mind. This is the greatest and the first commandment. The second is like it: You shall love your neighbor as yourself" (Matthew 22:37–39). Jesus goes even further in the Sermon on the Mount to say: "But I say to you, love [agape] your enemies, and pray for those who persecute you" (Matthew 5:44).

The only way we can possibly love our enemies is through *agape* love. Our ways of loving are limited and weak; God's way of loving is boundless. We are encouraged to strive for God's love. In the New Testament there is no greater explanation of *agape* love than in Saint Paul's First Letter to the Corinthians. Often read at weddings, this testimony to love forms the heart of that to which our final step calls us:

> If I speak in human and angelic tongues but do not have love, I am a resounding gong or a clashing cymbal. And if I have the gift of prophesy, and comprehend all mysteries and all knowledge; if I have faith so as to move

mountains but do not have love, I am nothing. If I give away everything I own, and if I hand my body over so that I may boast but not have love, I gain nothing.

(1 CORINTHIANS 13:1–3)

Neither a lofty degree of intelligence nor
imagination nor both together go to
the making of genius. Love, love, love,
that is the soul of genius.

—MOZART

Love is more than words. How often we find that people think words are enough. *I love you* is easy to say, but difficult to live. I remember once counseling a married couple. The husband was waxing eloquent about his love for his disgruntled wife who sat next to him, unimpressed. After his long poetic soliloquy she turned to him and said, "That's nice. But do you think maybe, just one night, you could do the damn dishes?"

Words are cheap. Deeds are not. We live in a culture that has cheapened love. The insincere platitudes that masquerade as love strike dissonant chords, like, as Paul says, gongs or clashing cymbals. They simply don't ring true. Hollywood leads this unharmonious symphony as it presents us with cinematic simplicities that hardly resemble real relationships born of struggle, rooted in true love. The dialogue on the big screen is often laughable because people sitting in the seats know that's just not the way it is.

Love is more important than prophesy and even faith. Without love these are empty. We cannot direct others what to do if we are not rooted in the charitable love of God who directs all else. Faith without love cannot exist because belief presupposes love of the one to whom I give myself. Boasting and bravado are not substitutes for an active love that places others before myself.

> Love is patient, love is kind. It is not jealous, (love) is not pompous, it is not inflated, it is not rude, it does not seek its own interests, it is not quick-tempered, it does not brood over injury, it does not rejoice over wrongdoing but rejoices with the truth. It bears all things, believes all things, hopes all things, endures all things.
>
> (1 CORINTHIANS 13:4–7)

Waiting is one thing we do not do well. We have become accustomed to the quick fix, the instant message, high-speed access, and no-wait check-in (if you happen to be a platinum member). But love can't be rushed. And it's willing to wait. A woman once told me that she had waited twenty years for the man she loved because she knew he was the only one for her. They had met at a benefit dinner at Tavern on the Green in Central Park and had talked the whole night; but he was engaged at the time and married his betrothed two months later. The woman, a nurse, was heartbroken but undaunted. She knew she was meant to be with this man—this, after only *one* night of conversation. The man's wife died after nineteen years of marriage, and the woman who had waited and the widower were married one year later. Love is patient.

Love by its nature is kind. To love like God means we embody a love rooted in generosity and kindness. "Let not kindness and fidelity leave you; bind them around your neck" (Proverbs 3:3). A woman parishioner once said to me, "What I wouldn't give for one kind word from that man." She was referring to her husband of thirty-three years who was not known to possess the milk of human kindness. He put her down constantly. Never an encouraging word. Nothing she did was ever good enough. The love, therefore, was hard to see. The pain in the relationship was not.

> *Love is the difficult realization that something*
> *other than oneself is real.*
> —IRIS MURDOCH

The character of Blanche DuBois in Tennessee Williams's *A Streetcar Named Desire* has a memorable closing line: "I've always depended on the kindness of strangers." While she utters the line to a doctor sent to escort her to a mental institution, the poignancy of the sentiment resonates. We do indeed depend on the kindness of strangers. Random acts of kindness delight and surprise us and sometimes get us through difficult circumstances. The anomoly is that we sometimes find it hard to exercise that same kindness with those whom we love most. Kindness with strangers can be easy; kindness with loved ones is not always. The exhortation to kindness in loving asks us to remember that no act of charity goes unnoticed, especially with those whom we love.

Jealousy is referred to as the green-eyed monster. Although Shakespeare coined the phrase, its aptness resounds with anyone who has been the captive or victim of jealousy. It can literally make us sick. As I've mentioned, jealousy is rooted in attachment. We become jealous when something that we think we own or have a right to is being usurped by someone else. Jealousy, however, cannot coexist with true love. Love suggests that there is no scarcity in the world of spirit. There is only abundance. What we love cannot be taken from us because we never really possess it in the first place. To be jealous in love refuses to acknowledge the abundant nature of love and the call in charity to love without possessing.

My cousin Michael once told me that his wife was going sailing in the Caribbean on a catamaran with some friends for a week.

"Without you?" I said.

"Yeah. She's going with a few girlfriends and some guy friends. I have to stay home and work."

"And that's okay with you? That she's going to be on a boat with some guys for a whole week."

"Sure, why not?" he said.

"Well, aren't you a little threatened? Or maybe jealous?"

"Absolutely not," he said. "I want Lori to be with me because she wants to be with me, not because she feels as though she *has* to be. I want her to stay with me because she loves me. If for some reason she didn't want to stay, or if she met someone else that made her happier, I'd have to let her go."

"Yeah, but you make it sound so easy. You'd be crushed, wouldn't you?"

"I'm not going to pretend it wouldn't be difficult. But the alternative would be worse. Why would I want her to stay if she'd rather be someplace else? That wouldn't be a marriage that I'd want any part of."

He refuses to be eaten up by the green-eyed monster.

Among those whom I like or admire,
I can find no common denominator,
but among those whom I love, I can:
all of them make me laugh.

—W. H. AUDEN

Love does not brood over injury. It is hard to heal when we've been hurt by a loved one. The wound inflicted by the beloved cuts more deeply. Forgiveness, therefore, must be at the core of any relationship of love. While being hurt in relationships is inevitable, if we hold on to the hurt, we never get beyond it. We wallow in resentment and diminishment. A friend of mine who was devasted by her husband's infidelity told me that for two years she held on to the pain, unable to forgive. "Until I realized it was hurting me more than him. If I wanted to stay in the marriage, I had to forgive him." Forgiveness opens our clenched fist again and allows the wound to heal. A scar may remain, but the wound no longer hurts.

"Then Peter approaching asked Jesus, 'Lord, if my brother sins against me, how often must I forgive him? As many as seven times?' Jesus answered, 'I say to you, not seven times but seventy times seven times'" (Matthew 18:21–22). The reason for boundless forgiveness is clear: It has never been withheld from us by God. In that same love, we cannot withhold it from one another.

Love never fails. If there are prophesies, they will be brought to nothing; if tongues, they will cease; if knowledge, it will be brought to nothing. For we know partially and we prophesy partially, but when the perfect comes, the partial will pass away. When I was a child, I used to talk as a child, think as a child, reason as a child; when I became a man, I put aside childish things. At present we see indistinctly, as in a mirror, but then face to face. At present I know partially; then I shall know fully, as I am fully known. So faith, hope, and love remain, these three; but the greatest of these is love.

(1 CORINTHIANS 13:8–13)

How wonderful to have something or someone in our lives that never fails us. Ideally, this is love and the person whom we love and who loves us. "Someone truly in love keeps before his mind's eye the face of the beloved and embraces it there tenderly. Even during sleep the longing continues unappeased, and he murmurs to his beloved. That is how it is for the body. And that is how it is for the spirit" (Climacus, Step 30).

Failure in romantic love is easy to witness. The high divorce rate is testimony enough. But true *agape* love doesn't fail us because it is rooted in a God who does not fail us. God is love. "For stern as death is love, relentless as the nether world is devotion; its flames are a blazing fire. Deep waters cannot quench love, nor floods sweep it away. Were one to offer all he owns to purchase love, he would be roundly mocked" (Song of Songs 8:6–7).

As human beings, we never perfect this love because we love imperfectly and "partially," as Saint Paul says. But we can love better as we mature, like a child who behaves better as he or she matures into an adult. Love is not primarily an emotion. It is an action. Immature love is based on how we feel; mature love is rooted in what we do. While emotions are involved, they cannot be the primary criteria for love. As a child learns to share, realizing that he or she is not the center of the universe, so, too, the lover puts aside childish ways and acts generously and lovingly.

Of course, the *agape* love to which Climacus refers is not limited to lovers or spouses. This is a love we are called to exhibit in *all* of our relationships. It is indeed a challenging goal. Each day we are presented with obstacles to loving. Bad moods, angry people, hurtful responses, betrayals, and cutthroat negotiations all serve to block love. These obstacles and others prevent us from clearly seeing the path of love because they obfuscate the nature of love. They trick us into responding in like manner. Saint Paul says we do so because we see indistinctly, as in a mirror. Because ancient mirrors were made of pieces of polished metal, the images were often "indistinct," or blurry or dim. Paul suggests that we view love that way. Love is not always clear for us. The task of living and loving is to grow in clarity and perception. As we do so, we love more like God.

So, how does this happen? It happens by doing it. Clear and simple. Loving is about action. It is a decision to act in a certain way because of a belief that there is no more powerful force in the universe than love. The teachings of Jesus are based on love of God and neighbor. The specifics of how that love occurs are not always easily executed. The decision to love is a refusal to be drawn into the negative pulls of competition, jealousy, wanton sexual gratification, racism, and all kinds of discrimination. The wars of the world would be eliminated if people and nations had the courage to live from a stance of love. But fear, mistrust, and insecurity often prevent this from happening. We can never live in love until we accept that we are all the same and are all called to the same God, who is love. Is this an oversimplification? Yes. But I still believe that it's true. The essence of love is simple.

> *Love thy neighbor as yourself,*
> *but choose your neighborhood.*
> —LOUISE BEAL

Spiritual writers have suggested that the opposite of love is not hate but fear. Fear sabatoges love. Most negative emotions are rooted in some kind of fear. The First Letter of John says: "There is no fear in love, but perfect love drives out fear because fear has to do with punishment, and so one who fears is not yet perfect in love" (1 John 4:18).

As we end our climb together, some helpful questions might be: What am I afraid of? What fear in me blocks me from loving more freely, as God calls me to love? Fear is about limitations. I am afraid I'm not good enough or not lovable enough. I am afraid to be vulnerable because I may get hurt. I am afraid to give more because then I will have less. I am afraid that if people really knew me, they wouldn't love me. I am afraid that you are more lovable than I am. I am afraid that I may disappoint you or even God.

Fear exists in the world of scarcity but has no place in the spirit world of abundance. Perfect love casts out all fear. There will never be less love if I give it away, because love by its very nature self-generates and increases. The more I give it, the more I receive it, and the more of it there is.

So, open your life. Let it be flooded by a love that knows no limits. Let your soul be provided for by the Love that is all-encompassing. For in the end, faith, hope, and love remain, but the greatest of these is love. And it really is *all you need.*

God speaks to each of us before we are,
Before he's formed us then, in cloudy speech,
But only then, he speaks these words to each
And silently walks with us from the dark:

Driven by your senses, dare
To the edge of longing. Grow
Like a fire's shadowcasting glare
Behind assembled things, so you can spread
Their shapes on me as clothes.
Don't leave me bare.

Let it all happen to you: beauty and dread.
Simply go—no feeling is too much—
And only this way can we stay in touch.

Near here is the land
That they call Life.
You'll know when you arrive
By how real it is.

Give me your hand.

—RAINER MARIA RILKE
(TRANSLATION BY LEONARD COTTRELL,
USED WITH PERMISSION)

Acknowledgments

There are many people who have provided for my soul during the writing of this book. I am particularly grateful to the following for their contributions to my life and to this work:

Karen O'Neill-Arredondo, Norma K. Asnes, Edward Beck (my father), Joan Cheever, Jean Cheever, Andrew Corbin (my editor at Doubleday), Blue Cullen, Father Philip Egitto, Maurie and Bob Flanagan, Peter Friedman, Henry and Ruth Garcia, Father Robert Joerger, C.P., Father Joseph Jones, C.P. (Provincial of the Passionists), Father Phil Kelly and the community of Saint Joseph of the Holy Family Church, Maura Kye-Casella (my agent), Monsignor Thomas P. Leonard, Héctor Lozada, Denise Marcil (my agent), Andrea Marcusa, Malia Scotch Marmo, Denise and Donald Mc-Manamon, Father Michael A. Perry, O.F.M., Winnie Philips, Debbie Phillips, Darya Porat (Doubleday), Father Columkille Regan, C.P., Steve Rippon, Judy Scheffler, Norman C. Simon, Father Melvin A. Shorter, C.P., Paul Wadell, Wendy M. Wright, and Judy Zucker.

And special thanks to Father Finbar Maxwell, SSC, a heroic missionary in Pakistan and a generous friend who, from afar, shared his thoughts about each of the steps of this ladder. I could not have made this climb without him.

© Ellen Barroso

EDWARD L. BECK, C.P., is a Roman Catholic priest of the
Passionist Community. In addition to giving retreats and
workshops on spirituality nationally and internationally, Father Beck writes and develops mainstream television and film
projects and is a commentator on religious and faith issues for
various media outlets. He lives in New York City. His Web site
is www.EdwardLBeck.com.